Lecture Notes in Computer Science 2604

Edited by G. Goos, J. Hartmanis, and J. van Leeuwen

Springer
Berlin
Heidelberg
New York
Barcelona
Hong Kong
London
Milan
Paris
Tokyo

Nicolas Guelfi
Egidio Astesiano
Gianna Reggio (Eds.)

Scientific Engineering for Distributed Java Applications

International Workshop, FIDJI 2002
Luxembourg-Kirchberg, Luxembourg, November 28-29, 2002
Revised Papers

Springer

Series Editors

Gerhard Goos, Karlsruhe University, Germany
Juris Hartmanis, Cornell University, NY, USA
Jan van Leeuwen, Utrecht University, The Netherlands

Volume Editors

Nicolas Guelfi
Institut Supérieur de Technologie
Départment d'Informatique Appliquée
6, rue Richard Coudenhove-Kalergi, 1359 Luxembourg, Luxembourg
E-mail: nicolas.guelfi@ist.lu

Egidio Astesiano
Gianna Reggio
Universitá di Genova-Italy
Dipartimento di Informatica e Scienze dell'Informazione (DISI)
Via Dodecaneso 35, 16146 Genova, Italy
E-mail: {astes/reggio}@disi.unige.it

Cataloging-in-Publication Data applied for

A catalog record for this book is available from the Library of Congress.

Bibliographic information published by Die Deutsche Bibliothek
Die Deutsche Bibliothek lists this publication in the Deutsche Nationalbibliografie;
detailed bibliographic data is available in the Internet at <http://dnb.ddb.de>.

CR Subject Classification (1998): D.2, C.2.4, I.2.11

ISSN 0302-9743
ISBN 3-540-00679-6 Springer-Verlag Berlin Heidelberg New York

Springer-Verlag Berlin Heidelberg New York
a member of BertelsmannSpringer Science+Business Media GmbH

http://www.springer.de

© Springer-Verlag Berlin Heidelberg 2003
Printed in Germany

Typesetting: Camera-ready by author, data conversion by PTP-Berlin, Stefan Sossna e. K.
Printed on acid-free paper   SPIN: 10872768   06/3142   5 4 3 2 1 0

Preface

FIDJI 2002 was an international forum for researchers and practitioners interested in the advances in, and applications of, software engineering for distributed application development. Concerning the technologies, the workshop focused on "Java-related" technologies. It was an opportunity to present and observe the latest research, results, and ideas in these areas.

All papers submitted to this workshop were reviewed by at least two members of the International Program Committee. Acceptance was based primarily on the originality and contribution. We selected for these postworkshop proceedings 16 papers amongst 33 submitted, two tutorials, and two keynotes.

FIDJI 2002 was aimed at promoting a scientific approach to software engineering. The scope of the workshop included the following topics:

- design of distributed Java applications
- Java-related technologies
- software and system architecture engineering and development methodologies
- development methodologies for UML
- development methodologies for reliable distributed systems
- component-based development methodologies
- management of evolutions/iterations in the analysis, design, implementation, and test phases
- dependability support during system lifecycle
- managing inconsistencies during application development
- atomicity and exception handling in system development
- software architectures, frameworks, and design patterns for developing distributed systems
- integration of formal techniques in the development process
- formal analysis and grounding of modeling notation and techniques (e.g., UML, metamodeling)
- industrial and academic case studies
- tool presentations

The organization of such a workshop represents an important amount of work. We would like to acknowledge all the program committee members, all the additional referees, all the organization committee members, the Luxembourg University of Applied Sciences administrative, scientific, and technical staff, the Henri-Tudor public research center and SITEC. FIDJI 2002 was mainly supported by the "Ministère de l'Enseignement Supérieur et de la Recherche" and by the "Fond National pour la Recherche au Luxembourg."

November 2002　　　　　Nicolas Guelfi, Egidio Astesiano and Gianna Reggio

Organization

FIDJI 2002 was organized by the Department of Applied Computer Science of the Luxembourg University of Applied Sciences (IST).

Program Chairs

Guelfi, Nicolas   IST, Luxembourg
Astesiano, Egidio   DISI Genoa, Italy
Reggio, Gianna   DISI Genoa, Italy

International Program Committee

Biberstein, Olivier	HTA, Bienne, Switzerland
Bouvry, Pascal	IST, Luxembourg
Di Marzo Serugendo, Giovanna	CUI, Geneva, Switzerland
Dubois, Eric	CRP Henri-Tudor, Luxembourg
Fourdrinier, Frédéric	Hewlett-Packard, France
Gengler, Marc	ESIL, Marseille, France
Guerraoui, Rachid	EPFL, Lausanne, Switzerland
Karsenty, Alain	JSI, Marseille, France
Kozaczynski, Wojtek	Rational Software Corporation, Boulder, USA
Molli, Pascal	LORIA, Nancy, France
Romanovsky, Sacha	DCS, Newcastle, UK
Rothkugel, Steffen	IST, Luxembourg
Rottier, Geert	Hewlett-Packard, Belgium
Sendall, Shane	EPFL, Lausanne, Switzerland
Souquières, Jeanine	LORIA, Nancy, France
Vachon, Julie	DIRO, Montreal, Canada

Organizing Committee

Amza, Catalin	IST/DISI, Genoa, Italy
De Colnet, Olivier	SITEC, Luxembourg
Dahaoui, Mustapha	IST, Luxembourg
Guelfi, Nicolas	IST, Luxembourg
Kies, Mireille	IST, Luxembourg
Lambeau, Bernard	SITEC, Luxembourg
Perrouin, Gilles	IST, Luxembourg
Reggio, Gianna	DISI, Genoa, Italy
Ries, Benoît	IST, Luxembourg
Sterges, Paul	IST, Luxembourg

Additional Referees

Brimont, Pierre
Eshuis, Rik
Foukia, Noria
Gautheron, Laurent
Khadraoui, Djamel
Oriol, Manuel

Perrouin, Gilles
Periorellis, Panayiotis
Razafimahefa, Chrislain
Ries, Benoît
Sterges, Paul

Sponsoring Institutions

This workshop was supported by the Luxembourg University of Applied Sciences, the Ministry for Culture, Higher Education, and Research, and the National Research Fund.

Table of Contents

Keynote Talks

Tutorials

A Java Coordination Tool for Web-Service Architectures: The Location-Based Service Context

P. Álvarez, J.A. Bañares, P.R. Muro-Medrano, J. Nogueras, and F.J. Zarazaga

Department of Computer Science and Systems Engineering
University of Zaragoza
María de Luna 3, 50015 Zaragoza (Spain)
{alvaper, banares, prmuro, jnog, javy}@posta.unizar.es
http://iaaa.cps.unizar.es

Abstract. The use of open technologies and standards have made easier the integration of Web services into end-applications. These interoperable services have been organized on distributed architectures over Internet in accordance with shared functional principles. But these Web-service architectures have not resolved the distributed computing difficulty in "gluing together" multiple and independent Web services. This paper presents an approach based on Java technology and Internet standard protocols and data formats for resolving coordination problems among Web services. Interaction models based on distributed events over HTTP are supported for providing the required coordination functionality. Cooperation problems and their solutions have been studied in the prototypical context of Location-Based Services.

Keywords: Web-service architectures, distributed service cooperation, Internet, Java and JavaSpaces Technologies

1 Introduction

Nowadays nobody doubts the Internet has become the most important global network infrastructure. Many companies are enclosing as software services their traditional computing tasks or introducing new tasks to connect them to Internet at a rapid pace searching new promising opportunities. However, this growth of services over the network has been faster than the formal efforts to agree on service-oriented architectures [6] and to identify the necessary support for enabling these distributed services to work together harmoniously [16].

First formal steps have progressed around the interoperability among systems (any Web service can interact with any other Web service [18]). This way, SOAP (http://www.w3.org/TR/SOAP/) has become a de facto standard for Web-service messaging and invocation, and for solving the problems of converting data between traditional distributed platforms such as CORBA, DCOM or EJB [19]. Additionally, many standardization initiatives have arisen in specific

N. Guelfi et al. (Eds.): FIDJI 2002, LNCS 2604, pp. 1–14, 2003.

research areas for defining open, ubiquitous and interoperable service interfaces, such as the area of the Location-based Services (LBS).

LBS extend the spatial processing capabilities of the Geographic Information Services (GIS) integrating wireless communications, location data and Internet technology [25,12]. In this context, two well-positioned organizations have emerged as the drivers of the LBS interoperability: LIF (Location-Interoperability Forum, http://www.locationforum.org/) and OGC (Open GIS Consortium, http://www.opengis.org/, and its Open Location Service Initiative (OpenLS), http://www.openls.org/). Both are promoting and defining standard interfaces for a collection of wireless, Location and GIS services for providing the required LBS functionality [2,26,29]. These public interfaces make easier the integration through Internet of these distributed services into end applications as individual computing entities, but in an isolated way, they have a very limited functional value. Therefore, LBS context may be considered as a prototypical technological-context where it may be evaluated the impact of the integration of industrial web-centric standards over the development of distributed applications.

Once services and their interfaces have been described, it arises the necessity of establishing an organization for supporting their use, interactions and automated discovery. This organization must define an architecture that provides a framework for making easier the collaborative work among the services and the access to them [14]. Past architecture experiences such as [24,31] could help us to define these future ones: problem in the use of the object technology in large-scale applications when it must be combined and recombined [23], and in building of component-based frameworks [21]. Besides, in order to integrate services implemented with different computational models, services must cooperate and to be ensemble over this architectural vision in an orthogonal way to their computing tasks [8], allowing to exploit the true value of services beyond independent computing entities.

This work presents a coordination Web-service for distributed architectures over Internet which has been used inside the LBS context as a prototypical domain. This support service has been implemented in Java so it could be used independently of the hardware platform and the operating system on which it is being executed. Internet is a distributed environment where many hardware and software configurations can be found (http://leb.net/hzo/ioscount/data/r.9904.txt). Therefore, Java as programming language of Web services, is the key for achieving the required platform portability and independence. Besides, it provides a number of built-in networking capabilities that make it easy to develop Internet-based and Web-based applications [10]. A more detailed description of our technological evolution towards this approach may be found in [4].

The paper is structured as follows. Section 2 presents a description of services provided by standards that constitute the LBS framework. It is shown in a succinct way the underlying conceptual model, the hierarchical levels of functionality, and the found problems in order to orchestrate these services. Section 3 justifies the adopted coordination-approach based on JavaSpaces technology and standards to develop web-centric solutions from XML and HTTP. Section 4 shows design and implementation details. Section 5 reviews the benefits of the proposal. Finally, future work and conclusions are presented.

2   A Web-Service Architecture for Providing LBS Functionality

2.1   Conceptual Model of Architecture

In general, a Web-service architecture is composed by a collection of services that are organized according to any functional aspects. An example of this kind of distributed architectures are the LBS frameworks, which integrate GIS and Location Services [26,28,32]. According to the functional aspects related to this LBS context, a conceptual model of architecture has been defined.

The proposed model is hierarchical and organized in relation to the level of intensity of data processing involved. Three functional levels of services have been identified:

- Data Management, which is responsible for data storage and recovery.
- Data Processing, which generates new data from raw data.
- Data Analysis, which provides high-level functionality from generated data by the lower levels.

It is important to underline that requirements of levels are not independent in this model. Processing level requires raw data storage, and analysis level is built on the lower levels.

2.2   Building a LBS Framework on the Basis of Web Services

The presented architectural model has been the conceptual base for the development of a LBS framework whose functionality may be integrated into end-applications through Internet (see fig. 1), such as ERP or CRM systems [4]. Required services are organized according to the proposed functional levels and built according to the Web-service philosophy: their operations are provided through a standard, published interface to ensure interoperability, and are accessible via ubiquitous Internet protocols and data formats, such as HTTP and XML.

The Data Management level is the base of the proposed architecture. Its services must be able of providing the necessary support for the storage and recovery of geodata. LBS frameworks require a wide variety of geodata: georeferenced maps; location descriptors such as street addresses, roads, place names or telephone numbers; sensor data such as immediate locations of mobile devices; or more specific data of the LBS context, such as traffic conditions or road repairs. A collection of services has been implemented for fulfilling these requirements. For example, basic GIS services: Web Map Server (WMS), for

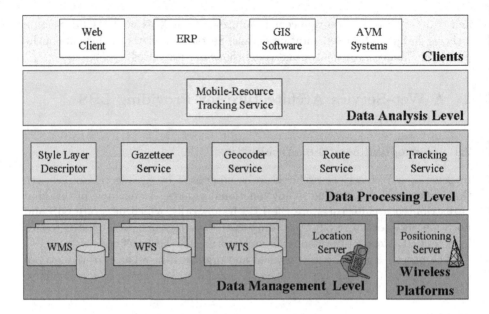

Fig. 1. LBS Web-service architecture

visualizing digital maps on the Internet as rendered raster data [3,13]; Web Feature Server (WFS), for storing, spatial and non spatial querying and discovering geographical features, such as the previously presented location descriptors [1]; and Web Traffic Server (WTS) [26], for providing traffic conditions of a specific region of interest. Interfaces of these services have been developed following the specifications proposed by the Open GIS Consortium (OGC).

Besides these GIS services, Location Services are required for communicating with remote sensors, an example could be services for acquiring location data from mobile devices throw wireless media to send and receive location requests and responses. These services define their interface according to the LIF (Location Inter-operability Forum) specification, which describes a Mobile Location Protocol (MLP) that can be used by an Internet application to request location information from a Location Server. As a part of this Location Services, it is possible to integrate the Mobile Positioning Servers provided by a telecommunication operator through its Location Service Platform.

Geodata provided by these Data Management services are not usually used in an isolated way, instead they are used by the Data Processing services for generating more complex and elaborate data. It is interesting to have services for combining different kinds of geodata, such as maps and location descriptors; for linking many location descriptors; or for calculating structured geodata, such as ideal routes from a set of mobile-device locations.

To achieve this functionality, geospatial services have been implemented for geodata presentation (such as, Style Layer Descriptor Server), utility (Gazetteers and Geocoders), and determination (Route Server and Tracking Server). Details about their specifications can be found in [26]. A Style Layer Descriptor Server (SLD) visualizes the result of a WFS query over a digital map returned by the WMS, applying a visualization style specified by the service client to the displayed geoinformation. On the other hand, the implementation of the WFS has been utilized as the baseline for developing another geoservices [11,4]: Gazetteers, used to link text-based location descriptions to geographic locations; Geocoders, used to transform a textual term or code, such as an address, place name, or telephone number, into a geographic location; Route Server, used to calculate ideal routes along a set of locations; and Tracking Server, used to store, query, retrieve the latest known geographic location of mobile device. The Tracking Server is not proposed in the OpenGIS specification. However we propose it as a natural way to provide mobile data.

Finally, at the higher level of the architecture, the Data Analysis level is composed by specific application services, such as the Mobile-Resource Tracking Service (MRTS), built on the lower-level services for integrating their functionality into end-applications through Internet. This service allows to make tracking tasks of mobile resources with an installed location-device (such as, vehicles or employees with a mobile phone with an integrated GPS-receptor), to visualize their real-time positions, to plan a route and tracking it, or to generate operational reports. To provide these operations through its interface, it is necessary that data and geoprocessing services of lower levels collaborate among them in an adequate way as an only global system.

2.3   Problems in the Real Implementation

The interoperability among built services is guaranteed by the use of Internet protocol and data format for accessing to services' operations, and by the definition of these operations according to widely accepted standards (OpenGIS and LIF specifications). Services may interoperate, making easier the integration of services provided by different suppliers. The need of cooperation has been already identified when the conceptual model was presented: "the requirements of levels are not independent".

But the problem is more complex. The remarked interoperability guarantees that services communicate and understand among them. However, from this standard-based interoperability, it is also necessary to have tools for orchestrating services: defining chains of services, synchronizing services and services with applications, or building more complex communication models than HTTP. This need becomes more apparent when the specific implementation of the proposed model is built. For example, the Mobile-Resource Tracking Service requires that services of lower levels collaborate among them for providing its application functionality.

A collection of restrictions has been found in the development of the presented LBS framework that could be extrapolated to other contexts. They are mainly related with the functional characteristics of Location Services and the difficulties for communicating them with other distributed services, such as data and geoprocessing GIS services:

1. Location Services have not persistence for storing received locations from mobile devices. If a service requests the geographic location of a device for processing it, a Location Service must communicate with the remote mobile-device for acquiring and providing it to the requester service.
2. Many location-data consumers are not simultaneously supported. Owing to the fact that a Location Service has not persistence and its interface's operations are invoked using the HTTP Internet protocol, the invoker service can only receive the requested location. If many services require the location-data of a same device, then each one must make an independent request.
3. Asynchronous responses for operations of the interface are more adequate. A service can request an immediate location of a device or a periodic collection of them, but a Location Service does not know in advance how long it is required for acquiring and receiving the requested location. This fact is owing to the introduced delay by communication networks. Therefore an asynchronous model for receiving location responses is more adequate. However, HTTP provides a synchronous request/response model.
4. A Location Service provides operations whose initiative comes from remote mobile-devices and not from the service client. For example, generation of emergency alarms or location events when a device comes into/out from a specific geographical region. Service clients must be able to subscribe to be notified when those alarms or events happen, instead of being continuously requesting to the Location Service to check their occurrence through its HTTP interface.

These restrictions show the need of a more complex communication mechanism among Web services than the one provided by the HTTP protocol:1) able to store exchanged data and to support many consumers and 2) an asynchronous and reactive communication model. Besides, these communication requirements involve matters of service synchronization too: services can be waiting for receiving new location data or being notified by alarms or events for doing their task, such as to update the vehicle location or to show a new alarm on a digital map, to track a predefined route or to recalculate a tracking report. Therefore, the particular target is to provide a high-level tool for coordinating (communicating and synchronizing) Location Services with GIS services. However, this target will be deal with a broader perspective, trying to provide a flexible tool to coordinate any Web service over Internet.

3   Coordinating Web Services

To make possible the coordination among services in an Internet-architecture, the proposed solution has been designed and implemented as a new support-service to provide coordination functionality. Using this new service, distributed services over Internet could communicate and synchronize among them. This coordination service has been built in accordance with the Web-service philosophy for making easier its integration into open architectures: coordination functionality must be accessible via ubiquitous Internet protocols and data format, such as

HTTP and XML; its open interface must hide the implementation details of the service, such as the hardware or software platform on which it is implemented or the programming language in which is written; and it must encourage a flexible and loosely-coupled interaction among Web services.

3.1   A Coordination Model for Distributed Environments

Before building the service, a coordination model for representing supported interactions must be defined. However, it has not been considered the possibility of creating a new model starting from scratch because there are some proposed solutions that can be used as starting points (the creation of a new one should be a different objective and involve other research areas different from our focus). A distributed shared memory (DSM) model for inter-process communication has been selected. This model provides the illusion of a shared memory allowing communicating processes to be uncoupled logically, temporally, and spatially. A well-known DSM model is the Generative Communication [17,7]. It is based on a so-called blackboard that is used as a shared data space. Entities communicate by putting messages into the blackboard, which can be retrieved later by other entities asking for a certain template message. In the model, senders do not have any prior knowledge about receivers and vice versa. This uncoupling is necessary in an open environment, such as Internet, because it is very important to reduce the shared knowledge between different entities to the minimum. Moreover, this model presents another basic advantage, entities can be replaced or added without adapting or announcing other entities.

The Generative Communication model is based on writings into and readings from a shared space. But it has a failure if writing and reading processes work in a hostile and not reliable environment, such as Internet. The reading operations are blocked if no desired message is available into the space yet. Besides, they may involve long waits.

An event-based approach suggests the possibility of improving the collection of operations proposed by the Communication Generative model, adding a more reactive coordination style. Processes subscribe their interest in receiving event notifications when other writing process insert specific messages into the shared space, instead of being blocked until messages are received.

This communication style, which is very prevalent for distributed systems [9], makes easier and loosely coupling communications [27]. Furthermore, this event-based communication style allows to model asynchronous data communications, identifying a read operation from the space as a subscription and a non-blocked waiting for the event notification.

3.2   Building the Coordination Service

A Java implementation of the Generative Communication model, called JavaSpaces Technology[15], has been used for building the coordination service. In JavaSpaces a collection of processes may cooperate via the flow of Java objects into and out of one network-accessible shared space. Besides, the Jini Distributed

Event model is incorporated into JavaSpace for firing events when entries that match templates are written into a space. It allows to react to the arrival of entries as they are placed in a space.

The built coordination Web-service encapsulates one or more spaces implemented by JavaSpaces, and provides through its interface the proposed operations by the extended Generative Communication model. In order to coordinate Web services through Internet, these operations are accessible through HTTP protocol.

Distributed services cooperate among them inserting and retrieving messages into/from the encapsulated space using the HTTP operations provided by the coordination service interface. Exchanged messages are encoded in XML format, and producing and consuming services must understand their content. Standards which define how to express the exchanged data (such as the MLP proposed by LIF that defines XML-Schemas for location, alarm or location-event data) are used for achieving this syntactic interoperability.

4   Design and Implementation of the Coordination Web-Service

According with the ideas proposed before, a coordination web-service has been implemented and tested in the LBS context. Its kernel consists of three software components (see fig. 2):

XML-Based Space Component. This component has been implemented as a Remote Method Invocation (RMI) server over the technological base of JavaSpaces. Its interface provides a collection of operations for writing XML-messages into and reading them from an interaction space and being notified of the writing of a new XML-message into the encapsulated space, according to the previously model presented.

The encapsulated interaction space is a Java space provided by the JavaSpaces implementation (see fig. 3). It allows storing and retrieving Java objects. Therefore, the XML-messages must be internally stored as Java objects. A generic object, called XMLEntry, has been defined for representing an XML-message. This object is able to parser the XML-message and stores the information of its nodes and vice versa, restoring the original XML-message.

The main problem to solve by the use of JavaSpaces is how to specify XML-templates for retrieving XML-messages from the space. The matching rules of JavaSpaces say that a template object and an inserted object can potentially match only if (1) they are from the same class and (2) for each field that is not wildcards in the template object, it must have the same value as its corresponding field in the inserted object. These rules have been extended for working with XML-messages: the XML-Schema is the class of an XML-message, and each node of the message is a field. At the present, simple Schemas are only considered. But in the future, a subset of the XQL language specification will be incorporated

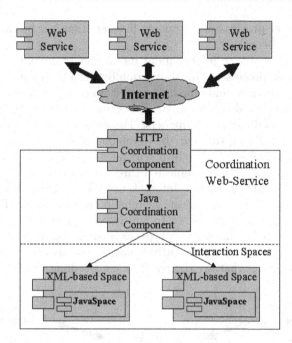

Fig. 2. Software Components of the coordination kernel

to the matching rules for supporting more complex XML queries. XQL is a path expression based query language proposed to the W3C query workshop (http://www.w3.org/TandS/QL/QL98/pp/xql.html).

Java Coordination Component. This Java component is the core of the coordination service. It has two different interfaces: Basic Coordination Interface (BCI), which provides the collection of writing and reading operations proposed by the Generative Communication model and encourages a cooperative style based on blocking readings; and Reactive Coordination Interface (RCI), whose operations allow a process advertising its interest to generate a specific type of XML-messages, publishing the advertised XML-messages and subscribing its interest to receive XML-messages of a specific type, encouraging a reactive style of cooperation among processes.

When an external process invokes an operation of the interface, a proxy of the invoker process is created inside the component for representing it (see fig. 3). External processes delegate their coordination tasks to their respective internal proxies, which cooperate among them exchanging XML-messages through one or more XML-based Spaces. Therefore, the coordination among external processes happens among their internal proxies, which communicate them the cooperation result. According to the invoked operation, a proxy expert on communication, synchronization or reactive behaviour is created. Proxies has been implemented as Java process able to act as clients of XML-based spaces for exchanging messages with another proxies and as remote listeners that can be called by spaces when a matching occurs.

Proxies must be able to inform about its internal state and to push data to respective external processes. This connection between both must be established when the proxy is created and remained until it is destroyed. The technique used to connect each other depends on the executing environment where is being used the Java Coordination Component. For example, if a collection of Java processes are cooperating through the developed coordination component and both are running inside a same Java Virtual Machine (JVM), processes and their respective proxies can be connected through message passing. However, in a distributed environment, such as Internet, the HTTP streaming technique can be used to connect them. It consists of remaining open an HTTP connection to push fresh data from the proxy to the remote process (see fig. 3). These processes may even be simple HTML-pages able to receive JavaScript events (for more details, http://www.pushlets.com/). In this case, exchanged data are the XML-messages that are the result of its coordination task.

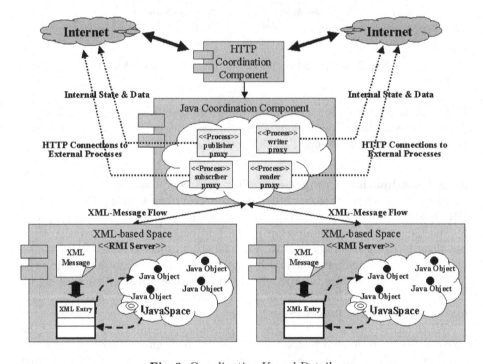

Fig. 3. Coordination Kernel Details

HTTP Coordination Component. This component plays as a web-accessible interface of the Java Coordination Component previously presented, providing through its HTTP interface the same collection of operations. This interface allows web-applications to cooperate independently of the hardware and software platform where they are running and independently of the programming language in which they are written.

The core of this component has been implemented as a Java Servlet, a Java program that resides and executes on a Web-Server, in this case on Apache Server (http://www.apache.org/) using Tomcat as a servlet container (http://jakarta.apache.org/tomcat/).

5   Benefits of the Proposed Approach

This section presents how the proposed coordination Web-service is able to solve the identified communication problems among Location Services and other distributed GIS services:

1. Spaces encapsulated into the coordination service are persistent and messages may be indefinitely stored into it. Therefore, Location Services can use it as a persistent repository of location data writing received locations from the mobile devices into it.
2. Many distributed services are simultaneously able to access to the coordination service for reading a stored message, such as a location data. So, a location that has been requested and stored into the coordination service may be shared by many consuming services.
3. The publishing and subscribing operations provided by the coordination service's interface support an asynchronous interaction model. It allows time-uncoupled interactions between producing and consuming processes.
4. Distributed services can be subscribed for retrieving messages instead of being making constant readings over the coordination service, being the server who has the notification-based initiative.

6   Conclusions and Future Work

In this work it has been presented an architectural model for organizing Web services and an implementation of it based on standards in the context of the LBS. Despite the lack of problems from a conceptual point of view, real restrictions arise when distributed services must work together harmoniously. For resolving them, it is proposed a coordination Web-service implemented using Java and Internet technologies. The coordination functionality provided by the service is orthogonal to the computing functionality offered by the coordinated entities. This fact keeps the independence between the computing and coordination models.

Open research issues are trying (1) to discover the real potential of the XML language to express synchronization restrictions and work flows among Web services, and (2) to add a new component that integrates thesaurus and ontologies for supporting the semantic interoperability among Web services. The underlying idea is to extend the concept of matching rules in the way that different values and XML representations will match if correspond to the same concept [22,30].

Finally, it is important to have a formal instrument for reasoning upon the behaviour of coordinated distributed-services and the coordination service. From a formal point of view, Petri nets are the most attractive formalism for modelling concurrent system that allows formal analysis, graphic representation and the execution/simulation of the system models. In this sense, advanced software development approaches for modelling, implementing and reasoning upon open parallel and distributed systems are based on principles presented in this paper, that is, concurrent object-orientation, generative communication, and Petri nets. In [20] it is presented a Petri net formalism to provide semantics for the Objective Linda language, and modelling the internal behaviour of concurrent objects; and in [5] it is presented transition merging as the main mechanism to represent the interaction between concurrent objects, providing a symmetric form of communication very close to generative communication that allows the cooperation of an arbitrary number of entities, and no direction of communication.

Acknowledgment. The basic technology of this work has been partially supported by the Spanish Ministry of Science and Technology through projects TIC2000-1568-C03-01, TIC2000-0048-P4-02 and FIT-0700002000B270827 from the National Plan for Scientific Research, Development and Technology Innovation, co-supported by FEDER resources.

References

1. OpenGIS Project Document 01-065, *Web feature server implementation specification (version 0.0.14)*, Tech. report, OpenGIS Consortium Inc, 2001.
2. OpenGIS Project Document 02-112, *The OpenGIS abstract specification. Topic12: OpenGIS service architecture (version 4.3)*, Tech. report, OpenGIS Consortium Inc, 2002.
3. OpenGIS Project Document 99-077r4, *OpenGIS Web map server interface specification (version 1.0)*, Tech. report, OpenGIS Consortium Inc, 2000.
4. P. Álvarez, J.A. Bañares, P.R. Muro-Medrano, and F.J. Zarazaga, *Integration of location based services for field support in CRM systems*, GeoInformatics **5** (2002), no. July/August, 36–39.
5. J.A. Bañares, P.R. Muro-Medrano, J.L. Villarroel, and F.J. Zarazaga, *Object-oriented programming and Petri nets*, Lecture Notes in Computer Science, no. 2001, ch. KRON: Knowledge Engineering Approach Based on the Integration of CPSs with Objects, pp. 355–374, Springer Verlag, Berlin Heidelberg 2001, 2001.
6. S. Burbeck, *The tao of e-business services. The evolution of Web applications into service-oriented components with Web-services*, Available in http://www-4.ibm.com/software/developer/library/ws-tao/index.html, October 2000.
7. N. Carriero and D. Gelernter, *Linda in context*, Communications of the ACM **32** (1989), no. 4, 444–458.

8. N. Carriero and D. Gelernter, *A computational model of everything*, Communications of the ACM **44** (2001), no. 11, 77–81.
9. A. Carzaniga, E. Di Nitto, D.S. Rosenblum, and A. Wolf, *Issues in supporting event-based architectural styles*, 3rd International Software Architecture Workshop (Orlando FL, USA), November 1998, pp. 17–20.
10. H.M. Deitel, P.J. Deitel, and T.R. Nieto, *Internet and world wide Web. How to program*, Pentice Hall, 2000.
11. V. Dessard, *GML & Web feature server. The baseline for online geoservices*, GeoInformatics **5** (2002), no. March, 38–41.
12. ESRI, *What are location services? the GIS perspective*, Available in http://www.geojava.com, December 2000.
13. P. Fernández, R. Béjar, M.A. Latre, J. Valiño, J.A. Bañares, and P.R. Muro-Medrano, *Web mapping interoperability in practice, a Java approach guided by the OpenGis Web map server interface specification*, EC-GIS. 2000, 6th European Commission GI & GIS Workshop (Lyon, France), May 2000.
14. P. Fingar, *Component-based frameworks for e-commerce*, Communications of the ACM **43** (2000), no. 10, 61–66.
15. E. Freeman, S. Hupfer, and K. Arnold, *Javaspaces. Principles, patterns, and practice*, Addison Wesley, 1999.
16. F. Friday, N. Davies, and E. Catterall, *Supporting service discovery, querying and interaction in ubiquitous computing environments*, Second ACM International Workshop on Data engineering for wireless and mobile access, Santa Barbara, California (USA), ACM Press, 2001, pp. 7–13.
17. D. Gelernter, *Generative communication in Linda*, ACM Transactions on Programming Languages and Systems **7** (1985), no. 1, 80–112.
18. G. Glass, *The Web services (r)evolution. Applying Web services to applications*, Available in http://www-4.ibm.com/software/developer/library/ws-peer1.html, November 2000.
19. S. Graham, S. Simeonov, T. Boubez, D. Davis, G. Daniels, Y. Nakamura, and R. Neyama, *Building Web services with Java. Making sense of XML, SOAP, WSDL, and UDDI*, SAMS, 2002.
20. T. Holvoet and P. Verbaeten, *Object-oriented programming and Petri nets*, Lecture Notes in Computer Science, no. 2001, ch. Using Petri Nets for Specifyin Active Objects and Generative Communication, pp. 38–72, Springer Verlag, Berlin Heidelberg 2001, 2001.
21. G. Larsen, *Component-based enterprise frameworks*, Communications of the ACM **43** (2000), no. 10, 25–26.
22. E. Mata, J.A. Bañares, J. Gutiérrez, P.R. Muro-Medrano, and J. Rubio, *Semantic disambiguation of thesaurus as a mechanism to facilitate multilingual and thematic interoperability of geographical information catalogues*, Proceedings of the 5th AGILE Conference on Geographic Information Science (Palma de Mallorca, Spain), April 2002, pp. 61–66.
23. M. Mattsson, J. Bosch, and E. Fayad, *Framework integration. problems, causes, solutions*, Communications of the ACM **42** (1999), no. 10, 81–87.
24. P.R. Muro-Medrano, D. Infante, J. Guilló, F.J. Zarazaga, and J.A. Ba nares, *A CORBA infrastructure to provide distributed GPS data in real time to GIS applications*, Computers, Environment and Urban Systems **23** (1999), 271–285.
25. H. Niedzwiadek, *All businesses are in pursuit of Java location services*, Available in http://www.geojava.com/, January 2000.
26. OpenLS, *A request for technology. In support of an open location services (OpenLS) testbed*, Tech. report, OpenGIS Consortium Inc, 2000.

27. D.S. Rosenblum and A. Wolf, *A design framework for Internet-scale event observation and notification*, Proceedings of the sixth European Software Engineering Conference (Zurich, Switzerland) (M. Jazayeri and H. Schauer, eds.), Springer-Verlag, September 1997, pp. 344–360.

28. J.C. Thill, *Geographic information systems for transportation in perspective*, Transportation Research Part C: Emerging Technologies **8** (2000), no. Issues 1-6, February-December, 3–12.

29. J. VanderMeer, *Ubiquitous wireless location interoperability*, Available in http://www.directionsmag.com/, July 2002.

30. U. Visser and H. Stuckenschmidt, *Interoperability in GIS. Enabling technologies*, Proceedings of the 5th AGILE Conference on Geographic Information Science (Palma de Mallorca, Spain), April 2002, pp. 291–297.

31. F.J. Zarazaga, P. Álvarez, J.A. Bañares, J. Nogueras, J. Valiño, and P.R. Muro-Medrano, *Examples of vehicle location systems using CORBA-based distributed real-time GPS data and services*, Computers, Environment and Urban Systems **25** (2001), 293–305.

32. A.K. Ziliaskopoulos and S. Travis Waller, *An Internet-based geographic information system that integrates data,models and users for transportation application*, Transportation Research Part C: Emerging Technologies **8** (2000), no. Issues 1-6, February-December, 427–444.

Critical Evaluation of the EJB Transaction Model

Raul Silaghi and Alfred Strohmeier

Software Engineering Laboratory
Swiss Federal Institute of Technology in Lausanne
CH-1015 Lausanne EPFL, Switzerland

{Raul.Silaghi,Alfred.Strohmeier}@epfl.ch

Abstract. Enterprise JavaBeans is a widely-used technology that aims at supporting distributed component-based applications written in Java. One of the key features of the Enterprise JavaBeans architecture is the support of declarative distributed transactions, without requiring explicit coding. In this paper, after a brief introduction of the concepts and mechanisms related to the EJB Transaction Model, we provide guidelines for their consistent use. We then evaluate the EJB Transaction Model on an Auction System case study. The encountered limitations are presented, and possible work-arounds are proposed for the auction system. We conclude with suggestions for enhancing the current EJB Transaction Model.

Keywords. EJB, Enterprise JavaBeans, Transactions, Concurrency, Deadlock, Auction System.

1 Introduction

For three decades, transaction processing has been a cornerstone of modern information technology: it is an indispensable asset in banking, stock trading, airline reservation systems, travel agencies, and so on. With the new millennium's proliferation of e-Commerce applications, business-to-business workflows, and broad forms of Web-based e-Services, transactional information systems are becoming even more important.

Transactions are a classic software structure for managing concurrent accesses to global data and for maintaining data consistency in the presence of failures. The notion of transaction was first introduced in database systems in order to correctly handle concurrent updates of data and to provide fault tolerance with respect to hardware failures [1]. A transaction groups an arbitrary number of operations on data objects (also referred to as *transactional objects*), making the operations as a whole appear indivisible to the application and with respect to other concurrent transactions. The classic transaction scheme relies on three standard operations: *begin*, *commit*, and *abort*, which mark the boundaries of a transaction. The properties of transactions are referred to as the ACID properties: *Atomicity, Consistency, Isolation,* and *Durability* [1].

Support for transactions is an essential component of the Enterprise JavaBeans architecture. The Enterprise JavaBeans architecture supports only *flat transactions*, despite the fact that the classic transaction model has been extended a long time ago to support nested transactions [2], and thus provides a more flexible support for concurrency and recovery.

N. Guelfi et al. (Eds.): FIDJI 2002, LNCS 2604, pp. 15–28, 2003.

By simply setting certain attributes in a deployment descriptor, a developer can make his or her enterprise bean be executed within a client's transaction context, within a new transaction context, or within no transaction context. This power of freeing the developer from writing transactional code, not to say to write his or her own transaction service, comes nevertheless at a price. The simplicity in using the EJB Transactional Model comes along with a certain rigidity that restricts the ways in which transactions may be used and constrains the developer to stick to a certain manner of building distributed transaction-enabled applications.

For most applications, the EJB Transaction Model is adequate and can be used in a straightforward way. For other applications, however, certain work-arounds are necessary and a very precise configuration of the deployment descriptors is needed. Based on a concrete case study, i.e., the auction system, we will present in this paper the limitations that were encountered in the EJB Transaction Model, pointing out certain features that would enhance the current model and would make it more open and flexible.

The rest of the paper is organized as follows: Section 2 provides an overview of the Enterprise JavaBeans Transaction Model, introducing concepts that define how transactions are handled and discussing some issues in using them; Section 3 briefly describes the auction system case study; Section 4 presents the implementation solution for the auction system on top of EJBs, highlighting some problems that may arise and proposing work-arounds when possible; Section 5 discusses some features that are missing in the current EJB Transaction Model, and Section 6 draws some conclusions.

2   Enterprise JavaBeans Transactions

This section presents an overview of the Enterprise JavaBeans Transaction Model, setting the scene for the analysis that will be performed on the auction case study.

The Enterprise JavaBeans architecture [3] is a component-based architecture for building distributed business applications. It aims at simplifying the development of complex systems in Java by defining six distinct roles in the application development and deployment life cycle. These roles may be performed by different parties.

One of the roles is the *Enterprise Bean Provider*. Typically performed by an application domain expert, the Bean Provider builds reusable components, called *enterprise beans*, that implement the business methods without concern for the distribution, concurrency, persistence, transaction, security, and other non-business-specific aspects of the application. Enterprise beans are further deployed in Containers on Application Servers. The *EJB Container Provider* together with the *EJB Server Provider* are the ones supposed to be experts in distributed systems, concurrency, persistence, transactions and security. They must deliver tools for the deployment of enterprise beans, and a run-time system that provides the deployed beans with transactions and security management, distribution, management of resources, and other services. The other roles defined by the EJB specification are the *System Administrator*, the *Application Assembler*, and finally the *Deployer*.

Even without knowing anything about transactions, the Bean Provider must somehow tell the Container which beans, or which methods of a bean, or which segments of code, must be executed under the control of a transaction. The Bean Provider can choose between *bean-managed transaction demarcation*, in which case the enterprise bean code demarcates transactions using the `javax.transaction.UserTrans-`

`action` interface, or *container-managed transaction demarcation*, in which case the Container demarcates transactions following the instructions received from the Bean Provider in the *deployment descriptor*. These instructions can be set for the enterprise bean as a whole (and they will apply to all enterprise bean methods) or selectively for individual methods in a bean.

The Enterprise JavaBeans architecture defines three types of enterprise bean objects: *session*, *entity*, and *message-driven* objects. Due to their one-to-one mapping to tables in a database, entity beans are the most interesting for concurrency and transactions. As a consequence, we will concentrate only on entity beans for the remainder of this paper.

We will introduce now some attributes that are part of the EJB Transaction Model and that guide the Container in providing transaction support. Some issues in using these attributes along with the concurrency support offered by the Container will also be presented.

2.1   Setting Transactional Attributes in the Deployment Descriptor

The EJB specification [3] does not require enterprise bean and EJB client developers to write any special code to use transactions. Instead, the Container manages transactions based on two deployment descriptor attributes associated with each enterprise bean or with each enterprise bean method in particular: the *transaction* attribute, and the *transaction isolation level* attribute.

While transaction attributes are well standardized by the EJB specification, the transaction isolation levels are not yet standardized. What the specification proposes, however, are a set of guidelines that should be followed by the EJB Container Providers. In what comes next we will present the transaction attributes and the transaction isolation levels as supported by the IBM WebSphere Application Server [5].

2.1.1   Setting the Transaction Attribute

The transaction attribute defines the transactional manner in which the Container invokes enterprise bean methods. The valid values for this attribute in decreasing order of transaction strictness are introduced in Table 1 together with their effect on the transaction context.

Table 1. Effect of the Bean's Transaction Attribute on the Transaction Context

Transaction attribute	Client transaction context	Bean transaction context
TX_MANDATORY	No transaction	Not allowed
	Client transaction	Client transaction
TX_REQUIRED	No transaction	New transaction
	Client transaction	Client transaction
TX_REQUIRES_NEW	No transaction	New transaction
	Client transaction	New transaction
TX_SUPPORTS	No transaction	No transaction
	Client transaction	Client transaction
TX_NOT_SUPPORTED	No transaction	No transaction
	Client transaction	No transaction

While the second column in Table 1 indicates whether or not the bean method is invoked from within a client transaction context, the third column indicates the exact transaction context in which the bean method will be executed, e.g., the client transaction context, a new transaction context, or no transaction context.

Another transaction attribute that is not presented in Table 1 is TX_BEAN_MANAGED; it notifies the Container that the bean class directly handles transaction demarcation by using the javax.transaction.UserTransaction interface. This attribute can only be set for session and message-driven beans, and not for entity beans, because entity beans must always be designed with container-managed transaction demarcation.

2.1.2   Setting the Transaction Isolation Level Attribute

The transaction isolation level determines how strongly one transaction is isolated from another. Within a transactional context, the isolation level associated with the first method invocation becomes the required isolation level for all other methods invoked within that transaction. If a method is invoked with a different isolation level from that of the first method, an exception is thrown. This constraint is mainly imposed by the underlying databases because most resource managers interpret a change in the isolation level in the middle of a transaction as an implicit *sync point*, committing the changes done so far (even if the transaction has not committed yet).

The possible values that can be set for the isolation level attribute (from strongest to weakest) are: TRANSACTION_SERIALIZABLE, TRANSACTION_REPEATABLE_READ, TRANSACTION_READ_COMMITTED, and TRANSACTION_READ_UNCOMMITTED.

None of these values permits two transactions to update the same data concurrently; one transaction must end before another one can update the same data. The values determine only how locks are managed for *reading* data. However, risks to consistency can arise from read operations when a transaction does further work based on the values read. For example, if one transaction is updating a piece of data and a second transaction is permitted to read that data after it has been changed but before the updating transaction ends, the reading transaction can make a decision based on a change that is eventually rolled back. Thus, the second transaction risks making a decision on transient data.

2.2   Issues in Using the EJB Transaction Model

Sequential Access within the same Transaction Context. An entity bean object may be accessed by multiple clients in the same transaction. A program A may start a transaction, and then call program B and program C in the same transaction context. If the programs B and C access the same entity bean object, the topology of the transaction creates a *diamond*. In this scenario, the programs B and C will access the entity object *sequentially*. Concurrent access to an entity object in the same transaction context would be considered an application programming error, and it would be handled in a Container-specific way.

The EJB specification requires that the Container provides support for *local diamonds*. In a local diamond, all components (here A, B, C, and the entity bean) are deployed in the same EJB Container. Distributed diamonds are not required to be supported by an EJB Container. However, if the EJB Container Provider chooses to support distributed diamonds, then the specification requires that it provides a consistent view of the entity bean's state within a transaction. Two ways of how this can be achieved are proposed in the specification.

Concurrent Access from Multiple Transactions. For concurrent access from multiple transactions, the EJB specification mentions two different strategies that the Container typically uses to achieve proper synchronization. In the first one, the Container acquires exclusive access to the entity object's state in the database. It activates a single instance of the entity bean and serializes the access from multiple transactions to this instance, as shown in Fig. 1.

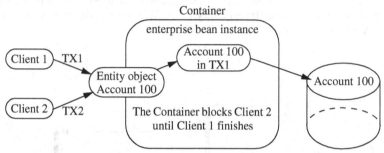

Fig. 1. Multiple clients can access the same entity object using a single instance

In the second one, the Container activates multiple instances of the entity bean, one for each transaction in which the entity object is being accessed, and relies on the underlying database to perform the transaction synchronization during the accessor method calls performed by the business methods, and by the ejbLoad, ejbCreate, ejbStore, and ejbRemove methods.

While the second strategy just passes the problem to the next in line, the first one might lead to deadlock, as presented in section 4.1.

Transaction Isolation Level Attribute Issues. The choice of the *transaction isolation level* attribute depends on several factors, which include: the acceptable level of risk to data consistency, the acceptable levels of concurrency and performance, the isolation levels supported by the underlying database. The first two factors are related. Decreasing the risk to consistency requires to decrease concurrency because reducing the risk to consistency requires holding locks for longer periods. The longer a lock is held on a piece of data, the longer concurrently running transactions must wait to access that data. The TRANSACTION_SERIALIZABLE value protects data by eliminating concurrent access to it. Conversely, the TRANSACTION_READ_UNCOMMITTED value allows the highest degree of concurrency but entails the greatest risk to consistency. These two factors need to be balanced appropriately depending on the application.

The third factor means that although the EJB specification allows one to request one of the four levels of transaction isolation, it is possible that the database being used in the application does not support all of the levels. Also, vendors of database products implement isolation levels differently, so the precise behavior of an application can vary from database to database.

Transaction Attribute Issues. Attention must be paid to the possible values of a transaction attribute. In particular, the TX_REQUIRES_NEW value, as shown in Table 1, directs the container to always invoke a bean method within a *new transaction context*, regardless of whether the client invokes the method within or outside of a transaction context. Please notice that by *"new transaction"* it is meant that a new, top-level transaction is started and no nesting, or overlapping is implied.

The scenario presented in Fig. 2 illustrates how misusing the TX_REQUIRES_NEW value for the transaction attribute might lead to the violation of the all-or-nothing property of transactions. We considered a bean method m1 with the transaction attribute set to TX_REQUIRED, and another bean method m2 with the transaction attribute set to TX_REQUIRES_NEW. For rendering the example more realistic, we supposed that the two methods belong to two different entity beans, deployed in different Containers on different Application Servers.

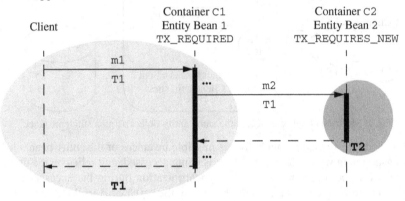

Fig. 2. Changing Transaction Contexts according to the Transaction Attribute

Imagine now that a client calls the bean method m1 from within a transaction context T1. Receiving the call to m1 together with the transaction context T1 that comes with the call, the container C1 follows the exact instructions found in the deployment descriptor for the invoked method, i.e., it will execute method m1 within the client transaction context T1 (see Table 1). When method m2 is called from within m1, the container C1 passes the transaction context with the invocation. Receiving the call to m2 together with the transaction context T1, it is the turn of the container C2 to follow the instructions found in the deployment descriptor for the invoked method, i.e., it will execute method m2 within a new transaction context. First of all, however, container C2 suspends the association of the transaction context T1 with the current thread, and only then, it will start a new top-level transaction T2 and it will invoke the business method m2. The container will resume the suspended transaction association after the business method m2 and the new transaction T2 have been completed.

In our example, performing certain operations in the new top-level transaction T2 will not guarantee the all-or-nothing property for T1. Why? Because once transaction T2 commits, there is no way to roll it back if later on transaction T1 aborts. The changes made on behalf of T2 will persist even if T1 rolls back. As a conclusion, all the operations that must be performed in a transaction context should not cross the boundaries of other transactions, not even if those transactions were created from within the main transaction. However, other operations that do not interfere with the main transaction could be invoked in separate transactions, e.g., garbage collection is independent of whether we commit or roll back our main transaction.

3   Case Study Description

The auction system is an example of an inherently dynamic, distributed, and concurrent application, with multiple auctions going on and with clients participating in several auctions at the same time. As a consequence, the auction system becomes an excellent case study for testing the performance of new transaction models, in our case the EJB Transaction Model.

The auction system runs on a set of computers connected via a network. Clients access the auction system from one of these computers. The system allows the clients to buy and sell items by means of auctions. In the *English auction*, which will be considered in this case study, the item for sale is put up for auction starting at a relatively low minimum price. Bidders are then allowed to place their bids until the auction closes. Sometimes, the duration of the auction is fixed in advance, e.g., 30 days, or, alternatively, a time-out value, which resets with every new bid, can be associated with the auction.

Any client interested in using the auction system services must first register with the system by filling out a *registration form*. All registered users must deposit a certain amount of money or some other security with the auction system at registration time. The money is transferred to an account under control of the auction system.

Once the registration process is completed, the client becomes a *member* of the auction system. Whenever a member wants to make use of the services provided s/he must first *login* to the system using his or her username and password, provided at registration time. Once logged, the member may choose from one of the following possibilities: start a new auction, browse the current auctions, participate in one or several ongoing auctions by placing bids, or deposit or withdraw money from his or her account. To bid on an item the participant simply has to enter the amount of the bid. A valid bid must fulfill all the following requirements:

- The bidder has sufficient funds on his or her account.
- The member placing the bid is not the member having started the auction.
- The auction has not expired.
- The new bid is higher than the current highest bid. If nobody has placed a bid yet, then the bid must be at least as high as the minimum price requested by the seller.

If the auction closes and at least one valid bid has been made, then the auction ends successfully and the participant having placed the highest bid wins the auction. The money is withdrawn from the account of the winning participant and deposited on the account of the seller, minus a commission, which is deposited on the account of the auction system for the provided services.

If an auction closes, and no participant has placed a valid bid, then the auction was unsuccessful and no charge is required for the provided services.

The auction system must be able to tolerate failures. Crashes of any of the host computers must not corrupt the state of the auction system, e.g., money transfer from one account to the other should not be executed partially.

4   The EJB Solution for the Auction System

In this section, we will present how the auction system was implemented on top of EJBs. Certain design decisions will be motivated by pointing out limitations that were encountered in the EJB Transaction Model. A deadlock situation that can arise in the EJB Solution will be presented and some possible work-arounds will be proposed.

Maybe the most important requirement for auctions is that they must be fault-tolerant. All-or-nothing semantics must be strictly adhered to. Either there is a winner, and the money has been transferred from the account of the winning bidder to the seller's account and the commission has been deposited on the auction system account, or the auction was unsuccessful, in which case the balances of the involved accounts remain untouched. Allowing the possibility of a total rollback while an auction is active and participants are placing their bids, would mean to place everything in a long-living transaction that would commit when there is a winner, or abort if something goes wrong during the lifespan of the auction. This idea is not at all in the spirit of the EJB Transaction Model, where transactions are supposed to last small time units; in this way, they do not block access to transactional objects from other ongoing concurrent transactions for a long time period. Since the auction system is inherently concurrent and very dynamic, with multiple auctions going on and with clients placing bids in several auctions, a long-living transaction acting on behalf of an auction would block the access to the accounts of several participants, thus blocking the other ongoing concurrent auctions from advancing.

Following the EJB specification and having in mind all the considerations presented in section 2.2, the solution that we came up with for implementing the auction system is to break the whole lifespan of an auction into small operations and execute them within separate transactions when their time comes.

Fig. 3 presents the entity beans used to model the auction system. Each entity bean represents an object view of data in different tables in the same or different databases: MemberBean handles the personal information of the members, AccountBean keeps the evidence of the accounts in the system, and AuctionBean manages the auctions in the system.

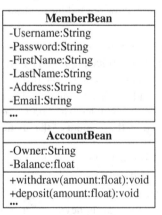

Fig. 3. The Entity Beans in the EJB Solution

In most of the cases, deposit and withdraw operations can very well be executed in two different transactions. A member would like to deposit some money in his or her account and the system will perform this operation within a transaction. Later on, s/he would like to withdraw some money from his or her account and the system will perform this new operation within a new transaction. In this case, a new transaction is needed because the two operations are not at all related and there is no reason of undoing the deposit operation if the withdraw operation fails.

However, when several operations are somehow inter-connected for achieving a certain goal, they can no longer be executed in separate transactions. They have to be executed in the same transaction for the sake of preserving the ACID properties. This is the case of the placeBid method which encapsulates small operations that have all to be executed in the same transaction context for preserving a consistent state of the auctions. When a participant places a bid in an auction we have to withdraw from his or her account the corresponding amount of money, protecting in this way the system from participants that would overdraw their accounts by placing bids in several auctions without actually having all that money. However, when s/he gets overbidden in the same auction, we are required to give the money back and make a new withdraw from the new bidder's account corresponding to the amount of the new bid. One possible solution to achieve this behavior is sketched in Fig. 4.

```
void AuctionBean::placeBid(bidder:String, bid:float) {
    ...
    //Withdraw the bidded amount of money
    getAccount(bidder).withdraw(bid);

    //Give back the money to the previous highest bidder
    getAccount(getHighestBidder()).deposit(getHighestBid());

    //Update the information in the AuctionBean entity bean
    setHighestBidder(bidder);
    setHighestBid(bid);
    ...
}
```

Fig. 4. The PlaceBid Method of the AuctionBean

In the placeBid method, we withdraw first from the new bidder's account the amount of money s/he wanted to bid, we give the money back to the previous highest bidder, and then we update the information in the current AuctionBean object, i.e., the new highest bidder and the new highest bid. If something goes wrong somewhere within this method, the new bid should not be considered valid and the state of all implicated transactional objects (here the AuctionBean object and the two AccountBean objects) should be restored. In order to have the Container execute the whole placeBid method within the same transaction context, the *transaction attribute* of all the involved enterprise beans must be configured accordingly. For this particular example we should have: TX_REQUIRED for the placeBid, setHighestBidder, and setHighestBid methods of the AuctionBean; and TX_REQUIRED for the withdraw, and deposit methods of the AccountBean.

In this way, when the placeBid method is first invoked, a new transaction context will be created (supposing that it is not already called from within a transaction context), and it will be passed around to all the other method invocations that are made within `placeBid`. If one of the invoked methods calls at its turn other methods of other enterprise beans, then those methods should also be configured with the transaction attribute set to `TX_REQUIRED` in the deployment descriptors of those beans.

Based on these considerations, the *English Auction*, as implemented on top of EJBs, is graphically presented in Fig. 5. We identified three main operations that must be executed in a transactional way: the creation of a new auction, placing a bid in an auction, and ending an auction.

By simply filling an *item form*, Member 1 will create a new `AuctionBean` object within a transaction `T1`, and, automatically, a new row will be added in the table of all auctions. In a few seconds the displays of all the logged members will be refreshed, and thus, they will see the new proposed auction. Member 2 decides to participate, and places his bid. Once the method `placeBid` has been invoked on the `AuctionBean` object, four operations will be executed within the same transaction context (`T2`) on different beans. First we will `withdraw` the new bid from the account of member 2. Then some money will be returned to the previous highest bidder (this is not the case here since member 2 is the first bidder). Finally, the information concerning the current highest bidder and current highest bid will be updated in the `AuctionBean` object. Later on, Member 3 decides to overbid member 2 in the same auction, thus it will invoke the `placeBid` method on the same `AuctionBean` object. Within the same transaction context (`T3`) we will: withdraw the new bid from the member 3's account, give back the money that member 2 has previously paid, and update the information in the `AuctionBean` object. In our example we considered that no other member overbids member 3. Once the auction closes, the `endAuction` method is invoked on the `AuctionBean` object. Here we considered that the member that created the auction closes it by invoking `endAuction`. If the auction terminates due to time limit, then it will be a separate auction system thread that will call the `endAuction` method. At least two op-

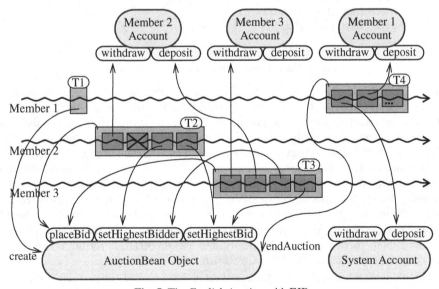

Fig. 5. The *English Auction* with EJBs

erations must be executed within the same transaction context (here T4) when closing an auction: deposit a certain percentage of the amount of the final bid on the system account as a commission, and deposit the rest of the amount of the final bid on the seller's account (here member 1's account). Another operation that might also be performed when an auction finishes is to mark it as closed, so no other bids can be made.

4.1   A Possible Deadlock in the EJB Solution

Due to all these withdraw-deposit operations that have to be done on several accounts, a deadlock situation might appear in the EJB Solution.

Consider for instance two auctions and two participants in both auctions. Suppose now that participant A is the current highest bidder in Auction 2, and that participant B is the current highest bidder in Auction 1, and that both overbid each other, i.e., participant A overbids participant B in Auction 1, and participant B overbids participant A in Auction 2. As already presented in the previous section, the placeBid method, together with all the four operations that are chained inside it, will be executed within the same transaction context. Fig. 6 presents the scenario where the placeBid method invoked by participant A is executed in the transaction context T1, and the placeBid method invoked by participant B is executed in the transaction context T2. We represented the last two operations inside the placeBid method, i.e., setHighestBidder and setHighestBid, under the name of update.

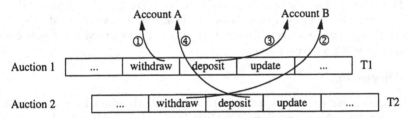

Fig. 6. Deadlock Situation in the EJB Solution

Due to the isolation between transactions (see section 2.2), when the withdraw operation will be performed on account A (Fig. 6 ①) from within transaction T1, access to this account will be locked until the transaction T1 finishes. The same happens with the withdraw operation on account B (Fig. 6 ②), which locks access to account B until the transaction T2 finishes. This situation ends in a deadlock since the two deposit operations (Fig. 6 ③ , ④) will wait for their target accounts to be unlocked, which will never happen since neither one of the two transactions can finish.

4.2   Proposed Work-Arounds for Avoiding the Deadlock Situation

One solution to avoid the deadlock situation would be to have a certain *random timeout* after which we abort a transaction. In our example, once transaction T1 aborts, transaction T2 can continue and commit. In this case, the participant A will have to re-issue a call to the placeBid method and hope that this time it would work.

Another solution is to have ordered access to the involved accounts. The order is dictated by the account numbers that are involved in the same placeBid method. We will introduce a new operation, called dummy, that will be the first operation executed inside a placeBid method. The dummy operation will target the account with the smallest number with the only purpose of getting its lock. If, for example, we have to `withdraw` from Account 2 and `deposit` in Account 1, then a `dummy` operation will be performed first on the account that has the smallest number (see Fig. 7).

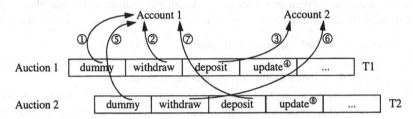

Fig. 7. Proposed Work-around for the Deadlock Situation

In this way, if two `placeBid` methods are dealing with the same two accounts, like in the deadlock situation, they will both try to perform first the `dummy` operation on the same account, i.e., the one with the smallest number, trying to get its lock until the end of the enclosing transaction. One of the transactions will get the lock first. The other one will have to wait, thus not performing other operations on other accounts and not blocking other transactional objects. The battle is done once, at the beginning, and after that everything should go on smoothly without other blockings.

The order in which the operations inside the two `placeBid` methods will be executed changes due to the anticipated blocking behaviour introduced by the `dummy` operation. In Fig. 7 we used encircled numbers to show the exact order in which those operations are going to be executed.

5   Discussion

In this section, we will discuss the drawbacks of the EJB Solution for the auction system, highlighting those limitations in the EJB Transaction Model that led to these drawbacks. We will also point out certain features that would enhance the current EJB Transaction Model.

First of all, the proposed EJB Solution for the auction system does not provide the desired *all-or-nothing* semantics of transactions. In an ideal case, we can imagine having one long-living transaction for each auction, which can be rolled back at any time while the auction is still open, returning the system in the previous consistent state. Such a solution is proposed by [7], where the same auction system is modeled on top of open multithreaded transactions (OMTTs) [8] in a very natural way. In the EJB Solution, we can roll back only small increments. For example, once a new `AuctionBean` object is created, there is no possibility to undo it, only by explicitly removing it from the table in the database. The same thing happens with the `placeBid` method. We can roll it back if something happens while inside, but once it finishes, there is no way to come back to the previous state. With this approach, the system is always in a consistent intermediate state and it will even persist to system crashes, which is not the case for the OMTT Solution, where everything is lost and has to be restarted from the beginning. In the EJB Solution, after a system crash, all the information about the created auctions, about the current highest bidders and bids in all auctions, about the balances of all accounts, will simply be restored from the corresponding tables in the database(s). In this way, all bids made by a member are remembered and s/he can continue exactly from the same state where the system crashed. So, we could say that fault tolerance is provided by the persistency of the underlying database, while in the OMTT Solution, fault tolerance is provided automatically by the underlying transaction support.

Due to the isolation between transactions, bean objects are locked until the transaction that has locked them commits or aborts. From this perspective, we can understand why the EJB Transaction Model does not encourage the usage of long-living transactions. A lot of bean objects can be involved in a long-living transaction, which can reduce system efficiency and throughput, as there is no support for partial rollbacks, early-release locks, savepoints, or compensating actions, like in Sagas [9]. It should be possible to release bean objects during a long-lasting transaction execution. Or, a method-commutativity table should be created for each bean, marking some methods as non-conflicting. This would increase the Container's knowledge about the bean, and, consequently, increase the potential for sharing a particular bean object with other transactions.

Another feature that is offered by OMTTs are nested transactions, which give the developer the possibility to make partial undos by rolling back a subtransaction and all its children, without causing abortion of the whole open multithreaded transaction. In the auction system, such partial undos are related to returning the money to a bidder once s/he gets overbidden. In the EJB Solution, we handle this by having compensation operations in the upcoming transaction. In the OMTT Solution, it is achieved using nested transactions. When a user places a bid, the money is withdrawn from his or her account inside a nested transaction. Later on, if someone places a higher bid, the money is returned to the account by simply aborting the nested transaction.

One step forward towards providing nested transactions in the EJB Transaction Model, would be to support abort-dependent and commit-dependent transactions. In this way, transactions would be able to change their behavior based on the state of another transaction. Once a transaction aborts, the corresponding abort-dependent transactions will also abort. A transaction commits if all its corresponding commit-dependent transactions have already committed. If applications are mostly based on transactions, it is desirable to express bindings and dependencies between them [10], [11].

The EJB specification is not clear regarding multithreaded transactions, contrary to the full support of multithreading in OMTTs. In the Java Transaction API (JTA) [12], however, it is mentioned that each thread has associated a transaction context, which is either *null* or refers to a specific global transaction. The transaction-to-thread association is managed transparently by the Transaction Manager. Multiple threads may concurrently be associated with the same global transaction. This can be achieved by creating or spawning threads from within an already existing transaction context. However, it is not clear how a newly created thread can be associated with a previously started transaction, i.e., how threads can join already existing transactions.

Some other limitations of the EJB Transaction Model that we will not enter into details in this paper are: transactions cannot manage their locks according to the application's requirements, the set of values for the transaction attribute is very limiting, bean methods cannot be associated with several transaction attributes, bean methods cannot be dynamically associated with a particular transaction attribute, no support for asynchronous operations, and no constraint for distributed diamond support.

6   Conclusions

Even if the EJB specification does not require the Bean Provider to have any programming knowledge for concurrency, transactions, and other services, s/he must first accomplish a detailed analysis of all the enterprise beans' methods before starting the configuration of all deployment descriptors. Any misuse of the values of the transaction and isolation level attributes might lead to incorrect applications. Changing the values defined by the Bean Provider for these two attributes is highly error-prone. Only the implementor of the bean knows exactly the semantics of the methods, and is qualified to select the appropriate policies.

By implementing the auction system on top of EJBs, a certain rigidity of the EJB Transaction Model was sensed. We discovered several limitations of the EJB Transaction Model and we proposed work-arounds when possible. A deadlock situation was identified in the EJB implementation, and some solutions to avoid it were proposed. We also presented certain features that are missing in the EJB Transaction Model and that, we believe, would enhance the current model and would make it more open and flexible.

References

[1]   Gray, J.; Reuter, A.: *Transaction Processing: Concepts and Techniques*. Morgan Kaufmann Publishers, San Mateo, California, 1993.

[2]   Moss, J. E. B.: *Nested Transactions, An Approach to Reliable Computing*. Ph.D. Thesis, MIT, Cambridge, April 1981.

[3]   Sun Microsystems: *Enterprise JavaBeans^{TM} Specification*, v2.0, August 2001.

[4]   Sun Microsystems: *Java^{TM} 2 Platform, Enterprise Edition Specification*, v1.4, Proposed Final Draft, August 2002.

[5]   IBM: *WebSphere® Application Server*. http://www.ibm.com/websphere/

[6]   Vachon, J.: *COALA: A Design Language for Reliable Distributed Systems*. Ph.D. Thesis #2302, Swiss Federal Institute of Technology, Lausanne, Switzerland, December 2000.

[7]   Kienzle, J.; Romanovsky, A.; Strohmeier, A.: *Auction System Design Using Open Multithreaded Transactions*. Proceedings of the 7th International Workshop on Object-Oriented Real-Time Dependable Systems, San Diego, California, USA, January 2002. IEEE Computer Society Press, Los Alamitos, CA, 2002, pp. 95–104.

[8]   Kienzle, J.: *Open Multithreaded Transactions: A Transaction Model for Concurrent Object-Oriented Programming*. Ph.D. Thesis #2393, Swiss Federal Institute of Technology, Lausanne, Switzerland, April 2001.

[9]   Garcia-Molina, H.; Salem, K.: *Sagas*. Proceedings of the SIGMod Annual Conference, San Francisco, California, USA, May 1987. ACM Press, pp. 249–259.

[10]   Elmagarmid, A. K.: *Database Transaction Models for Advanced Applications*. Morgan Kaufmann Publishers, 1992.

[11]   Jajodia, S.; Kerschberg, L.:*Advanced Transaction Models and Architectures*. Kluwer Academic Publishers, 1997.

[12]   Sun Microsystems: *Java^{TM} Transaction API (JTA) Specification*, v1.0.1, April 1999.

[13]   Sun Microsystems: *Java^{TM} Transaction Service (JTS) Specification*, v1.0, December 1999.

[14]   Software Engineering Laboratory: *Open Multithreaded Transactions - The Auction System Case Study*. http://lglwww.epfl.ch/research/omtt/auction.html

[15]   Weikum, G.; Vossen, G.: *Transactional Information Systems: Theory, Algorithms, and the Practice of Concurrency Control and Recovery*. Morgan Kaufmann Publishers, 2002.

Automated Prototyping of CORBA-Based Distributed Object-Oriented Systems

Stephan Philippi

Bielefeld University, Faculty of Technology,
P.O.Box 100131, 33501 Bielefeld, Germany
stephan.philippi@uni-bielefeld.de

Abstract. The CORBA international standard is developed by the Object Management Group to provide means for handling the inherent complexity of distributed systems development. On the one hand, the availability of a standardized middleware which decouples distribution related aspects from the application development is undoubtedly very helpful in heterogeneous settings. On the other hand, the constantly growing complexity of the CORBA standard is accompanied by only basic support in todays modeling tools and integrated development environments. Therefore, the design and implementation of distributed systems is still a time consuming task which needs the expertise of specialists. In order to support the rapid prototyping of distributed systems and to make the CORBA technology more accessible to developers who are not experts in this area, the focus of this article is on concepts and tool support for the automated prototyping of CORBA distributed systems with special emphasize on Java as target programming language.

1 Introduction

Due the advent of the internet and affordable network technologies, the development of distributed systems is an important area of software engineering today. Distributed systems (potentially) have many advantages in comparison to local ones, like the sharing of resources over networks, fault tolerance, increased performance, scaling of applications, and others. Unfortunately, these advantages do not come for free, since the development of distributed systems is very demanding. Problems in this context arise from the heterogeneity of hardware platforms, operating systems, and programming languages, as well as the use of unreliable networks for reliable communication between components, real concurrency, security issues with respect to the (mis-)use of services, and the need for location transparency. In order to support the development of distributed systems in the light of these problems, the CORBA (Common Object Request Broker Architecture) international standard is developed by the OMG (Object Management Group) [OMG02]. The idea behind this standard is to specify a middleware which decouples distribution related aspects from application development. In order to support arbitrary combinations of operating systems, programming languages and underlying hardware, the CORBA standard is specified in a platform independent manner. Today, CORBA is the most widely used middleware

N. Guelfi et al. (Eds.): FIDJI 2002, LNCS 2604, pp. 29–38, 2003.

with implementations for almost every environment. Even if the wide range of availability of CORBA compliant implementations clearly indicates that the services provided by this middleware are in principle useful for the development of distributed systems, there are also some problems. In detail, the still growing complexity of the standard leads to a situation in which a straight forward understanding of the underlying ideas and their details is difficult, especially for software developers with little or no experience in distributed systems. In addition, todays modeling tools and integrated development environments only offer basic CORBA support. Out of this, the development of distributed systems is still a demanding task which needs the experience of specialists to handle the additional complexity introduced by the CORBA standard.

> *"CORBA's flexibility gives the developer a myriad of choices, and requires a vast number of details to be specified. The complexity is simply too high to be able to do so efficiently and quickly."* [OMG99]

As not every computer scientist is specialized in distributed systems, but more and more such systems have to be build nowadays, the above described situation motivates the work presented in this article. The main idea is that it should be possible without *detailed* knowledge of the CORBA specification to develop prototypes of CORBA enabled systems. This article therefore focuses on concepts and tool support for the automated prototyping of CORBA-based distributed object-oriented systems.

The structure of the presentation is as follows. The next section gives a brief survey on the CORBA standard and how distributed systems are developed with it. Section three describes concepts for the automated prototyping of distributed object-oriented systems. A prototypical CASE tool which implements these concepts is then used to develop a simple example with Java as target programming language. Finally, related work is discussed and perspectives for further developments are given.

2   CORBA-Based Development of Distributed Systems

Due to the wide spread availability of CORBA implementations, former problems with the development of distributed systems in heterogeneous environments have been overcome. The core concept of CORBA is the *object management architecture* (OMA) which describes in an abstract way how distributed components communicate with each other. The idea is that a so called *object request broker* (ORB) transparently handles communication between objects offering services and objects requesting services, independently from their particular location. Client and server objects are bound to an ORB by means of *interface definition language* (IDL) descriptions. The IDL is used to specify the interfaces of distributed services in a standardized and programming language independent way. If an object requests a distributed service, it only needs to know the particular interface definition. The locating of the object providing the service and the communication with it is transparently handled by the ORB. Therefore, the ORB is often referred to as *software bus* (fig. 1).

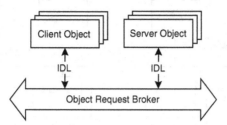

Fig. 1. Reference Model of the *Object Management Architecture* (simplified).

In the following, the CORBA development process is sketched for a single server and a single client component (fig. 2). Starting with the development of the server, and given that the services to offer in the distributed environment have already been identified, *interfaces* have to be build which are semantically meaningful groups of services. These interfaces are then specified with the IDL in an operating system and programming language independent way. In addition, it has to be decided in which way the interfaces have to be published in the distributed environment in order to be usable by clients. Together with the documentation on how to use them, the IDL specified interfaces and the chosen publication scheme form the contract between client and server. As this contract is the only common part of both, client and server components may be developed separately by different teams using different hardware platforms, operating systems, programming languages, and ORBs. The development of the server continues with the translation of the IDL descriptions into statements of the programming language the server is to be implemented with. Therefore, an IDL compiler is incorporated which creates so called *skeletons* from IDL descriptions according to a specified mapping to the target programming language. At the run-time of a system, skeleton code receives requests for services from the ORB, transparently translates the call and the arguments into the implementation specific format of the server object, invokes the method which implements the requested service, and returns the result to the client, if any. The next step of the server development is that so called *servants* have to be provided which are implementations of the specified server interfaces. In addition to this application specific code, administrative parts of the server have to be implemented, like creating and initializing of an ORB object, CORBA object instantiation, publishing of objects, hand-over of control to the ORB which then waits for service calls from remote clients, and shut-down functionality to free resources. In the last stage of the server development, code and libraries have to be compiled and linked.

The development of the client roughly follows a similar pattern. First of all, the IDL descriptions of the remote services to be used have to be translated into constructs of the implementation language of the client. Therefore, the IDL

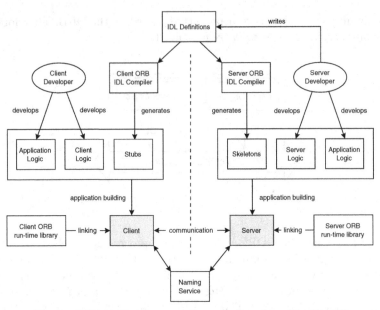

Fig. 2. CORBA Development Process (based on [HenVin99]).

compiler of the ORB used by the client is called to generate so called *stubs* according to a specified target programming language mapping. At the run-time of a distributed system, stubs serve as proxies for calls to remote services. Therefore, the client side stubs are the counterparts of the server side skeletons, i.e. the stub code is responsible for the transparent call of the remote service in question. In addition to the application logic, the client also needs to implement administrative functionality for creating and initializing of an ORB object and finding of CORBA objects and services. The last step of the client development is that all classes have to be compiled and linked together with the libraries needed. If a naming service is available to client and server which provides initial access to remote object references, both are ready then to communicate in a distributed environment.

Even if the use of a CORBA compliant middleware as outlined above is un-doubtedly a great help for the development of distributed systems in general, there are still drawbacks. The most severe problem is that the modeler/pro-grammer can not concentrate on his main interest which is the development of application logic. In addition, further non-trivial tasks have to be fulfilled in order to integrate a CORBA compliant distribution middleware into a sys-tem. Especially for designers and programmers with little or no background in CORBA technology, or distributed systems in general, this is a difficult task due to the complexity of the standard and the implementing products. In order to make the basic CORBA functionality more accessible even for non experts in this area, the next section introduces concepts for the automation of CORBA-based distributed systems development.

3   Automation Concepts

For the purposes of an easier access to the basic CORBA functionality for the prototyping of distributed systems, we propose to introduce automation techniques into the above described development process. Ideally, such techniques fully encapsulate distribution related aspects and allow developers to focus on the application logic. As a prerequisite, we assume that the application development is model driven (see [OMG01a]) and UML class diagrams [OMG01b] are used for the specification of distributed system components. Starting from this assumption, the following three areas of CORBA-based systems development can be identified to benefit from the use of automation concepts:

IDL support: The first step of the server development is the specification of its remotely accessible interfaces by means of IDL descriptions. With a model driven development process for the architectural specification of a server, interfaces are described with constructs of the underlying modeling language. Obviously, publicly available CORBA interfaces and internally used ones have to be distinguished, e.g. by making use of 'CORBA_Interface' and 'CORBA_Struct' stereotypes in UML class diagrams. With the help of a predefined IDL mapping of specific elements of UML class diagrams, this approach enables automatic derivation of IDL descriptions from architectural models. In addition, the compiler which translates the IDL descriptions of the server into target programming language skeletons is ideally invoked transparently.

During the development of a client component the server specified remote interfaces have to be known, i.e. the automatically generated IDL descriptions of the server have to be imported into the architectural model of the client. Ideally, this import is fully automated after the selection of the IDL descriptions needed, i.e. the interfaces should be visualized automatically within the UML class diagram of the client. Analogue to the server development, the IDL compiler of the client for the translation of the interface descriptions into target programming language stubs should be invoked transparently.

Implementation and run-time support: As described with the CORBA development process in the last section, the integration of a CORBA compliant middleware into a distributed component demands for the manual development of non-trivial server and client side administrative parts. Automation support in this area has potentially the greatest impact to help the development of distributed systems. The main idea here is to provide an own API which is automatically extended with application specific code in order to encapsulate the CORBA interface from the application.

Server objects are usually created and destroyed by means of so called *homes* which implement the factory method design pattern [Gamma95] and which are CORBA objects themselves. These homes are initially created in the server and their references are published within a naming service for client access. In addition, so called *portable object adapters* (POAs) are needed by the ORB for run-time administration of servants. Ideally, the factory classes and the POAs are generated automatically together with their implementations. Moreover, a server framework should be provided in order to transparently assemble the automatically generated parts of the server with the manually developed application logic. At run-time this framework is responsible e.g. for ORB initializations and publishing of home references within a naming service.

A client needs to know the references of server factory objects published in the naming service in order to be able to create remote objects which are then used to serve client requests. The communication of the client with the naming service to retrieve these references is ideally encapsulated by automatically generated code which upon request returns the reference of the factory object needed. Analogue to the server, the described means to support the client development are ideally completed with a client framework which transparently handles ORB initializations and then passes control to the client application logic.

Build support: As the compilation and linking of components in a distributed system is not always straight forward due to complexity of configuration options, this task should be automated, too. Especially the differences in application building which have their origin in ORB implementations from different vendors with differing configuration parameters should be handled transparently by the supporting development environment.

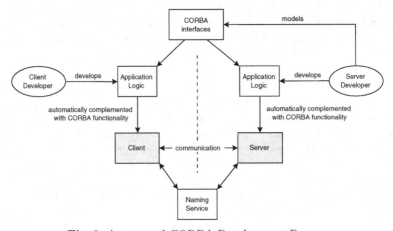

Fig. 3. Automated CORBA Development Process.

With the above described automation concepts, the original development process given in figure 2 is considerably simplified and results in the process shown in figure 3. The introduced approach for the automation of CORBA-based systems development almost completely frees the developer from CORBA-specific tasks, only the modeling of CORBA-interfaces remains. Consequently, developers can concentrate on the application logic as their main interest. Furthermore, also non-CORBA experts are able to develop distributed systems with the simplified development process, given that the described concepts are properly supported by an integrated development environment. The next section therefore introduces a prototypical implementation of the introduced automation concepts targeted towards Java as an example programming language.

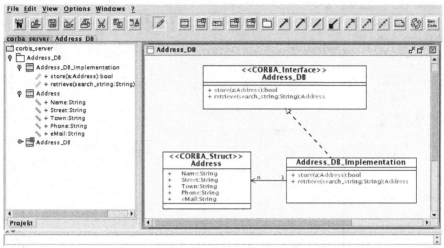

Fig. 4. Screenshot with the Architectural Model of the Address Database Server.

4   Tool Support for Automated Prototyping

The integration of the introduced automation concepts in a prototypical CASE tool is described in the following with the development of a simple distributed address database. The example consists of a single server and a single client component. The task of the CORBA server is to store addresses of individuals sent to it by clients. Clients not only send addresses to the server, but also requests to retrieve them. Starting from this scenario, the first step of the development is the specification of the remote server interface to be used by the client. As described above, we assume that the development is model driven in a way that UML class diagrams are used for the architectural specification of the distributed system components. Figure 4 gives the class diagram of the CORBA server which consists of a 'CORBA_Struct', which defines the data structure of the addresses to store, and a 'CORBA_Interface', which specifies the signatures of the remotely available methods 'store' and 'retrieve'. Textual IDL descriptions may be generated and exported automatically from this architectural model for client side use. The server developer then has to provide the application logic for both methods of the interface using Java as implementation language. After the implementation of the application logic has been completed, the server may be generated. The generation then transparently creates skeletons, servant homes, POA administration code, a tie-based binding of interface implementations to the POAs, and an application framework with the 'main' method of the server which performs initializations and then waits for remote service calls. The building of the application is integrated into the generation process and therefore fully automated. A prerequisite to this is that the particular ORB to be used is preconfigured in the development environment.

The development of the address database client starts with the import of the IDL descriptions of the CORBA interfaces to use into the client project

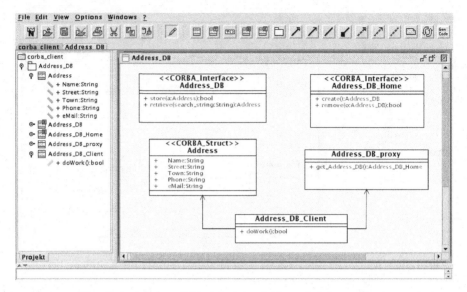

Fig. 5. Architectural Model of the Address Database Client.

of the CASE tool. The IDL descriptions are then automatically transformed into representatives of the client UML class diagram. Figure 5 gives the result of this process for the example. In detail, the CORBA structure 'Address' as well as the CORBA interfaces 'Address_DB' and 'Address_DB_Home' are automatically generated from the IDL import. Moreover, the additional proxy class 'Address_DB_proxy' is generated automatically which is used to encapsulate the communication with the naming service needed in order to get the initial reference to the servant home. After the application logic of the client has been provided by the developer in class 'Address_DB_Client', the client component may be generated. While the build support is the same as for the server, the generation transparently provides implementations for the proxy class and a client framework which performs ORB initializations and then passes the control to the application logic. Assuming that a naming service is running on a default port, server and client can be started with automatically provided scripts and then communicate in a distributed environment.

A more detailed description of the implementation of the automation concepts into the experimental CASE tool platform NEPTUN [Phil02] is given in [Brands02].

5   Discussion, Related Work, and Further Perspectives

Automation concepts to support the development of CORBA-based distributed systems have been introduced in this article together with a prototypical implementation which focuses on Java as target programming language. The development process of such systems is significantly simplified by this approach (fig. 3), as only the modeling of CORBA interfaces and the application logic development remain as manual tasks to fulfill. However, this high degree of automation also has some limitations. Due to the fact that almost all decisions on how to statically and dynamically bind an ORB to the application logic are hidden from the developer, he also loses the flexibility of a non-automated development process. This is not necessarily a drawback, as it depends on the area of use if highly efficient development or high flexibility are more important. From our point of view, especially the rapid prototyping of distributed systems benefits from the introduced approach, as in most cases a prototype is developed as a 'proof of concept' and hence efficiency of development is more important than bells and whistles. In addition, the described approach offers benefits for developers which are not familiar with distributed systems development in general and the CORBA standard specifically. In such a case the developer loses some flexibility but also the accompanying complexity of choice.

While there is a plethora of work on distributed systems modeling, automation concepts to be used in this area are only rarely discussed in the literature. A proposal which is similar in focus to the approach presented in this article is introduced in [AleKor02]. However, the idea described by the authors fundamentally differs from our concept, as they propose to enrich IDL specifications during their manual development with additional semantic information as a prerequisite to automatic Java code generation. Another area of related work are the automation concepts offered by existing tools for (Java) systems modeling, roundtrip engineering, and more traditional integrated development environments. As will be pointed out in the following, all these tools only offer limited support for the automation of distributed systems development. Considering for example 'Rational Rose' [Rati02] and 'Together' [Toge02] as popular tools for the model driven software development, we find that they only offer automatic generation of IDL descriptions from UML class diagrams and some application building support. Integrated development environments like e.g. 'JBuilder' [Borl02], 'Visual Age for Java' [IBM02], and 'NetBeans' [Net02] are programming language centered and thus do not make use of modeling languages for systems development, i.e. interface descriptions have to be written manually. Often, such environments have an ORB integrated out of the box which (potentially) simplifies application building. Interestingly, the open source project 'NetBeans' offers the most sophisticated support for the development of CORBA-based distributed systems today. A wizard driven approach to distributed application development allows for the automatic generation of CORBA-specific client and server side code fragments, which have to be completed manually by the developer. In summary, the existing tools either offer automatic IDL generation from class diagrams or they are programming language centered and thus mainly concentrate on application building. Therefore, none of the tools available today offers a seamless automation support ranging from high-level systems modeling to low-level application building as proposed in this article.

Future work on the presented approach for the automated prototyping of CORBA-based distributed systems will enable the developer to individually choose the appropriate level of tool support, i.e. if either flexibility or efficiency of development is more important in a particular stage of a project. Also, the introduced automation concepts will be further refined to be able to provide support for more complex application scenarios. Furthermore, the transparent use of CORBA *or* RMI for distributed Java applications is also a topic of interest.

Acknowledgements. The author would like to thank the NEPTUN team and especially Holger Brands for their contributions to the project, as well as Jacob Köhler and Dion Whitehead for commenting an earlier version if this paper.

References

[AleKor02]   M. Aleksy and A. Korthaus. *'Automatic Java Code Generation Based on CORBA IDL plus Semantic Comments'. 'Proceedings of the International Conference on Computer Science, Information Technology, e-Business, and Applications (CSITeA '02)'.* Foz do Iguazu, Brasil, 2002.

[Borl02]   Borland. *'JBuilder Documention'.* 'www.borland.com', 2002.

[Brands02]   H. Brands. *'Modellierung and Generierung von CORBA-Anwendungen'.* Diploma Thesis, Koblenz University, 2002.

[Gamma95]   Erich Gamma, Richard Helm, Ralph Johnson and John Vlissides. *Design Patterns.* Addison Wesley, Reading, MA, 1995.

[HenVin99]   M. Henning and S. Vinoski. *'Advanced CORBA Programming with C++'.* Addison-Wesley, Reading, 1999.

[IBM02]   IBM. *'Visual Age for Java Documentation'.* 'www.ibm.com', 2002.

[Net02]   NetBeans. *'NetBeans Documentation'.* 'www.netbeans.org', 2002.

[OMG99]   OMG. *'CORBA Components Vol. I, Joint Revised Submission'.* 'www.omg.org/corba', 1999.

[OMG01a]   OMG. *'Model Driven Architecture (MDA)'.* 'www.omg.org/mda', 2001.

[OMG01b]   OMG. *'UML 1.4'.* 'www.omg.org/uml', 2001.

[OMG02]   OMG. *'CORBA Specification 3.0'.* 'www.omg.org/corba', 2002.

[Phil02]   S. Philippi. *'A CASE-Tool for the Development of Concurrent Object-Oriented Systems based on Petri-Nets'.* Petri-Net Newsletter 62, 2002.

[Rati02]   Rational. *'Rational Rose Documenation'.* 'www.rational.com', 2002.

[Toge02]   Togethersoft. *'Together Documentation'.* 'www.togethersoft.com', 2002.

Jawa: A Java Tool-Kit for Mobile Objects Applications

Eko Mursito Budi, Geoff Roy, and Graeme Cole

Murdoch University, School of Engineering,
Dixon Road Rockingham, Western Australia, 6168
{mursito, geoff, graeme}@eng.murdoch.edu.au

Abstract. Jawa is a Java tool-kit for distributed applications development. It provides an infrastructure for automatic management of remote computers, and a framework for mobile objects applications development. The scheduling and migration of mobile objects to remote computers utilizes the parallelism and scheduling principles; in which a Jawa based application may expect performance improvements. More over, Jawa also simplifies the development cycle of its respective application.

1 Introduction

Users always demand the fastest and the most accurate results from software applications. A faster computation may be achieved by dividing the applications into several small units and then distributing the units to several computers. However, a distribution introduces complexity for the application itself as well as the development cycle; and thus threatens the correctness of the application [19].

The Standard Java SDK provides distributed services based on Remote Methods Invocation (RMI). Despite being powerful, RMI is only suitable for static distributed client-server architectures. The RMI development cycle is also somewhat tedious. Therefore, a tool-kit called Jawa is designed with the following features:

- Simple development: The application's classes are compiled and deployed as a single Java archive (jar) for easy and statically correct development. However, it contains several mobile objects, representing distributable computational units.
- Auto dynamic distribution: The application is initiated on a local computer, and then it automatically discovers the remote computers and distributes the mobile objects.
- Clean termination: The application terminates completely from all computers, therefore it safe for repetitive executions and iterative development.
- Robust sharing: Several Jawa based applications may run simultaneously in the network, along side with other applications in well separated processes.

This paper begins by reviewing the background theories and the standard Java distributed services. The next section presents the Jawa architecture, followed by the descriptions of Jawa packages. Finally, the paper discusses some comparison and related works, then concludes with the main characteristics and benefits of Jawa.

N. Guelfi et al. (Eds.): FIDJI 2002, LNCS 2604, pp. 39–48, 2003.

2   Background Theories

The main inspirations of Jawa are parallel computing [7] and scheduling theories [4]. In parallel computing, several processors work cooperatively to execute application software. The fundamental concepts of parallel computing are:

- Scalability: the management of all possible computers as a set of machines.
- Modularity: the decomposition of the application into a set of small jobs.
- Locality: the grouping of related jobs to minimize communications.
- Concurrency: the simultaneous executions of many jobs in the machines.

To be efficient, parallelism requires a good scheduling; to assign the right processor for the right job. The scheduling consists of three main concepts:

- Measurement: the determination of machines resources capabilities and the jobs resources requirements.
- Optimization: the assignment of a set of machines to complete a set of jobs under particular objectives and constraints.
- Dispatching: the loading and unloading of the jobs onto the machines (depending on the assignment).

3   Standard Java for Distributed Computing

The distributed object technology recognizes several basic architectures such as code-on-demand, remote evaluation, client-server, mobile objects/agents [11], and replicated objects [3]. So far, the best architecture supported by standard Java from Sun Microsystems is client-server architecture with an automatic discovery. It uses Jini + RMI activation framework [8][17] that works as follows (see Figure 1):

a. The environment consists of one local and several remote computers in a wide area network (Internet). Every remote computer runs an RMI activation daemon (RMID), and there must be at least one Jini lookup service (Reggie).

b. The application is developed as separated servers and client archives (collection of classes) that share a common interface definition language (IDL). The programmers must make sure that the clients match the servers.

c. The server archives have to be installed and started on several remote computers as necessary. To enable access by any clients, the servers register themselves to the RMI daemon and the Jini lookup service. After that, the client archive can be started on the local computer.

d. On operation, the client objects discover the server objects from the Jini lookup service. Client objects will receive the server stubs, and can use it to access the server objects.

e. On termination, the clients close the connections and shut themselves down. However, the server objects are kept running on the remote computers.

Additional tool-kits are required to support mobile objects and replicated objects, for example Aglets [12], Voyager [21], JavaThread [7], Brake [18], JGroup [2], and FilterFresh [3].

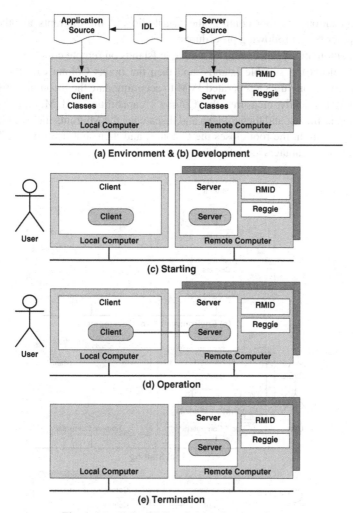

Fig. 1. Java Jini + RMI activation framework.

4 Jawa Architecture

Jawa is developed as a tool-kit to support automatic distribution of an application, and simplifies the development cycle. It works as a mobile-objects architecture with additional services as follows (see Figure 2):

a. The environment is a local area network (LAN) that consists of a local and several remote computers. Every remote computer runs a Jawa Island daemon.

b. The application's source consists of several classes of mobile objects, but they are compiled together and deployed as a single archive.

c. The application is started on the local computer. It contains a Root that controls several Residents (non movable objects) and Migrants (movable objects).

d. On operation, the root controls the distribution of the migrants to other remote computer by the following procedures:
  - It automatically discovers all available Islands on remote computers.
  - It selects the suitable Islands, and then the books Colonies on those Islands. Each Colony uses a separated JVM to accommodate the incoming Migrants.
  - It dynamically measures the Colony's capabilities and Migrant's resources requirements, and then assigns and dispatches the Migrants into the Colonies.
e. On termination, the root closes the Colonies and then shut itself down. Therefore, the remote computers are left clean.

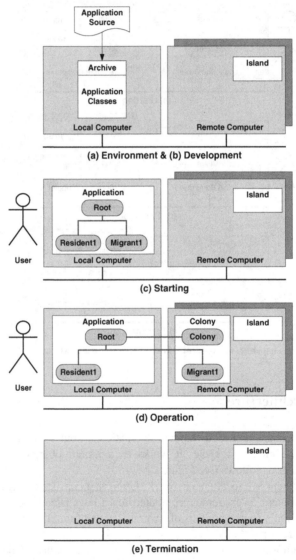

Fig. 2. Jawa architecture.

5 Jawa Packages

Jawa is built on top of the standard Java using the layering as shown in Figure 3. The tool-kit consists of seven packages (Island, Application, Scheduling, Discovery, Measurement, Mobile and Local) and one executable (Island daemon). The Island daemon is installed on each remote computer. The programmer builds custom applications by importing the packages. The Jawa services are comparable to grid computing [10].

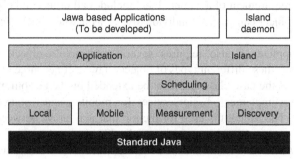

Fig. 3. Jawa packages.

5.1 Island Package

The Island Package provides automatic management of remote computers. Jawa assumes that the target system contains ordinary non-dedicated computers in a local area network; for example, a computer laboratory. Therefore, the infrastructure should be generic, light and robust.

Jawa uses identical Islands for every remote computer. The Island is responsible for these minimum generic services:

- Being prepared to be discovered.
- Providing the measurements for remote computer capabilities, such as CPU, memory, hard disk, network, and java virtual machine.
- Providing the list of local resources, such as file and input/output; and the necessary service to access the resources locally.
- Creating a Colony when a booking occurred, and controlling it.

The Colony is launched only when required, so it is light. It is also robust because it is a new JVM, which is separated from other applications and has independent resource management. More importantly, each Colony has its own codebase and security policy to allows dynamic class loading from the application's local computer. The Colony main services are:

- Providing the measurement of the actual capability of the virtual machines.
- Receiving and executing the incoming Migrants.
- Monitoring and reporting the actual performance of the Migrants.
- Terminating cleanly on normal or exceptional condition.

5.2   Application Package

The application package supports the framework to build a parallel application that can be distributed into the Colonies efficiently. For job partitioning, it uses the idea of hierarchical mobile agents [15]. The characteristics of the package are as follows:

- The mobile objects are organized in a tree structure. Each mobile object can nest other mobile objects within itself and can only be nested by one other mobile object.
- The resource requirement of a parent object includes all of its child objects.
- Each mobile object can migrate individually, or as a whole including all its child objects.

However, the application also requires several non-mobile objects and ordinary objects. To support these different types of objects, Jawa defines three basic classes:

1. *Jawa.migrant* is the base class that must be extended by the custom mobile objects. This base class implements basic services for mobility and resource requirement measurement. The Migrant is used for the job that may move between Colonies. A Migrant may contain other Migrants or serializable objects.
2. *Jawa.resident* is the base class for non-mobile objects. The base class implements the services for remote access and resource requirement measurement. The resident is used to wrap the job that must stay in a computer, but accessible from other computers, for example: databases or input/output device. A Resident may contains some Migrants or serializable objects, as well as Residents or non-serializable objects.
3. *Jawa.root* is the base class for the main object of the application. The programmer must extend this class and add the necessary code to initialize the application, such as the first level Migrants and Residents.

Under that framework, the programmer must carefully design the job partitioning of the application by exploiting parallelism. The programmer should arrange a dividable job as a Migrant, and group highly related Migrants under a parent Migrant. For a simple example, Figure 4 shows a possible job partitioning of an application to calculate the following formula:

$$A = \sum_1^n X + \sum_1^m Y$$

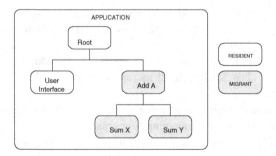

Fig. 4. Sample job partitioning

5.3 Scheduling Package

The scheduling package defines the interface and implements some implements some base class for scheduling. Scheduling itself is a broad topic, thus this package is a flexible framework that provides the skeletons for:

- The selection mechanism of the machines and the jobs. Jawa has a defined machine capabilities matrix that includes platform information and benchmarking result (see section 5.4). Programmers may define a custom job resource requirements matrix, and the selection policy, such as random, least loaded, etc.
- The dispatching mechanism. Jawa supports initial placement (by dynamic class loading) and preemption migration (by weak mobility, strong mobility is still under development).
- The scheduling algorithm. The scheduling algorithms may be static or dynamic with any search mechanism (enumeration or heuristic). Jawa provides generic static-table scheduling and dynamic-list scheduling.

5.4 Measurement Package

The Measurement package provides the services for benchmarking, organized as follows:

- Generic: integer, floating point, array, vector, hash table
- Concurrency: multithreading, synchronization
- Memory: memory space, memory allocation
- Input/Output: sequential read, sequential write, random read, random write
- Network: latency (ping), bandwidth (average throughput)

The benchmark algorithms were taken from many open sources on the Internet, including from Java Grande [16]. The algorithms have been adapted to minimize the effect of just-in-time compiler on JVM [19].

5.5 Discovery Package

The discovery package provides the services to discover remote computers (Islands) in the network automatically. A standard package for this function is Jini [8]. However, Jini does not support unequal comparison for search criteria. The applications can search, for example, all computers that have memory *equal to* 128 MB. However, it cannot ask for all computers that have memory *greater than* 128 MB. Therefore, the applications have to search all possible combinations or seek all remote computers then test it one by one.

As the alternative options, Jawa use the light RMI-discovery protocol [5]. The application sends the discovery request directly to the Islands using a multicast communication. The Island evaluates the request; and on acceptance, answers it directly to the application using unicast communication. This technique greatly simplifies and improves the speed of discovery process.

5.6 Mobile Package

The mobile package provides the service for the movement of computation units between computers. As noted by Fuggeta [11], a complete mobility should carry data, code, execution state, and reference. Standard Java, however, does not provide execution state and reference mobility. The Jawa Mobile package add the necessary mobility services on top of the standard Java as follows:

- The data and code mobility uses the standard Java RMI. Each application's Root includes a custom class server. At the other end, the Colonies are configured to use codebase from that class server. The more efficient data and code migration was discussed in [14].
- The execution state mobility uses several approaches. For the basic, Jawa provides weak mobility with a state machine like Aglets [12] or Voyager [21]. The support for strong mobility is not stable yet. The first option is using portable thread migration (Brakes) [18]; but the application must be recompiled for some byte code modification. The other option is using thread serialization tool-kit (Java Thread) [7]; however, it uses non-standard Java virtual machines.
- The reference mobility using a smart proxy that wraps the standard RMI stub, and add the functionality to reconnect itself when the referenced Migrant moves. The basic idea of smart proxy is taken from [13][22]. Another example of mobile reference is MobileRMI [1].

5.7 Local Package

The local package provides the necessary services to access the local resources on the remote computers, such as files or input/output devices. Usually, they are platform dependent and may involve some native code. The local package classes are installed on the remote machines and managed by the Islands. If the Migrants need to access any local resources, it may get the necessary classes from the Island and instantiates it within the same JVM (the Colony). Therefore, the Migrants can access the resources directly without the overhead of inter-process communication.

6   Comparisons and Related Works

Jawa has several advantages over the standard Java RMI + Jini as shown in Table 1. In short, the Java RMI + Jini supports the basic client-server distributed architecture and the automatic server objects management. As a more advance tool-kit, Jawa supports the mobile objects architecture, completed with the automatic remote machines management, hierarchical jobs structuring, and autonomic scheduling.

Jawa is similar with many projects. The international project for Java high performance computing is Java Grande (www.javagrande.org). From another block, the new paradigm about the automatic environment is emerging as grid computing (www.gridcomputing.org).

Table 1. Comparison of Jawa and Java RMI + Jini

Requirements	Jawa	RMI + Jini
Functional		
Auto remote computers management	Yes	Yes
Single development and deployment	Yes	No
Application starts from one local computer	Yes	No
Dedicated remote processes for each application	Yes	No
Dynamic load distribution	Yes	No
Clean termination	Yes	No
Auxiliary		
Statically correct (from versioning problem)	Yes	No
May improve performances	Yes	Yes
Robust (from other applications)	Yes	No
Reliable (from partial failures)	No	No
Security	Medium	High
Safe for repetitive execution	Yes	No
Safe for iterative development	Yes	No

7 Conclusion

Jawa provides a toolkit that simplifies the distributed application development. The programmers can compile and deploy the application in a single archive. The application then started on a local computer, but will automatically distributed into the available remote computers in the network. After completing the execution, the programmer may modify the program and repeat the execution without class versioning problems. Several Jawa based applications may run on the same network with minimum interference on each others, except for the shared resources.

The Jawa based applications that are carefully designed with parallelism may gain performance improvements. Jawa also provides load balancing for overall system. However, the cost of communication, migration, and scheduling are relatively high. Therefore, Jawa is more appropriate for big applications.

For future works, Jawa should consider other aspects such as distributed scheduling and fault tolerance. The distributed scheduling is necessary to ensure that the overall system is convergent when several Jawa based applications run simultaneously. The fault tolerance feature is an assurance for possible partial failures in the networks or remote computers.

References

1.   Avvenuti et al., MobileRMI: a Toolkit to Enhance Java RMI with Mobility, 6th ECOOP Workshop on Mobile Object Systems: Operating System Support, Security and Programming Languages, June 13, Sophia Antipolis, France, 2000.
2.   Ban, B., JavaGroups-Group Communication Patterns in Java, http://www.javagroups.com/javagroupsnew/docs/papers/Patterns.ps.gz, November 2002

3.   Baratloo, A., P. E. Chung, Y. Huang, S. Rangarajan, and S. Yajnik, Filterfresh: Hot Replication of Java RMI Server Objects. In Proc. of the 4th Conf. on Object-Oriented Technologies and Systems, Santa Fe, New Mexico, April 1998.
4.   Berg, Clifford J., Advanced Java 2 Development for Enterprise Application, 2nd ed., Sun Microsystems Press, Prentice Hall, 2000
5.   Bishop, Philip, Nigel Warren, Jini-like discovery for RMI, http://www.javaworld.com/javaworld/jw-11-2001/jw-1121-jinirmi.htmp, September 2002
6.   Blazewicz, J. et al, Scheduling Computer and Manufacturing Processes, Springer-Verlag, Berlin, 1996
7.   Bouchenak, S., Making Java Applications Mobile or Persistent, 6th USENIX Conference on Object-Oriented Technologies and Systems (COOTS'01), San Antonio, Texas, USA, 2001
8.   Edward, W.K., Core Jini 2nd Edition, Prentice Hall, 2001
9.   Foster, Ian, Designing and Building Parallel Programs: Concepts and Tools for Parallel Software Engineering, Addison-Wesley, USA, 1995
10. Foster, I., Carl Kesselman, Steven Tuecke, The Anatomy of the Grid: Enabling Scalable Virtual Organizations, http://www.globus.org/research/papers/anatomy.pdf, Nov. 2002
11. Fuggeta, Alfonso, Gian Pietro Picco, Giovanni Vigna, Understanding Code Mobility, IEEE Transaction on Software Engineering, vol 24 no 5, May 1998
12. Lange, Danny B., Java Aglet Application Programming Interface (J-AAPI) White Paper - Draft 2, http://www.trl.ibm.com/aglets/JAAPI-whitepaper.htm, September 2002
13. Loton, Tony, The Smart Approach to Distributed Performance Monitoring with Java, http://www.javaworld.com/javaworld/jw-09-2000/jw-0901-smart.html, September 2002
14. Nester, C., M. Philippsen and B. Haumacher, A more efficient RMI for Java, Proceedings of the ACM 1999 conference on Java Grande, June 1999
15. Satoh, Ichiro, "Hierarchically Structured Mobile Agents and their Migration", Workshop on Mobile Object Systems (MOS'99), Lisbon Portugal, 1999
16. Smith, L.A., J.M.Bull, A Parallel Java Grande Benchmark Suite, ACM, November 2001
17. Sommers, Frank, Activatable Jini Services, Part 1: Implement RMI Activation, http://www.javaworld.com/javaworld/jw-09-2000/jw-0915-jinirmi.html, September 2002
18. Truyen, Eddy, Bert Robben, Bart Vanhaute, Tim Coninx, Wouter Joosen, Pierre Verbaeten, Portable Support for Transparent Thread Migration in Java, Proceedings of International Symposium on Agent Systems and Applications/Mobile Agents, Zurich, Suisse, 2000
19. Twang, Writing Micro-Benchmarks for Java Hotspot JVM, http://www.concentric.net/~Ttwang/tech/microbench.htm, September 2002
20. Waldo, Jim, Geoff Wyant, Ann Wollrath, Sam Kendall, A Note on Distributed Computing, Technical Report, Sun Microsystems, http://research.sun.com/techrep/1994/smli_tr-94-29. pdf, October 2002
21. Wheeler, Thomas, Reducing Development Effort Using the Voyager ORB, http://www.recursionsw.com/products/voyager/whitepapers/Ease of Development.pdf, Sept. 2002
22. Wilson, M. Jeff, Get Smart with Proxies and RMI, on-line article, http://www.javaworld.com/javaworld/jw-11-2000/jw-1110-smartproxy.html, September 2002
23. Wilson, S., Jeff Kesselman, Java Platform Performance: Strategies and Tactics, Addison Wesley, USA, 2000

Performance Analysis of Java Group Toolkits: A Case Study*

Roberto Baldoni, Stefano Cimmino, Carlo Marchetti, and Alessandro Termini

Dipartimento di Informatica e Sistemistica,
Università di Roma "La Sapienza"
Via Salaria 113, 00198, Roma, Italy
{baldoni,cimmino,marchet,termini}@dis.uniroma1.it

Abstract. *In this paper we present a performance evaluation of three Java group toolkits (JavaGroups, Spread and Appia) with respect to a specific application scenario: software replication using a three-tier architecture. We also compare performances of these Java group toolkits with Maestro/Ensemble which has been developed in C++. Results show that performances of Java group toolkits are becoming comparable with the ones of Maestro/Ensemble, once selected a well tailored configuration for a given application.*

Keywords: *Group Communications, Java, Software replication, Performance.*

1 Introduction

There is an emerging demand for Java-oriented reliable software for distributed applications due to Java platform independence, the dynamic plug-in of Java components (e.g. downloading Java applets) and the simplicity of application programming just to name some of the Java features. One of the well-known way to add reliability to a distributed application is through software replication. However there are only a few systems that implement replication in Java.

Software replication is a well known technique allowing to increase the availability of a service exploiting specialized software running on COTS (Commercial-Off-The-Shelf), cheap hardware. The basic idea underlying software replication is to replicate the server of a given service on different hosts connected by a communication network so that the service's clients can connect to different server *replicas* to increase the probability of getting replies to their requests. When dealing with a replicated service, it arises the problem of guaranteeing *consistency* among the local states of the replicas despite crashes. *Active* [1] and *passive* [2] replication are well-known approaches to increase the availability of a stateful service. These approaches employ group communication primitives and services such as *total order multicast, view synchronous multicast, group membership,* etc. Implementations of such primitives are provided by *group communication toolkits* e.g., ISIS [3], TOTEM [4], Maestro/Ensemble [5]. Previous group

---

* This work has been partially supported by a grant from EU IST Projects "EU-PUBLI.COM" (#IST-2001-35217) and "MIDAS" (#IST-2001-37610), and by a grant from MIUR on the contexts of projects "DAQUINCIS" and "MAIS"

N. Guelfi et al. (Eds.): FIDJI 2002, LNCS 2604, pp. 49–60, 2003.

toolkits have been implemented in C and/or C++. Only recently Java group toolkits have emerged e.g. JavaGroups [6], Spread [7] and Appia [8]. However, to the best of our knowledge, there does not exist a performance comparison among these toolkits, and the evaluation of Java implementations is a critical point as distinct Java designs of the same application can lead to huge differences in performance due to the interaction between the virtual machine and the bare operating system and the network. Furthermore, a performance comparison among such group toolkits cannot prescind from a specific application, otherwise the comparison risks to be useless.

In this paper we present a performance evaluation of Java group toolkits in the context of a specific architecture for software replication, namely the three-tier (3T) software replication, based on group toolkit. More specifically, in a three-tier architecture for software replication, clients (the client-tier) interact with a middle tier (the middle-tier) that forwards client requests to replicas (the end-tier) maintaining consistency. To achieve this, the middle-tier embeds two basic components, namely the *sequencer* and the *active replication handler*. The first component assigns, in a persistent way, consecutive and unique sequence numbers to client requests. This is based on the classical "one-shot" total order multicast provided by group toolkits[1], while the second masters the client/server interaction enforcing atomicity on the end-tier.

Therefore to evaluate Java group toolkits we realized an implementation of the sequencer component, one for each group toolkit, and measured their performance in terms of client latency and sequencer component latency. We show how the performance of a given Java group toolkit is heavily influenced by the protocol implementing the total-order primitive. To evaluate the gap between a C++ group toolkit and Java ones, we also show the performance results of the same 3T architecture whose sequencer is based on Maestro/Ensemble. This performance comparison points out that, once selected the "one-shot" total order protocol well tailored for the underlying application, the gap between a Java group toolkit and Maestro/Ensemble is acceptable.

The rest of the paper is structured as follows: Section 2 introduces main features of Java group communication toolkits. Section 3 presents the application scenario, namely software replication based on a three-tier architecture, where group toolkits will be evaluated and finally Section 4 shows the performance results.

2   Group Communication Toolkits

Group Communication Toolkits (GCTs) have proven to be an effective tool for building reliable software in partially synchronous distributed systems[2]. They provide a rich set of services and primitives (e.g., total order multicast, group membership etc) which help

---

[1] "One-shot" means that there is no relation between any two consecutive runs of a total order protocol.

[2] A partially synchronous distributed system alternates stable and unstable intervals. During a stable interval there is a bound (know or unknown) on (i) communication transfer delays and (ii) on the time a process takes to execute a step. During unstable intervals the system becomes purely asynchronous. If the duration of stable intervals tends to zero, the group toolkit does not longer guarantee its services. Conditions verifying partial synchrony can be easily ensured on a LAN.

developers in adding specific *properties* to their application. As an example, they can be used to build highly available systems through software replication. The advent of Java has raised the need to provide Java GCTs, which exploit the advantages of this language. However, advantages like portability, ease of programming and adaptivity often negatively impact performance; in particular, for a Java application, the way the virtual machine interacts with the underlying operative system and network can greatly influence performance. In order to compare different toolkits from a performance point of view, we focus on differences in their architecture and implementations. To this end, as a first abstraction level, we identify two basic building blocks in the architecture of a GCT, namely *(i)* the API and *(ii)* the core system, as shown in Figure 1(a). The first one is the set of interfaces used by the application to use the GCT services; the second is the part that actually implements such services. With respect to these building blocks, GCTs can be classified according to *(i)* the programming language used and to *(ii)* the deployment of the two blocks. In fact the API and the core system can be implemented in different languages; moreover, they can either reside in the same process, thus sharing the same address space, or they can run in two different processes on the same host, communicating through IPC, or they can be even deployed on different hosts, communicating through the underlying network. Moreover as we are interested in Java toolkits, it is important to consider where the Java Virtual Machine (JVM) is located with respect to a given deployment. In the case in which only the API is written in Java, the JVM is collocated under this block, while the core is free to exchange messages with the network using native system calls. On the contrary, if even the core is written in Java, the communication with the network passes through the JVM, which is collocated under the core. Let us remark that for every invocation of a service done by an application through the API, the core system often needs to exchange several messages. Therefore, having the core written in Java can yield some performance penalties. Concerning the collocation of the

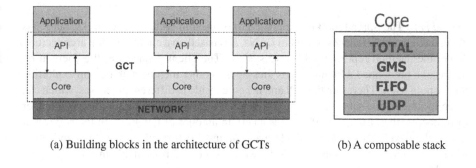

(a) Building blocks in the architecture of GCTs   (b) A composable stack

Fig. 1. Architecture of group communication toolkits

two blocks, we should note that if they reside in different processes or in different hosts, there are two additional hops in the communication between any two processes of a group, thus yielding an additional overhead that results in a performance degradation.

Another abstraction level regards the core system itself; in particular, we consider the protocols implemented within the core and the way in which they interact. From this point of view, GCTs can be classified into two distinct types: one is characterized by a *fixed* set of protocols, which interact always in the same way; the other is based on the concept of a *composable* protocol stack (see Figure 1(b)), where each specific functionality, e.g. total ordering of messages, is confined in a *micro-protocol*, which can be placed above another to form a stack. The developer is also free to add new semantics, by encapsulating them in a new micro-protocol, which can be used to compose another protocol stack. Moreover, this composition can be done dynamically, giving the possibility to build *adaptive systems*. As an example, an application sending totally ordered messages using the stack depicted in Figure 1(b), can decide, at some point in time, to add an encryption layer, defined by the developer, to obtain confidentiality. This behavior is not possible if the core system is built as a fixed predefined set of protocols, because it allows the developer to choose only among a static set of GCT services, whereas every additional functionality must be added at the application level, which is not easy and sometimes even impossible. In contrast, from a performance viewpoint, composable protocol stack can yield penalties due, for example, to arbitrary delays introduced by micro-protocols and to the growth of the message size due to layering.

We now give a brief description of the GCTs we used in the experiments, focusing on aspects that allow to classify them on the basis of the previous discussion.

Maestro/Ensemble [5]. Ensemble is a flexible and efficient toolkit written in the Objective CAML language. It is based on the concept of composable protocol stack, but also implements some optimizations, trying to overcome the performance degradation that results from a layered architecture. Maestro is an interface to Ensemble written in C++, and thus can be considered the API of the toolkit with respect to our framework defined above. Maestro starts Ensemble in a separate thread, therefore the API and the core reside in the same process, sharing the same address space.

Spread [7]. The Spread toolkit is intended to be used in wide area networks, but it has also excellent performances if used in LANs. It is based on a client-daemon architecture, where the daemon represents the core system. The client connects to the daemon by means of a predefined API, and sends messages to other members of a group exploiting the daemon itself. Therefore the API and the core reside in different processes, which can be collocated on the same host, or in distinct ones. The daemon employs a fixed number of protocols, therefore, even if it gives a certain amount of flexibility in the services it offers, the developer is forced to add every additional functionality at the application level. The daemon is written in ANSI C, whereas the API is available in C++, Java and other languages.

Appia [8]. As Ensemble, the Appia toolkit is based on a protocol stack, but it is more flexible than Ensemble as it provides the possibility to extend not only the protocols that compose the stack, but also the events used for intra-stack communication. In Appia there isn't a clear separation between the API and the core system, because an application will make use of the toolkit by providing it's own micro-protocol, and collocating it on the top of the stack. It follows that the application reside in the same process of the core system. The entire toolkit is written in Java.

JavaGroups [6]. JavaGroups is also entirely written in Java, with the aim to exploit as much as possible all the benefits of this language. It can be considered as an API at all, because it can be easily extended to be integrated with any group communication toolkit. As an example, it provides interfaces to Ensemble as well as its native core system. It is thus based on a protocol stack. In this configuration, the application and the core system run in the same process. An important remark on JavaGroups is that it is heavily based on *patterns*.

Table 1 summarizes previous discussion.

Table 1. Classification of some group communication toolkits

Toolkit	API language	Core language	Collocation of the JVM	Core design
Maestro/Ensemble	C++	OCaml	-	Composable
Spread	Java	ANSI C	Under the API	Fixed
Appia	Java	Java	Under the core	Composable
JavaGroups	Java	Java	Under the core	Composable

3   A Case Study: Software Replication

In this section we present the case study used for the group toolkits evaluation. We first briefly introduce software replication. Then we present the notion of three-tier replication, an overview of a protocol for three-tier *active* replication that has been used as a testbed of the performance evaluation of GCTs.

3.1   Software Replication

Software replication is a well-known technique to increase the availability of a service. The basic idea underlying software replication is to replicate the server of a given service on different hosts connected by a communication network so that the service's clients can connect to these different server *replicas* to increase the probability of receiving replies to their requests. The problem with the replication is to guarantee the *consistency* of the replicas; to this aim, it is firstly necessary that every replica produces the same result to the same client request. This is what the *linearizability* [9] consistency criterion formally states. Under a practical point of view, sufficient conditions to linearize the executions of a stateful replicated service are *(i) atomicity* and *(ii) ordering*. Atomicity means that either all or none of the replicas execute each state update; ordering means that replicas execute updates in the same order. Group toolkits help developers to enforce these conditions. As an example, a total order primitive ensures that every message is delivered to all or none of the members of a group and that all members receive messages in the same order.

3.2   Three-Tier Replication

The idea behind three-tier (3T) software replication is to free clients and replicas from participating to protocols that guarantee linearizability. This is achieved by embedding the replication logic (handling atomicity and ordering) within a software middle-tier *physically detached* from both clients and replicas . In other words, the middle-tier encapsulates all the synchrony necessary to get linearizable executions of a stateful replicated service. In this architecture, a client sends it's request to the middle-tier, which forwards it to replicas according to the replication logic implemented by the middle-tier. Then some replica processes the request and returns a result to the middle-

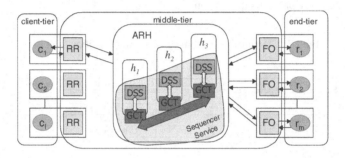

Fig. 2. A Three-tier Architecture for Active Replication

tier that finally forwards the result to the client. The middle-tier has to be fault tolerant to ensure the termination of a client/server interaction in presence of failures. In particular, if a middle-tier entity that was carrying out a client/server interaction crashes, another middle-tier entity has to conclude the job in order to enforce end-tier consistency despite failures. Interested readers can find additional details on 3T replication in [10,11,12]. Figure 2 shows the components of the three-tier architecture for active replication (i.e., each replica executes the same set of client requests in the same order). In the remainder of this section we introduce a brief functional description of each component.

Retransmission/Redirection (RR). To cope with ARH replica failures and with the asynchrony of communication channels, each client process $c_1, \ldots, c_l$ embeds a RR message handler. Clients invoke operations through RR that issues uniquely identified request messages to ARH. After the elapsing of a timeout set upon the request sending, RR retransmits the request, until a result is eventually received.

The Active Replication Handler (ARH). ARH component is the core of the replication logic: by exploiting the *sequencer service*, it orders all incoming client requests and ensures that at least one copy of each ordered client request is eventually delivered at every available end-tier replica. Requests are sent to end-tier replicas along with the sequence numbers provided by the sequencer. Replicas execute requests according to these sequence numbers. Once replicas return results, ARH returns the latter to clients.

Sequencer Service. The sequencer service is available to each ARH replica. In particular, each ARH replica has access to the distributed sequencer service (DSS) class
which is a distributed and fault-tolerant implementation of the persistent sequencer
service. This service returns an unique and consecutive sequence number for each
distinct client request through the invocation of the $GetSeq()$ method. As shown
in Figure 2, each DSS component uses a GCT module as communication bus: in
particular our implementation is based on the usage of a *"one-shot" total order multicast* primitive. DSS uses this primitive to assign a sequence number to a client
request. In other words the DSS component manages a persistent state composed
of pairs $\langle client\ request, sequence\ numbers \rangle$ that allows, for example, to retrieve,
upon the failure of some component of the 3T architecture, a client request given a
sequence number or viceversa [13].

Filtering and Ordering (FO). FO is a message handler placed in front of each end-tier
replica *(i)* to ensure ordered execution of client requests according to the number
assigned by DSS to each request, and *(ii)* to avoid repeated execution of the same
client request (possibly sent by ARH).

Figure 3 illustrates a simple run of the protocol in which no process crashes. In this
scenario, client c_1 invokes the method op_1. Upon receiving req_1, h_1 invokes the DSS
component ($GetSeq()$ method) to assign it a unique sequence number (1 in the example).
This method embeds an invocation to the total order primitive of the group toolkit. Then
h_1 sends a message containing the pair $\langle 1, op_1 \rangle$ to all end-tier replicas and starts waiting
for the first result from an end-tier replica. When this reply arrives, h_1 sends, in its turn, a
reply message back to c_1. h_1 discards further replies to operation op_1 produced by end-
tier replicas (for simplicity these messages are not shown in Figure 3). Concurrently, h_2
serves req_2 sent by c_2. A prototype of the 3T architecture for software replication, namely
the Interoperable Replication Logic (IRL) [14], based on a CORBA infrastructure, has
been developed in our department. This prototype has been used as a testbed for the
performance comparison among the group toolkits presented in the next section.

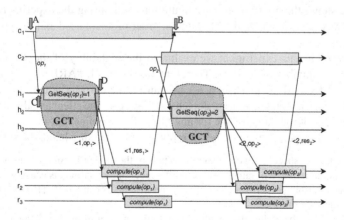

Fig. 3. A failure-free run of the 3T protocol for active software replication.

4   Performance Results

In this section we describe the performance analysis we carried out on the current IRL prototype. In particular, we first introduce the testbed platform and then explain the set of experiments done.

Testbed Platform. The testbed platform is composed by eight Intel Pentium II 600Mhz workstations that run Windows 2000 Professional as operative system. Each workstation is equipped with Java 2 Standard Edition version 1.3.0_01 ([15]) and IONA's ORBacus 4.1 for Java ([16]); also each PC is equipped with Appia version 1.5 ([8]), Spread version 3.16.2 ([7]) and JavaGroups 2.0.2 ([6]); the workstations are interconnected by a 100Mbit Switched Ethernet LAN. The replicated CORBA object used for the experiments is a simple hello-server that accepts requests and immediately replies. We measured the client latency and the DSS latency varying the number of replicas (#R, varying in {2,4,6,8}), the number of clients invoking the replicated server (#C, varying in {2,4,6,8}) and the number of the ARH components (#ARH). As depicted in Figure 3, the client latency is the time elapsed between points A and B, whereas the DSS latency is the time elapsed between points C and D.

Table 2. Group Toolkits Configurations.

GCT	API/Core colocation	Protocol Name	Protocol Type
Spread	same host	Ring	token based
Appia (AB)	same process	TotalABcast	based on Skeen protocol [17]
Appia (SB)	same process	TotalSequencer	sequencer based
JavaGroups (TB)	same process	TOTAL_TOKEN	token based
JavaGroups (SB)	same process	TOTAL	sequencer based
Maestro/Ensemble	same process	Seqbb	sequencer based

Table 2 shows the group toolkit configuration used during the experiments i.e., the relative deployment of core and API, the total order protocol used and its type[3].

Experiment 1. In this experiment we evaluated the scalability of the 3T architecture in terms of the number of replicas. Therefore we set #C=1, #ARH=2 (minimum fault tolerance), and varied #R in {2, 4, 6, 8}, measuring the corresponding client and DSS latency. The experimental results are depicted in Figure 4. The client and the DSS latency are independent of the value of #R for any GCT. This implies that the 3T architecture is scalable with respect to the number of replicas[4]. On the other hand, the selection of a

---

[3] Due to the lack of space, we won't enter the details of the total order algorithms, which can be found in literature. We will rather focus on differences among protocols causing performance gaps while describing experimental results. Interested readers can refer to [18] for a nice survey on total order algorithms.

[4] The scalability of the architecture with respect to the number of replicas is a consequence of the replication handling protocol run by the middle-tier, which awaits only for the *first* reply before sending it to the client.

particular GCT has an important role in the client latency. In fact the latency introduced by the DSS falls between 30% (Spread and Maestro/Ensemble) and 95% (JavaGroups (TB)) of that experienced by the client. From Figure 4 it can be devised that different

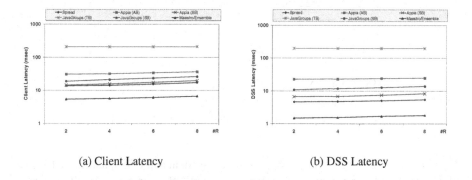

(a) Client Latency   (b) DSS Latency

Fig. 4. Client and DSS Latency as a Function of #R (#C=1, #ARH=2)

implementations of the same protocol (namely the total order primitive) can yield huge differences in the performance of the toolkit. More specifically, JavaGroups (TB) gets total ordering through the circulation of a token (as in TOTEM [4]) among the members of the group. This of course introduces an additional latency, not present in JavaGroups (SB) which is based on the notion of a sequencer i.e., each invocation of a total order primitive is redirected to a coordinator of the group that orders them. Also Appia shows different performance when using Appia (AB) or Appia (SB) to get total order[5]. Finally, the results also confirms that toolkits with a non-Java core has better performances. In particular, Spread gives better performances than the two other Java toolkits, despite of the collocation of it's API and core in distinct processes.

Experiment 2. In this experiment we evaluated the scalability of the 3T architecture in terms of the number of ARH (DSS) components (and then of the group toolkit); to this end, we measured client and DSS latency as a function of #ARH, and thus we set #C=1, #R=2 (minimum fault tolerance), and varied #ARH in $\{2, 4, 6, 8\}$.

As depicted in Figure 5(a) and Figure 5(b), the client latency has the same behavior of the latency introduced by the DSS component. Appia (AB) and JavaGroups (TB) don't scale well implementing protocols that have a time complexity that notably grows with the number of ARH. More precisely the token implementing JavaGroups (TB) have to touch all ARH replicas before delivering a message while Appia (AB) has to wait in the first phase replies from all the ARHs.

---

[5] While Appia (SB) is based on a sequencer similar to JavaGroups (SB), Appia (AB) follows a two phase protocol: the sender of a total order multicast message first gathers information concerning the messages delivered by other processes (first phase), then it multicasts the message by piggybacking control information (devised by the information received in the first phase) which allows other processes to totally order it with respect to the other concurrent messages.

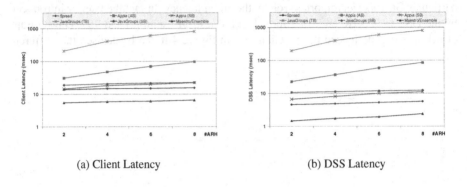

(a) Client Latency   (b) DSS Latency

Fig. 5. Client and DSS Latency as a Function of #ARH (#C=1, #R=2)

Experiment 3. In this experiment we evaluated the client and DSS latency as a function of the number of concurrent clients. Therefore we set #R=2 (minimum fault tolerance), #ARH=4, and varied #C in $\{1, 2, 4, 8\}$.

Figure 6 points out the experimental results. The client latency grows almost as the DSS latency does until the number of clients reaches 4; then it roughly doubles, while the DSS latency continues to increase smoothly. This is due to the additional synchronization required within each ARH replica to serve multiple concurrent clients. With 8 clients, indeed, each ARH replica receives requests from two clients, and the access to the DSS component is serialized within each ARH. As a consequence, the GCT works in the same conditions as there were only 4 clients. The little growth of the DSS latency is due to the small growth of network traffic due to the additional replicas, and it is almost independent from the toolkit, as confirmed in Figure 6(b). In contrast, synchronization

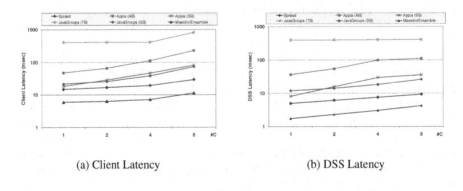

(a) Client Latency   (b) DSS Latency

Fig. 6. Client and DSS Latency as a Function of #C (#ARH=4, #R=2)

within each ARH causes the doubling of the client latency with respect to that observed with 4 clients. Therefore, overall performances are mainly influenced by the GCT when the number of clients is less than or equal to the number of ARH replicas. Figure 6(b) also confirms the gap between JavaGroups (SB) and other toolkits with a non-Java core. Let us finally remark that in all the experiments Maestro/Ensemble outperforms Java implementations, which lay on a virtual machine. However, pure Java GCTs like Appia (SB) and JavaGroups (SB) can be configured to perform close to Spread, which is comparable with Maestro/Ensemble in terms of efficiency.

5   Conclusions

In this paper we have first identified some architectural properties that influence the performance of a GCT, and then we have compared the performances of three Java GCT and a C++/OCAML toolkit, in the context of a three-tier software replication. Results are promising, as the expected performance degradation due to Java can be considered acceptable with respect to all the advantages due to the use of this language. However, a gap with C++ still exists, and optimizations are required in order to reduce it.

References

1. Schneider, F.B.: Replication Management Using the State Machine Approach. In Mullender, S., ed.: Distributed Systems. ACM Press - Addison Wesley (1993)
2. Budhiraja, N., Schneider, F., Toueg, S., Marzullo, K.: The Primary-Backup Approach. In Mullender, S., ed.: Distributed Systems. ACM Press - Addison Wesley (1993) 199–216
3. Birman, K., van Renesse, R.: Reliable Distributed Computing With The ISIS Toolkit. IEEE Computer Society Press, Los Alamitos (1993)
4. Moser, L.E., Melliar-Smith, P.M., Agarwal, D.A., Budhia, R.K., Lingley-Papadopoulos, C.A., Archambault, T.P.: The Totem System. In: Proc. of the 25th Annual International Symposium on Fault-Tolerant Computing, Pasadena, CA (1995) 61–66
5. Vaysburd, A., Birman, K.P.: The Maestro Approach to Building Reliable Interoperable Distributed Applications with Multiple Execution Styles. Theory and Practice of Object Systems **4** (1998) 73–80
6. Ban, B.: Design and implementation of a reliable group communication toolkit for java. Cornell University (1998)
7. Amir, Y., Stanton, J.: The Spread Wide Area Group Communication System. Technical Report CNDS-98-4, Center for Networking and Distributed Systems, Computer Science Department, Johns Hopkins University (1998)
8. Miranda, H., Pinto, A., Rodrigues, L.: Appia, a flexible protocol kernel supporting multiple coordinated channels. In: Proceedings of The 21st International Conference on Distributed Computing Systems (ICDCS-21), Phoenix, USA, IEEE Computer Society (2001) 707–710
9. Herlihy, M., Wing, J.: Linearizability: a Correctness Condition for Concurrent Objects. ACM Transactions on Programming Languages and Systems **12** (1990) 463–492
10. Marchetti, C.: A Three-tier Architecture for Active Software Replication. PhD thesis, Dipartimento di Informatica e Sistemistica, Università degli Studi di Roma "La Sapienza" (2002)
11. Baldoni, R., Marchetti, C., Tucci-Piergiovanni, S.: Asynchronous Active Replication in Three-tier Distribuuted Systems. In: Proc. of the IEEE Pacific Rim Symposium on Dependable Computing (PRDC02), Tsukuba, Japan (2002) to appear, also available as Technical Report at http://www.dis.uniroma1.ir/~irl.

12. Baldoni, R., Marchetti, C., Termini, A.: Active Software Replication through a Three-tier Approach. In: Proc. of the 22th IEEE International Symposium on Reliable Distributed Systems (SRDS02), Osaka, Japan (2002) ,pp. 109–118
13. Baldoni, R., Marchetti, C., Tucci-Piergiovanni, S.: Fault-tolerant Sequencer: Specification and an Implementation. In Ezhilchelvan, P., Romanovsky, A., eds.: Concurrency in Dependable Computing. Kluwer Academic Press (2002)
14. IRL Project Web Site: ⟨http://www.dis.uniroma1.it/~irl⟩
15. Java Sun website: ⟨http://java.sun.com⟩
16. IONA Web Site: ⟨http://www.iona.com⟩
17. Birman, K., Joseph, T.: Reliable Communication in the Presence of Failures. ACM Transactions on Computer Systems 5 (1987) 47–76
18. Dèfago, X.: Agreement-Related Problems: From Semi Passive Replication to Totally Ordered Broadcast. PhD thesis, École Polytechnique Fédérale de Lausanne, Switzerland (2000)

A Java-Based, Distributed Process Management System for Collaborative Design and Manufacturing

Moon Jung Chung[1], Sangchul Kim[2], Hyun Kim[3], and Ho Sang Ham[4]

[1] Department of Computer Science, Michigan State University, East Lansing, Michigan, U.S.A.
chung@cse.msu.edu
[2] Department of Computer Science and Engineering, Hankuk University of Foreign Studies, Yongin, Korea
kimsa@hufs.ac.kr
[3] Concurrent Engineering Team, ETRI, 161 Kajong-Dong, Taejon, Korea
hyunkim@etri.re.kr
[4] Mobile Distributed Processing Team, ETRI, 161 Kajong-Dong, Taejon, Korea
hsham@etri.re.kr

Abstract. Process management serves as a central mechanism for supporting collaborative design and manufacturing. In this paper, a Java-based, distributed process management system for collaborative design and manufacturing is presented. The system called MIDAS employs the process grammar to support the efficient representation of process alternatives and to facilitate the collaboration among users. The main features of our system are: *Java-based*, *distributed architecture*, and *XML-based*. Java applets and RMI increase the portability of our system, enabling the client-side module of our system to run at any location without the pre-installation of additional software. Process databases, servers, and external applications that are distributed over various companies can be integrated into the system transparently to users. XML is utilized to represent the execution status, data visualization, and task knowledge, increasing the scalability and customizability of the system functionalities. The system is shown to be efficient when we applied it to several real processes.

1 Introduction

Collaborative manufacturing enables a group of design and manufacturing companies to work on a large product that cannot be carried out by an individual company alone. Much work has been done on process management to provide system support for coordination among collaborative companies [3, 8]. Through contacts with a group of manufacturing companies, we have identified that the process management should provided the following requirements for collaborative design and manufacturing:

☐ Users need to access the process management system easily at any platform without prior work, such as the pre-installation of additional software.

N. Guelfi et al. (Eds.): FIDJI 2002, LNCS 2604, pp. 61–72, 2003.

❑ The engineering process is tentative and iterative by nature. Alternatives for designing and manufacturing are explored until a satisfactory solution is reached. The system needs to support users for exploring the alternatives easily.

❑ The process should be easily reconfigured when changes, such as new user requirement or the identification of configuration errors, are imposed on the process in execution

❑ Scalability is needed for large-scale process. New processes and tools should be added to the system in a modular way.

❑ The distributed data server is required. Since each individual company specializes in a certain part of the overall design and manufacturing process, the knowledge and data about the overall process is naturally distributed over companies.

❑ Each individual company has its own proprietary process during collaboration so that data protection from unauthorized use is essential.

We present a distributed process management system, called MIDAS (The Manufacturing Integration and Design Automation System), which facilitates the support for the requirements mentioned above. Modules of MIDAS, written in Java, communicate with each other using RMI. Process databases, servers, and external applications that are distributed over various companies can be integrated into the system transparently to users. XML is utilized to represent task knowledge and execution status. To our survey, little work has been published on distributed process management systems for collaborative design and manufacturing.

For many years researchers have had a strong interest in process management since it has been recognized as a key vehicle for process planning and process monitoring in order to improve productivity [4], [10]. In previous process management systems, XML is typically used to represent process information and the interface between subsystems [7], [12]. We utilize XML to represent various kinds of information, such as process and task knowledge, the status of a process in execution, and visualization data. It is shown that XML allows collaborative parties to communicate in common and simple terms, provides scalability required for large-scale collaboration, and enhances the protection of proprietary data from the unauthorized access. There are many XML-based standards for the representation of business processes, such as ebXML [12], RosettaNet [13], etc. Tasks in our system have generic interface for input and output. Therefore, their input and output can be in arbitrary format and there is no restriction on transaction protocol and data format. Other types of tools, such as ebXML, can easily interface with our system.

The distributed architecture of MIDAS facilitates organizing processes. It supports two types of distribution: resource and execution. The first type of distribution is that since collaborative companies may have their own database and a set of application tools at their own site, the transparent access to them is needed independently of their location. The second type of distribution is client-server style. The server is likely to be overloaded in case a very large number of clients. MIDAS moves much of the processing overhead from the server side to the client for increased performance. WfMC [16] is a standardization activity for the interoperability between workflow systems by defining the major subsystems and their interfaces. It seems like there has been little follow-up effort in the commercial market, but our system paper basically follows the architecture suggested by WfMC.

Many distributed process (or workflow) management system have been proposed which integrate the works of different organizations [5, 11]. Most of the systems [9 17] use CORBA to provide the interoperability between remote applications. The CORBA-based architecture enforces ORB to be installed at every site running CORBA-based applications. This enforcement is a great obstacle to the development of a portable client in the client-server style system, where the client is usually dedicated to the user interface while the server (or servers) provides application logic. This is the reason that MIDAS uses RMI (Remote Method Interface).

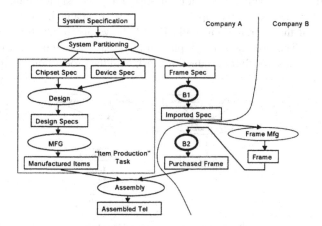

Fig. 1. A Process Flow Graph after Elaborating "Item Production" Task

2 Grammar-Based Process Representation and Execution

The core of the MIDAS is a process grammar, which provides the theoretical foundation to represent, manipulate and execute design and manufacturing processes [1]. In the MIDAS system, Design and Manufacturing processes are modeled as a collection of tasks. Each task can be decomposed into a set of subtasks. Our process flow graph depicts tasks, data and the relationships among them, describing the sequence of tasks for a larger D&M activity. Four basic symbols are used to represent the process flow: *Logical Tasks* (represented using oval), *Atomic Tasks* (two-concentric oval nodes), *Specifications* (rectangular nodes) and *Selectors* (diamonds nodes). A logical task can be decomposed into subtasks, while an atomic task cannot. A selector selects a specification or a parameter for a task. These elements can be combined into a process flow graph using directed arcs to indicate the specifications used and produced by each task.

Using these graphical elements, a process flow graph can be created in a top-down fashion. Fig. 1 shows a simple outsourcing arrangement, where company A produces a telephone by manufacturing all items, except the frame, and assembling all items, and company B manufactures the frame only. Process flow graphs can describe processes in varying degrees of detail. The overall process can be seen because the details are hidden within the tasks. A graph containing many logical nodes describes what should be done without describing how it should be done (for example, specifying which tools to use). Conversely, a graph in which all task nodes are either atomic or selectors fully describes a complete methodology for a design.

The process grammar provides a mechanism for transforming a high-level process flow graph into progressively more detailed process flow graphs. The grammar consists of a set of production rules. A production is a substitution that permits the replacement of a logical task node with a flow graph that represents a way of performing the task. If there are several production rules for a logical task, it implies that there are alternatives for the task. This capability is critical to maintaining the usability and effectiveness of the overall framework. Fig. 2 shows one production for "Item Production" task. The process flow graph of Fig. 1 has been obtained from a process flow graph by replacing "Item Production" task with the production of Fig. 2.

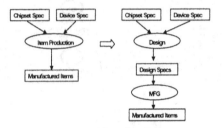

Fig. 2. A Production "Item Production"

3 The Overall Architecture of the MIDAS

Fig. 3 illustrates the architecture of MIDAS. The system consists of various components, and links external tools to design and manufacturing processes. The system is partitioned into the client side and the server side. The database, the connection server, the user information server, the site proxy server are in the sever side. The cockpit is in the client side. The cockpit is a Java applet, increasing the portability, and all other components are Java applications. All components communicate with each other using RMI connections.

Cockpit: The cockpit controls the interactions between the user and the other components. It allows multiple users to collaboratively edit and execute a process flow by sharing the execution status and visualization data. The collaborative process execution is carried out in a way that each of collaborative cockpits executes some part of the whole process. Also, the task manager is a part of the cockpit that schedules a sequence of tasks and invokes each task. Pre-evaluation functions estimate the possibility of success for each alternative. It calls post-evaluation functions to determine if task's outputs meet the specified requirements.

For the efficient, concurrent execution of independent tasks, multithreading is employed as follows. Initially a thread is created for the top-level description of process, and then the thread creates a thread for each constituent task if the task is ready for execution.

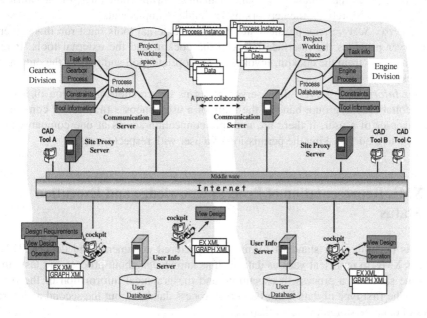

Fig. 3. The Architecture of MIDAS

Communication Server: This server is in charge of group communication. Each company has at least one communication server. Each user cockpit needs to be connected to a communication server (called *hooked connection server*). When a group of cockpits collaborate on a process, their hooked communication servers communicate the information to be shared by the group. The information includes events, such as the joining of a new cockpit or the leaving of a cockpit, the run-time status of tasks, and the visualization data of the flow graph. The hooked communication servers of all the users in a group cooperate as a multicasting network.

Process Database and Workspace: The communication server also manages the process database and the workspace. The process database contains the knowledge about processes and tasks. The working space archives the execution status of a process, and also keeps the data generated by a process. The knowledge and the runtime status of a process are represented in XML. Any site (or company) that has its own process database should run a communication server. A personal workspace exists separately for each user at their site, and a group workspace for each process in execution exists at a connection server. To enable accessing the process database and the workspace irrespectively of their physical location, the communication servers operate in a distributed way. Precisely speaking, all of the communication servers involving in collaboration for a group of cockpits form a Gnutella-style P2P network [6]. This kind of networking is adequate for the data management of our system since its operation is little affected by the joining of a new server or the leaving of an existing server. Considering a company may go bankrupt or a new company joins the supply-chain that typically requires the collaboration among manufacturing companies, the network is very attractive. Moreover, the networking is simple to implement.

Site Proxy Server: Any physical site that hosts external tools must run this server. The server provides the interface between the cockpit and the external tools. It receives requests from the cockpit, invokes an appropriate tool, and returns the output to the cockpit.

User Information Server: This server performs the creation or deletion of a user and a collaborating group, handles the login of a user, chooses the hooked communication server of a user, if there are multiple connection severs at one company, and responds to a query asking the permission of a user with respect to a task.

4   XML Representation of Process Knowledge and Execution Status

XML is becoming the standard format for structured documents and data. MIDAS utilizes XML to represent various data such as knowledge about process and task, the run-time status of a process in execution, and the graphical information of the flow graph. The first type of data is stored in the process database, but the second and third types of data are stored in the workspace.

4.1   Process Database

The process database keeps three types of XMLs (called PROCESS XML, TASK XML, and PRODUCTION XML, respectively) that encode the knowledge about processes and tasks. The PROCESS XML is to encode the top-level description of a manufacturing or design process. The PRODUCTION XML is to encode a production of a logical task. The TASK XML is a repository of the information about a task, including constraints, a set of production names for a task if the task is a logical one, and an external tool for accomplishing a task if the task is an atomic one. Using XML enables collaborative companies to share this knowledge more easily since XML allows common and simple items. XML makes it easy to integrate our system with other XML-enabled manufacturing tools, where the number of such tools is expected to grow rapidly. Moreover, the simple syntax of XML increases system scalability. Enterprise systems are constantly evolving: new processes and products are added to the system, and new technology makes old constraints obsolete. In a truly scalable enterprise system, processes, tools, machines should be added in a modular way. New information is simply added by introducing a new XML tag or a new attribute of an existing XML tag.

We use a three-step approach to generating XML schemas of the three XMLs from process and task specifications. The first step is to capture and represent those specifications in form of conceptual UML diagrams. Those diagrams correspond to ER diagrams in the designing of the database. The second step is to convert the conceptual diagrams to logical UML diagrams, and the last step is to convert the logical diagrams to XML schemas. The motivation for the three-step approach is that instead of devising XML schemas directly from the specifications, the conceptual modeling is an easy way to capture the complete knowledge about the process and to verify the correctness of the captured knowledge.

The second and the last step can be carried out algorithmically. The conversion at the second step can be done by an extended version of a method suggested by Routledge, et. al   [14]. The extension is needed since their method does not support the generalization relationship that is necessary for process grammar-based specifications. The extension is simple in that a super-class is not mapped to a complex-type object, but its attributes are reflected in the complex-type objects mapped to its sub-classes. The conversion at the third step can be done by a method suggest by Booch, et. al [2]. For more detail of our UML/XML modeling, refer to [15].

4.2 EX XML and GRAPH XML

The EX XML keeps track of the run-time status of a process from the start of execution. The information kept by the EX XML includes a list of productions ever used for the elaboration of logical tasks, the readiness of inputs and outputs, whether a task is being executed or not, etc. When the process flow graph gets elaborated with a production, the elaboration is recorded in the EX XML. Thus, the EX XML keeps the history of process execution, which is needed to find an unexplored alternative way when a task fails in some way of execution. The GRAPH XML keeps only the current status of a process in execution and the geometry of the process flow graph. The process flow graph is visualized using a XSL style sheet. Each cockpit is allowed to apply its own XSL style sheet for customized view.

The reasons for using XML to keep the execution status and visualization data of a process are many-folded:

☐ The simplicity of XML facilitates the development of external applications for additional services, such as the analysis or monitoring of the result of process execution.

☐ The run-time status of a process is inherently represented hierarchically since the elaboration of a process flow graph is hierarchically performed. That is, after a task of a process flow graph is elaborated with a production, the tasks of the production are elaborated afterwards. The hierarchical structure of XML is suitable for representing the hierarchical information.

☐ XML facilitates integrating MIDAS with other process management systems. It will be easy to develop tools that convert the execution status of a process into the formats understandable by those systems.

In MIDAS, there is a separate EX XML for each individual task. The EX XML for the top-level description of a process has almost the same content as the one for a logical task. In their EX XMLs, an attribute, called *status*, for a constituent task exists to tell the execution status of the task. For a logical task that has already been elaborated, the productions that have been explored are also specified. If a logical task (i.e. a production being selected) is failed, the failure and a new production, if any, are also specified.

There is one GRAPH XML for each cockpit in collaboration. The GRAPH XML serves as a mechanism for sharing the current status of a process in execution. After an EX XML is updated by an operation (Apply or Rollback, to be mentioned later) at a cockpit, the GRAPH XML of the cockpit is also updated accordingly and then sent, through "communication servers", to other collaborating cockpits.

The GRAPH XML needs to be constructed so as to protect the proprietary information of companies from unauthorized use by hiding the detail information. MIDAS allows two types of permission with respect to tasks: read and execute. The user with "execute" permission with respect to a task can execute the task. A user with "read" permission with respect to a task is able to view all the information on the task, including how the task, if it is a logical one, has been elaborated and to access the outputs of the task. Before the communication server forwards a GRAPH XML to a cockpit, it modifies the GRAPH XML in a way that the information on a task is masked out if the user of the cockpit has no "read" permission with respect to the task. For example, for such a logical task, the elaboration of the task is masked out so that the task appears as one node in the process flow graph. That is, the user cannot see how the task has been performed.

5   Cockpit and Process Execution

The cockpit finishes the execution of a process when an initial process flow graph gets fully elaborated. Applications bound to atomic tasks and selector tasks are executed during execution. The task scheduling of the thread for a logical task or the top-level representation of a process is performed basically in a data flow fashion. That is, as soon as all inputs of a constituent task are available, the task is scheduled to be ready for execution. When the execution of a task is done successfully, all outputs of the task become available to other tasks. The data flow style allows the concurrent execution of multiple tasks.

5.1   Various Ways of Process Execution

The knowledge about manufacturing and design processes is sometimes so complicated that representing all of it in a machine-executable form is not easy. For example, the precondition of a logical task is based on heuristics. Also, a new process needs to be executed before the knowledge about the process is fully captured due to the pressure on the delivery time of a product. Such a process needs to be reconfigured manually as the new knowledge is added. Therefore, MIDAS supports two modes of process execution: *manual mode* and *auto mode*. In manual mode, MIDAS interacts with users on during process execution to make decisions for task scheduling and production selection. That is, in manual mode, the user can determine which task to be executed next, and select a production. However, in auto mode, these decisions are made automatically by MIDAS.

Two styles of collaboration among cockpits are supported: *screen sharing style* and *client-server style*. These two styles reflect the two way of collaboration among companies. The screen sharing style is for CSCW (Computer Supported Collaborative Work) style collaboration. Each user can view how other users perform their own work. In the client-server style, a client cockpit sends a server cockpit a request for the execution of a task. Then the sever cockpit performs the task, and notify the client cockpit of the termination of the task. The client cockpit cannot see how the task has been done and the server also cannot see the execution of all other tasks except for its own task.

5.2 Multi-threaded Execution

Since there can be more than one ready task (a task whose all inputs are available), multi-threaded process execution is conceptually natural in that a thread takes care of one ready task. Sometimes backtracking, called "rollback", occurs to a previous point of execution. In case of the failure of a task, rollback occurs to either its predecessor or parent task. The thread of a task to which rollback occurs is asked to find the other alternative to explore different way of execution. The failure of a task occurs when all the alternative ways of executing the task have been explored but failed. For example, when all the productions of a logical task have been explored but none have lead to a fully elaborated flow graph, the task is said to fail. When a task fails, the thread for the task dies without heavy interaction with other threads. When the task is considered for execution again, a new thread is created for the task.

A thread does not die even though it has succeeded, because a rollback may happen to the thread afterwards. In case of the failure of a thread, it is difficult to determine to which rollback needs to occur if the thread has multiple predecessor threads. Rollbacks cannot occur to those predecessor threads concurrently since those threads do not share the internal detail of their work. For example, when a task with two predecessor tasks fails, we need to ask the threads of two predecessors to find an alternative way one after the other. Otherwise, it is very hard to enumerate all the combinations of the alternatives that can be done by the two threads.

5.3 Classes of the Cockpit

Fig. 4 illustrates the classes that implement the Cockpit. The key classes are
- Apply, Rollback: An Apply operation is to execute a task. Apply operation to a logical task performs the following operation: First evaluate the pre-evaluation function of the logical task to select the best production of the task. Once a production is chosen, the task is elaborated with the flow graph of the production. If this operation is applied to an atomic task, the designated work, such as external tool invocation, is performed on the task. A Rollback operation is the reverse of

the Apply operation. When this operation is applied to a task, the task is forced to fail. There are two choices of rollback points: predecessors and parents. In manual mode, the user is able to select one of the two choices. In auto mode, the second choice is made only if the task has no predecessor. Apply and Rollback operations modify the EX XML and the GRAPH XML.

- Shrink, Expand: There are two operations provided by the cockpit for enabling the user to change the presentation of the process flow graph. They are Shrink and Expand. Shrink is only applied to a logical task in the flow graph. The operation updates the flow graph in a way that the detail process flow of a logical task is hidden, and instead one task node is shown. Expand is the reverse of Shrink. It replaces a shrunken node by its underlying flow graph. These two operations are recorded in the GRAPH XML.

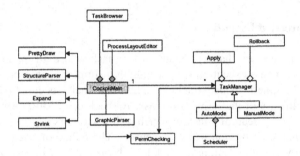

Fig. 4. An UML Model of the Client Side

6   Implementation and Benchmark

VisualCafe and IBM XML parser was used to implement MIDAS. MIDAS was applied to a gearbox manufacturing process and a pulley (a mechanical equipment) manufacturing process. The process grammar was shown to naturally capture the process knowledge since it facilitates the succinct representation of alternatives and abstraction. Support for manual mode together with auto mode of execution made engineers explore the D&M space more efficiently. The cockpit, a Java applet, enabled engineers to work continuously independently of their physical locations while they visit other companies for collaboration and work there, resulting in the speed up of the manufacturing process.   MIDAS showed reasonable performance even in case of many clients due to the distributed architecture.

7   Conclusions

Recently, system support for collaboration has been interesting research field in business, design, and manufacturing. As more manufacturing devices become computers-controlled and the network technologies have advanced, the demand for a system that facilitates collaborative design and manufacturing is increasing rapidly.

In this paper, we presented a process management system for collaborative design and manufacturing, called MIDAS. The core of MIDAS is the process grammar, which provides the theoretical foundation to represent, manipulate and execute D&M processes. The contribution of this paper is to propose a methodology for developing the process management system that efficiently supports the process grammar. Core technologies employed by the methodology are *Java, the distributed architecture* and *XML*.

The advantages of our system over previous ones are summarized as follows;

1. New process knowledge, external applications, and process engines (servers) can be easily incorporated into the system transparently of their location. Since the cockpit, the client-side component, is implemented as a Java applet, the cockpit can be started from any location without the pre-installation of any communication module.
2. MIDAS, with process grammar in its engine, supports the iterative nature of engineering process and provides a layered approach to information modeling.
3. MIDAS supports a flexible work process. Tasks can be performed automatically or manually, and alternative processes can be generated in mid-stream. By supporting search for alternative process, rather than simply searching for alternative design parameters, the system encourages truly a flexible approach to design process management.
4. The use of XML facilitates the sharing of process knowledge by collaborative organizations, system scalability, and the protection of proprietary process information from unauthorized access.
5. Our distributed task scheduling makes the architecture of our system more modular. Little previous effort has been published on the distributed scheduling in which rollback is considered for exploring the search space.

Our system can be viewed as an extension of agent-based approach. Each task behaves as an agent that carries out a specified task by selecting an appropriate tool based on constraints, input data and assigned resources. If the result of the task does not meet the requirements, the agent must select other alternative or input data.

References

1. Baldwin, R. and Chung, M.J., "Design Methodology Management: A Formal Approach", *IEEE Computer*, February 1995, pp. 54-63.
2. Booch, G., Christerson. M, Fuchs, M., and Koistinen. J., "UML for XML Schema Mapping Specification",
   http://www.rational.com/media/uml/resources/media/uml xmlschema33.pdf
3. Chung, M.J., Kwon, P. and Pentlan, Brian, MIDAS: A Framework for Integrated Design and Manufacturing Process, Proc. of SPIE Intelligent Systems in Design and Manufacturing III, 2000.

4. Dornfeld D., Wright P. K., Wang F-C., Sheng P., Stori J., Sundararajan V., Krishnan N., and Chu C-H, "Multi-Agent Process Planning for a Networked Machining Service," By North American Manufacturing Research Conference, 1999.
5. Georgakopoulos, Diimitrios and Hornick, Mark, "An Overview of Workflow Management: From Process Modeling to Workflow Automation Infrastructure", *Distributed and Parallel Databases*, 3, 119–153, 1995.
6. Ripeanu, M., Peer-to-Peer Architecture Case Study: Gnutella Network, http://www.cs.uchicago.edu/files/tr_authentic/TR-2001-26.pdf
7. Shiau, J., Y., Ratchev, S., and Valtchanov, G., "Distributed Collaborative Design and Manufacturability Assessment for Extended Enterprise in XML-based System, School of Mechanical, Material, Manufacturing Engineering and Management", Univ. of Nottingham, UK. Technical Report, 2002.
8. Lavana, H., Khetawat, A., Brglez, F., and Kozminski, K., "Executable Workflows: A Paradigm or Collaborative Design on the Internet", Proceedings of the 34th ACM/IEEE Design Automation Conference, June 1997.
9. Miller, J.A., Sheth, A.P., Kochut, K.J. and Wang, X., CORBA-Based Run-Time Architectures for Workflow Management Systems, Technical Report, Large Scale Distributed Information Systems Lab, Dept of Computer Science, Univ. of Georgia.
10. Sadeh, N., Hildum, D., Laliberty, T., McANulty, J., Kjenstad, J., and Tseng, A., "A Blackboard Architecture for Integrating Process Planning and Production Scheduling", *Concurrent Engineering: Research and Applications*, Vol 6, No 2, June 1998.
11. Papazolgou, M. P., Jeusfeld, M. A., Weigand, H., and Jarke, M., "Distributed, Interoperable Workflow Support for Electronic Commerce," http//infolabwww.kub.nl/infolab, 2002,
12. Riemer, K., ebXML Business Process, http://www.gca.org/papers/xmleurope2001/papers/s18-1.html
13. RosettaNet, http://www.rosettanet.org
14. Routledge, N., Bird, L., and Goodchild, A., "UML and XML Schema", Thirteenth Australasian Database Conference (ADC2002), Melbourne, Australia.
15. Quin, Y., Process Modeling and Presentation for Collaborative Design and Manufacturing, master thesis (draft), Department of Computer Science and Engineering, Michigan State University, 2002.
16. Workflow Management Coalition, http://www.wmfc.org.
17. Whiteside, R. A., Pancerella, C. M., Klevgard, P. A., "A CORBA-Based Manufacturing Environment", Hawaii International Conf on System Sciences, Maui Hawaii, January 7-10, 1997.

Structured Handling of Online Interface Upgrades in Integrating Dependable Systems of Systems

Cliff Jones, Panos Periorellis, Alexander Romanovsky, and Ian Welch

School of Computing Science, University of Newcastle upon Tyne
Newcastle upon Tyne, NE1 7RU, UK

Abstract. The integration of complex systems out of existing systems is an active area of research and development. There are many practical situations in which the interfaces of the component systems, for example belonging to separate organisations, are changed dynamically and without notification. Usually systems of system (SoS) developers deal with such situations off-line causing considerable downtime and undermining the quality of the service that SoSs are delivering [Romanovsky & Smith 2002]. In this paper we propose an approach to on-line handling such upgrades in a structured and disciplined fashion. All interface changes are viewed as abnormal events and general fault tolerance mechanisms (exception handling, in particular) are applied to dealing with them. The paper outlines general ways of detecting such interface upgrades and recovering after them. An Internet Travel Agency is used as a case study throughout the paper. An implementation demonstrating how the general approach proposed can be applied for dealing with some of the possible interface upgrades within this case study is discussed.

1 Introduction

A "System of Systems" (SoS) is built by interfacing to systems which might be under the control of organisations totally separate from that commissioning the overall SoS. (We will refer to the existing (separate) systems as "components" although this must not confuse the question of their separate ownership). In this situation, it is unrealistic to assume that all changes to the interfaces of such components will be notified. In fact, in many interesting cases, the organisation responsible for the components may not be aware of (all of) the systems using its component. One of the most challenging problems faced by researchers and developers constructing *dependable* systems of systems (DSoSs) is, therefore, dealing with on-line (or unanticipated) upgrades of component systems in a way which does not interrupt the availability of the overall SoS.

It is useful to contrast evolutionary (unanticipated) upgrades with the case where changes are programmed (anticipated). In the spirit of other work on dependable systems, the approach taken here is to catch as many changes as possible with exception handling mechanisms.

Dependable systems of systems are made up of loosely coupled, autonomous component systems whose owners may not be aware of the fact that their system is

N. Guelfi et al. (Eds.): FIDJI 2002, LNCS 2604, pp. 73–86, 2003.

involved in a bigger system. The components can change without giving any warning (in some application areas, e.g. web services, this is a normal situation). The drivers for on-line software upgrading are well known: correcting bugs, improving (non-) functionality (e.g. improving performance, replacing an algorithm with a faster one), adding new features, and reacting to changes in the environment.

This paper focuses on evolutionary changes that are typical in complex web applications which are built out of existing web services; we aim to propose a generally applicable approach. As a concrete example, we consider an Internet Travel Agency (TA) [Periorellis & Dobson 2001] case study (see Figure 1). The goal of the case study is to build a travel service that allows a client to book whole journeys without having to use multiple web services each of which only allows the client to book some component of a trip (e.g. a hotel room, a car, a flight). To achieve this we are developing fault tolerance techniques that can be used to build such emergent services that provide a service which none of its component systems are capable of delivering individually. Of course, the multiplicity of airlines, hotel chains etc. provides redundancy which makes it possible for a well-designed error-recovery mechanism to survive temporary or permanent interruptions of connection but the interest here is on surviving unanticipated interface changes. As not all the systems in our system of systems are owned by the same organisation, it is inevitable that they will change during the lifetime of the system and there is no guarantee that existing clients of those systems will be notified of the change.

When a component is upgraded without correct reconfiguration or upgrading of the enclosing system, problems similar to ones caused by faults occur, for example: loss of money, TA service failures, deterioration of the quality of TA service, misuse of component systems. Changes to components can occur at both the structural and semantic level. For example changes of a component system can result in a revision of the units in which parameters are measured (e.g. from Francs to Euro), in the number of parameters expected by an operation (e.g. when an airline introduces a new type of service), in the sequence of information to be exchanged between the TA and a component system (e.g. after upgrading a hotel booking server requires that a credit card number is introduced before the booking starts). In the extreme, components might cease to exist and new components must be accommodated.

Although some on-line upgrading schemes assume that interfaces of components always stay unchanged (e.g. [Tai et al. 2002]), we believe that in many application areas it is very likely that component interfaces will change and that this will happen without information being sent to all the users/clients. This is the nature of the Internet as well as the nature of many complex systems of systems in which components have different owners and belong to different organizations as shown in Figure 1. In some cases of course, there might be an internal notification of system changes but the semantics of the notification system might not be externally understood.

Although there are several existing partial approaches to these problems, they are not generally applicable in our context. For example, some solutions deal only with programmed change where all possible ways of upgrading are hard-wired into the design and information about upgrading is always passed between components. This does not work in our context in which we deal with pre-existing component systems but still want to be able to deal with interface upgrading in a safe and reasonable fashion. Other approaches that attempt to deal with unanticipated or evolutionary change in a way that makes dynamic reconfiguration transparent to the TA integrators[1] may be found in the AI field. However, our intention is not to hide changes from the application level. Our aim is to provide a solution that is application-specific and reliant on general approaches to dealing with abnormal situations. In particular, we will build on existing research in fault tolerance and exception handling which offer disciplined and structured ways of dealing with errors of any types [Cristian 1995] at the application level.

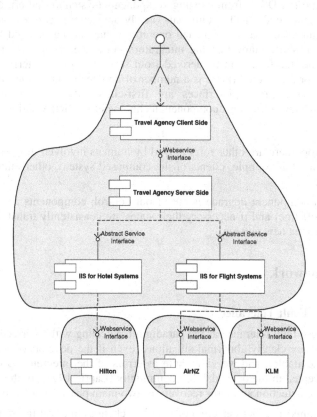

Fig. 1. UML Component diagram showing the component systems that make up the Internet Travel Agency (TA). The grey areas indicate the fact that the component systems are under the control of different organisations. A user is shown interacting with the Travel Agency Client Side component that validates client side inputs and passes requests to the Travel Agency Server Side component. The Travel Agent Server Side component handles each request by invoking multiple Intermediate Interfacing Subsystems (IIS). Each IIS provides an abstract service interface for a particular service type, for example the Flight Systems IIS provides an abstract service interface for booking flights with systems such as AirNZ and KLM even though each of these systems has different webservice interfaces.

---

[1] We use terms TA integrators and TA developers interchangeably.

Our overall aim is to propose structured multi-level mechanisms that assist developers in protecting the integrated DSoSs from interface changes and, if possible, in letting these DSoSs continue providing the required services.

2 System Model

Integrators compose a DSoS from existing components (systems) that are connected by interfaces, glue code and additional (newly-developed) components where necessary. An interface is a set of named operations that can be invoked by clients [Szyperski 1997]. We assume that the integrators know the component interfaces. Knowledge of the interfaces can be derived from several sources: interfaces can be either published or discovered (there is a number of new techniques emerging in this area), programmer's guides, interfaces are first-class entities in a number of environments such as interpreters, component technologies (CORBA, EJB), languages (Java).

Besides integrators there are other roles played by humans involved in the composed system at runtime, for example: clients of the composed system, other clients of the components, etc.

We assume that component upgrade is out of our control: components are upgraded somehow (e.g. off-line) and if necessary their states are consistently transferred from the old version to the new version.

3 The Framework

3.1 Structured Fault Tolerance

We propose to use fault tolerance as the paradigm for dealing with interface changes: specific changes are clearly abnormal situations (even if the developers accept their occurrence is inevitable), and we view them as errors of the integrated DSoS in the terminology accepted in the dependability community [Laprie 1995]. In the following we focus on error detection and error recovery as two main phases in tolerating faults.

Error detection aims at earlier detection of interface changes to assist in protecting the whole system from the failures which they can cause. For example, it is possible that, because of an undetected change in the interface, an input parameter is misinterpreted (a year is interpreted as a number of days the client is intending to stay in a hotel) causing serious harm. Error recovery follows error detection and can consist of a number of levels: in the best case dynamically reconfiguring the component/system and in the worst with a safe failure notification and off-line recovery.

Our structured approach to dealing with interface changes relies on multilevel exception handling which should be incorporated into a DSoS. It is our intention to "promote" multilevel structuring of complex applications to make it easier for developers to deal with a number of problems, but our main focus here is structured handling of interface changes. The general idea is straightforward [Cristian 1995]:

during DSoS design or integration, the developer identifies errors that can be detected at each level and develops handlers for them; if handling is not possible at this level, an exception is propagated to the higher level and responsibility for recovery is passed to this level. In addition to this general scheme, study of some examples suggests classifications of changes which can be used as check lists.

3.2 Error Detection

In nearly all cases, there is a need for meta-information to detect interface changes. Such meta-information is a non-functional description of the interfaces (and possibly of their upgrades), which may capture both structural and semantic information. Some languages and most middleware maintain structural meta-information, for example Java allows structural introspection and CORBA supports interface discovery via specialised repositories. However, at present there is little work on handling changes to semantic meta-information.

Meta-information for a component includes descriptions of:

- call points (interfaces), including input parameters (types, allowable defaults), output parameters (types, allowable defaults), pre- and post-conditions, exceptions to be propagated

- protocols: the sequences of calls to be executed to perform specific activities (e.g. cancel a flight, rent a car). A high-level scripting language can be used for this.

Interface changes can be detected either by comparing meta-description of old and new interfaces or if a component supports some mechanism to notify clients of changes. Another, less general, and as such less reliable, way of detecting such changes is by using general error detection features (some reasonable run-time type checking; pre- and post-conditions, or assertions of other types of checking parameters in the call points; protective component wrappers, etc.).

The intention should be to associate a rich set of exceptions with structural and semantic interface changes (changing the type of a parameter, new parameters, additional call points, changing call points, changing protocols, etc.); this would allow the system developers to handle them effectively.

3.3 Error Recovery

Error recovery can be supported through the use of:

- different handlers (at the same level) for different exceptions related to different types of interface changes

- multilevel handling.

3.3.1 Different Handlers

System developers should try and handle the following types of exception:

- changes of types of parameters, new parameter, missing parameter, new call point

- changes of the protocols, re-ordering, splitting, joining, adding, renaming and the removal of protocol events
- change of the meta-description language itself (if components provide us with such a meta-description of its interface)
- raising of new exceptions, if the protocol changes then new exceptions may also be raised during its execution.

To provide some motivational examples, consider the Travel Agent case study.

- A very simple interface change is where the currency in which prices are quoted changes. In this case, simple type information could show, for example, that the TA system requires a price in Pounds Sterling and the Car rental is being quoted in Norwegian Crowns. An exception handler can ask for a price in Euros which might be countered with an offer to quote in Dollars. Note that this process is not the same as reducing everything to a common unit (dollars?), finding agreement earlier can result in real savings in conversions.
- A previously functioning communication from the TA system to a hotel reservation system might raise an exception if a previously un-experienced query comes back as to whether the client wants a non-smoking room. Either of two general strategies might help here: the query could come marked with a default which will be applied if no response is given (an exception handler could accept this option) or the coded value might (on request from the exception handler) translate into an ASCII string which can be passed to the client for interpretation.
- Some of the most interesting changes and incompatibilities are likely to be protocol changes. An airline system might suddenly start putting its special offers before any information dialogue can be performed; the order in which information is exchanged between the TA and its suppliers of cars, flights etc. might change. Given enough meta-information, it is in principle, possible to resolve such changes but this is far more complex than laying out the order of fields in a record: it is the actual order of query and response which can evolve.
- In the extreme, the chosen meta-language might change. Even here, a higher-level exception handler might be able to recover if the meta-language is from a know repertoire.
- When an airline ceases to respond (exist?) the TA system must cope with the exception by offering a reduced service from the remaining airlines.
- Communication with new systems might be established if there is some agreement on meta-languages which can be handled.

In all of the above cases, the attempt is to use exception handling to keep the TA system running. Of course, notification of such changes might well be sent to developers; but the continuing function of the TA should not await their availability.

3.3.2 Multilevel Handling

Exceptions are propagated to a higher level if an exception is not explicitly handled or an attempt to handle the exception fails. This leads to a recursive system structuring with handlers being associated with different levels of a system. Possible handling strategies are:

- request a description of the new interface from the upgraded component
- renegotiate the new protocol with the component
- use a default value of the new parameters
- pass the unrecognised parameters to the end client (e.g. in ASCII)
- involve system operators into handling
- exclude the component from the operation
- execute safe stop of the whole system.

When designing handlers DSoS developers can apply the concepts of backward recovery, forward recovery or error compensation [Laprie 95]. Backward recovery restores the system to its state before the error, for example the TA abandons (aborts) a set of partial bookings making up an itinerary if one of the components cannot satisfy a particular booking. Forward recovery finds a new system state from which the system can still operate correctly, for example where DSoS developers decide to involve people in handling interface changes: TA support/developers, TA users/clients, component support. Error compensation relies upon the system state containing enough redundancy to allow the masking of the error. An example of error compensation is the use of redundant components. For example, in the TA case study if the KLM server changes its interface and TA cannot deal with this, it ignores it but continues using servers of BA and AirFrance.

After the TA has been safely stopped or a component has been excluded, the TA support and developers can perform off-line analysis of the new interface of the component (cf. fault diagnosis in [Laprie 95]). To improve the system performance and to make better use of the recent interface upgrades the TA application logic can be off-line modified when necessary following the ideas of fault treatment [Laprie 95].

4 Representing Meaning

In order to communicate semantic information between two computers or in the case of the TA between the SoS and its providers we need a structured collection of information (meta-data) as well as a set of inference rules that can be used to conduct automated reasoning. Traditionally knowledge engineering [Hruska & Hashimoto 2000], as this process is often called, requires all participants to share the same definitions of concepts. In our case, for example, definitions of what is a trip or a flight as well as the parameters for each of these have to be defined and shared. The protocol for booking and paying for a trip or an item is also required. Detailed descriptions of the parameter types and their semantic information also need to be held in a shared knowledge base. Knowledge bases however and their usage does not necessarily make the system more flexible; quite the contrary. Requests would have to be performed under strict rules for inference and deduction. The SoS would have to process its metadata (globally shared data descriptions) in order to infer how to make a request for a particular method (i.e. booking a flight) and further more infer what parameters accompany this method and what is their meaning.

This process requires a well defined globally shared description of the domain in which the SoS operates. Such a definition is usually called ontological definition and the process is referred to as ontological modeling. Current developments in web architectures and distributed systems are working towards communicating meta-data information across components systems. XML for example allows us to define our own tags in order to structure web pages and it is also widely used for structuring SOAP [W3C-SOAP] messages sent to components systems (web services). XML effectively allows the user to define its own tags the process of which is shared via a common document type definition which in turn enables both client and servers to interpret them. In order however to comprehend the semantics behind it then we need human intervention. To put it simply; a user for a share price component that accepts a string and returns the price of the share represented by the string may have a tag type stock price. So within the tags <stockprice> and </stockprice> the price of the share would be returned. Via XML we could communication between a provider and a consumer that a certain tag is of type String or Integer but that does not encapsulate its semantic information. This is where the resource definition framework (RDF) [W3C-RDF 2000] may help as it provides a technique for describing resources on the web. It is a framework for specifying metadata using XML syntax.

In conjunction with RDF interface descriptions could also bear and communicate their semantic information. All these technologies and disciplines however have not yet being put together for any meaningful application. They exist separately as hypertext and TCP/IP for example existed before the Internet. Using the current API's our choices are limited. The next section presents a general framework for dealing with interface upgrading and discusses the range of possible implementation technologies.

5   Interface Upgrading

In this section we provide a framework for implementing interface upgrading. The problem addressed by this framework is how to detect if the interface offered by a server has changed and how to dynamically load a new interface and continue interacting with the server.

We assume that in our distributed system there is a client, server and registry. The registry maintains a reference to the server, and a description of its interface. Note that the description of the interface may contain both structural and semantic information and we do not specify how this is represented.

When a client is implemented we assume that a copy of the server's interface is stored with it. This seems reasonable, as the client must make use of the interface in order to implement its program. We also assume that someone ensures that the reference to the server, and the description of the interface held at the registry is up to date. This may be the responsibility of the server provider, the client themselves, or a third-party. We also assume that the registry may be a separate entity or even collocated with the server, what is important is its function rather than its location.

When a client interacts with a server we assume that it goes through the following steps. The client contacts the registry and uses a symbolic name to look up both a reference to the server and a description of its interface. The client compares the description it retrieved from the registry to the cached description, if there is a difference then an exception is raised locally and handled locally. Assuming that there is no difference then the client invokes the operation on the server using the interface and the server's location. We assume that there may be a series of interactions and this series of interactions may represent a long lived task. The long lived nature of the task raises the possibility that the server may change its interface while the task is active. In this case, we assume that not-understood exception is raised at the server due to it no longer being able to understand the client's invocation or a not-understood exception is raised at the client due to the client no longer being able to understand the server's reply. This exception is handled locally at the client.

When the client or the server raises a not-understood exception then the following steps take place. The client contacts the registry again and looks up the server's interface. The client then compares the (hopefully updated) interface with its cached interface and raises an interface change exception.

Associated with each interface change exception there is an appropriate handler as described in Section 2.3.3.2. We assume that some handlers will wish to still keep interacting with the server but using the new interface, and therefore we require some means to take the new interface and dynamically invoke operations using it. The degree to which this is possible is directly related to the way that client-server interaction is implemented in the target middleware.

There majority of approaches to implementing client-server interactions can be classified using two dimensions: whether the client-server protocol sent across the wire is fixed or not, and whether the middleware tries to make distribution transparent or not. The following are examples classified using these two dimensions:

Fixed protocol for communication between clients and servers, the middleware provides an interface for dynamically composing invocations using the protocol (for example, CORBA's Dynamic Interface Invocation facility which allows the client to dynamically create invocations using the fixed protocol).

Potentially server-specific protocols for communication between clients and servers but a fixed protocol description language for describing the server-specific protocols, the middleware provides an interface for discovering the server-specific protocol and dynamically composing invocations using the protocol (for example, SOAP [W3C-SOAP] which allows the client to dynamically create invocations using server-specific protocols that are expressed using a fixed protocol description language).

Fixed protocol for communication between clients and servers, the middleware hides the protocol and allows communication with servers as if they were local objects (for example, Java RMI [JAVA RMI] which provides a local proxy that implements the fixed client-server protocol).

Potentially server-specific protocols for communication between clients and servers, the middleware hides the protocol and allows communications with the servers as if they were local objects (for example, Jini [Waldo 2001] with its "code-by-wire" approach where proxy objects that encapsulates the server-specific protocol are downloaded dynamically from a type of registry).

Note that some middleware uses a combination of approaches. For example, the Java webservices toolkit [JAVA-WEBSERVICES] allows the complexity of SOAP to be hidden using proxies but also allows dynamic invocation if required. There also extensions which complicate the picture. For example, Java RMI now provides the ability to download proxies as required that can be invoked dynamically using the standard Java reflection features since they are just local objects. Although this makes Java RMI appear like Jini it still makes use of a fixed protocol for communication between clients and servers.

Implementing our framework using middleware that provides transparent distribution can only be done if the middleware exposes aspects of the how the transparent distribution is achieved. Usually, transparent distribution is implemented through the use of a local stub object that the client uses to communicate with a remote server as if it was a local object. Should the server's interface change then there must be a facility of updating the local stub object that is used by the client. This requires that the local stub object can be reloaded dynamically. In addition since the stub object has changed then there must be some way to dynamically invoke its operations as there may be new operations or the signature of the operations may have changed from what existed when the client program was compiled. If any of these features is not provided by the middleware then our framework cannot be fully implemented.

Our framework is most easily implemented using middleware that supports dynamic invocation of server operations. It is harder to use because each invocation has to be explicitly constructed but there are none of the problems of updating and reloading proxies or requiring a feature allowing dynamic invocation of local objects.

In the next section we discuss our experiences with the Java RMI implementation, which highlight some of the problems faced when using a middleware that only supports transparent distribution.

6   Java RMI Implementation

This section discusses how some part of the general framework presented above is being applied within our ongoing experimental work on implementing Internet TA [Periorellis & Dobson 2001]. Current API's allow us to carry out some work towards dealing with online dynamic upgrades, although there is significant work to be done not just in programming terms at the application level but in terms of providing an adequate API that would allow us to overcome certain technical difficulties.

Java RMI does not offer a full API for dynamic interfaces. However, it does support dynamic invocation when used in conjunction with the standard Java reflective API. The client does not need to maintain a local copy of a stub for a remote service, and neither does it need to maintain a local copy of the interface for the remote service. This is because Java RMI supports the automatic downloading of RMI stubs on demand, and once the stub has been downloaded then the standard Java reflection API can be used to discover and invoke the methods supported by the stub and therefore the remote service. The limitation of this approach is that if the stub changes during the lifetime of the client then a replacement stub cannot be downloaded. This is due to caching at the client side, as the replacement stub has the same name as the original stub then the cached copy is used instead of downloading the stub again.

The TA prototype is using Java RMI and the standard Java reflective API to dynamically compose the emerging service out of participating components. As the stubs can be downloaded and the interface of the stubs discovered at runtime this allows the SoS to determine the composition of the emerging service at runtime. In order to implement such a structure we need four machines: one to act as an RMI server that accepts requests for component systems (e.g. playing a role of a KLM server), a client (IIS in our case, see Figure 1) and a stub repository that makes the stubs available via the network (this could be a web server or an anonymous FTP server), and a machine that hosts the RMI registry. In our implementation we maintain the stubs at the web server while the RMI server holds the actual implementations of the component systems, supporting classes and the interface description.

Each IIS only holds the names of the SoS component systems that it wraps. Each name is a human readable, implementation-independent reference that is registered with the RMI registry. This allows the location of SoS components to change without forcing changes to the implementation of the IIS. When the IIS invokes a SoS component service it queries the RMI registry for the stub that represents the SoS component service. The stub is transparently downloaded from the stub repository by the RMI infrastructure as the stub does exist locally. The IIS then uses the Java reflection API to discover and invoke methods on the stub and via RMI the SoS component system.

As each IIS provides a fixed abstract interface to the TA SoS then any changes to SoS component systems are localised to the IIS. The TA SoS and, via the TA SoS, any clients may be informed of unexpected changes to the component systems if extra information that is not captured by the abstract interface is required in order to complete a request. We foresee this being handled via our distributed exception handling scheme.

We already have an initial prototype that does not deal with server upgrading which can be accessed at http://ouston.ncl.ac.uk/main.htm. There are several avenues we are exploring right now that would allow some handling of online dynamic upgrades to SoS component systems. Although, changes to SoS component system interfaces that take place during the lifetime of a IIS are not visible via changes to the stub we can detect that some change has occurred by catching marshalling/unmarshalling or connection refused exceptions that will be caused by an upgrade. At present the best course of action that we can suggest is to restart the IIS and thereby force the local copy of the stub for the SoS component system to be refreshed. Once it has been refreshed then we can compare the interface of the new stub with a cached description of the old stub, this would allow the exact nature of the change to be detected and the appropriate handlers to be invoked. In this approach the actual stubs represent the meta-information used for handling interface upgrades. Assuming that we can find some technical solution to the caching problem then it would be possible to avoid restarting the IIS and therefore handling the effect of the upgrade would be more transparent.

Under some assumptions (e.g. the registry is updated before the server has been replaced with a new one) several scenarios are possible with respect to handling interface changes. For example:

- if a marshalling/unmarshalling exception is raised while accessing a KLM server we force the refresh of the local stub for the KLM server and compare its interface with a cached description of the KLM server in order to discover what has changed.

- if a connection refused exception is raised we can find out if we are trying to access the server in the middle of upgrading by going to the registry. This case clearly needs additional features because there is no guarantee that KLM updates the registry and the server atomically.

Our experience shows that Java and the RMI architecture in particular are not the most appropriate technologies for evaluating and implementing dynamic interface updates even though additional features such as the Java reflection API can be used to implement a limited form of dynamic interface discovery and remote. In particular, they do not allow us to call an updated service as a means for handling because of local caching of the stubs. By catching some RMI service exceptions we can infer that a service upgrade has occurred and this can drive manual clearing of the cache via a restart of the RMI client. Alternatively another way of handling such situation is to exclude the upgraded service from the following execution until the client logs off.

There are two directions in which we can progress from here. The first one is to see if we can modify the Java/RMI infrastructure to force local refresh of the stub cache. The second one is to use modern Web technologies which offer much more flexible features for on-line dealing with interface descriptions and provide dynamic discovery and invocation as first-class features.

7 Related Work

The distributed computing community has considered the problems of maintaining meta-information for service discovery within the context of loosely coupled distributed systems such as DSoSs. Most middleware systems implement some form of object trading service, for example CORBA has an Object Trader Service, Jini has a Lookup Service, and .NET uses services provided by the Universal Discovery, Description and Integration (UDDI) project. Furthermore recent developments supported by the World Wide Web Consortium (W3C)[2] include a number of XML-base languages complementing UDDI and allowing Web service interfaces [W3C-WSDL 2001] and business-level conversations supported by such services (e.g. [W3C-WSCL 2002]) to be described. Object traders enable providers to advertise

---

[2] http://www.w3.org/

services by registering offered interfaces with a trading service. Clients locate a service by querying the trader using descriptions based on the structure of an interface and quantitative constraints [Szyperski 1997]. As with our proposed solution, object traders provide the ability to associate some meta-information with services. However, there is an assumption that once a client has found a service that uses a particular interface then that interface will remain static. Another difference is that we plan to maintain a richer set of meta-information with services that capture both structural and semantic information about interfaces such as versioning information, protocols, meta-information related to ontology and knowledge representation, dealing with abnormal situations while using the service, associating typical scenarios with the protocols, etc.

On the other hand, the object oriented database community has explicitly considered system evolution. They have developed schemes for schema evolution, schema versioning and class versioning. For example, in [Amann et al. 2000] schemata of multiple DBs are expressed in XML. In this approach the user's queries are written using a domain standard, that identifies the various entities and relationships, and for each data-source/base there is a mapping from that source entities to the domain standard. So, that a rewriting of the user's query to the various source formats can be done automatically. Our work differs in that in addition to structural changes we consider semantic changes such as protocol mismatches that occur when evolution takes place. Also the solutions proposed by this community tend to assume the existence of a centralised authority for enforcing control whereas we are working in the context of decentralised authority.

There has been some work on resolving protocol mismatches in the area of component-based development. In [Vanderperren 2002] the concept of a component adaptor is introduced. It describes adaptations of the external behaviour independently of a specific API. When the adapter is applied to a composition of components the required adaptations can be automatically inserted. This is achieved through the application of algorithms that are based on finite automata theory. Our work differs in that we consider dynamic rather than build-time changes to protocols and we consider more wide ranging adaptation than just the renaming or addition of protocol events.

In our future work on the TA case study we intend to exploit this related work and some other features provided by modern component-oriented technologies and Internet technologies. Other useful features that can be used are language support for runtime reflection [Welch 2002], interface repositories and type libraries, and services such as CORBA's Meta-Object Facility that defines standard interfaces for defining and manipulating meta-models.

8 Concluding Remarks

This paper has not proposed a totally general or efficient solution; our interest is in providing a pragmatic approach that explicitly uses a fault tolerance framework. Our work is motivated by real problems encountered when considering a case study where mismatches due to evolution must be dealt with at runtime. Although there are some existing approaches to this problem we do not try to hide evolution from the application developer but provide a framework for dealing with it dynamically.

Acknowledgements. This work is partially supported by European IST DSoS Project and by Dependability Interdisciplinary Collaboration funded by EPSRC/UK. Ian Welch is supported by European IST MAFTIA Project.

References

[Amann *et al.* 2000] B. Amann, I. Fundulaki, M.Scholl. Integrating ontologies and thesauri for RDF schema creation and metadata querying. International Journal of Digital Libraries, 3, 3, pp. 221–236, 2000.

[Cristian 1995] F. Cristian. Exception Handling and Tolerance of Software Faults. In Lyu, M.R. (ed.): Software Fault Tolerance. Wiley, pp. 81–107, 1995.

[Hruska & Hashimoto 2000] T. Hruska and H. Hashimoto (eds), Knowledge Based Software Engineering, Ios Press June 2000.

[JAVA RMI] Java™ Remote Method Invocation (RMI), technical documentation, Sun Corporation, http://java.sun.com/j2se/1.4/docs/guide/rmi/, last accessed October 2003.

[JAVA WEBSERVICES] Sun Microsystems Limited, "Web Services Made Easier", technical white paper, June 2002 revision 3, http://java.sun.com/xml/webservices.pdf

[Laprie 1995] J.-C. Laprie. Dependable Computing: Concepts, Limits, Challenges. Proc. of the 25th Int. Symposium On Fault-Tolerant Computing. IEEE CS. Pasadena, CA. pp. 42–54. 1995.

[Periorellis & Dobson 2001] P. Periorellis, J.E. Dobson. Case Study Problem Analysis. The Travel Agency Problem. Technical Deliverable. Dependable Systems of Systems Project (IST-1999-11585). University of Newcastle upon Tyne. UK. 37 p. 2001.

[Romanovsky & Smith 2002] A. Romanovsky, I. Smith. Dependable On-line Upgrading of Distributed Systems. In Proc. of COMPSAC 2002. 26-29 August 2002, Oxford, UK. IEEE CS Press. pp. 975–976. 2002.

[Szyperski 1997] C. Szyperski. Component Software. ACM Press. 1997.

[Tai *et al.* 2002] A.T. Tai, K.S. Tso, L. Alkalai, S.N. Chau, W.H. Sanders. Low-Cost Error Containment and Recovery for Onboard Guarded Software Upgrading and Beyond. IEEE TC-51, 2, pp. 121–137. 2002.

[Vanderperren 2002] W. Vanderperren. A Pattern Based Approach to Separate Tangled Concerns in Component Based Development. Proc. of the 1st AOSD Workshop on Aspects, Components, and Patterns for Infrastructure Software, held in conjunction with the 1st International Conference on Aspect-Oriented Software Development. pp. 71–75. 2002.

[Waldo 2003] J. Waldo. The End of Protocols. October 2003. http://developer.java.sun.com/developer/technicalArticles/jini/protocols.html

[Welch 2002] I. Welch. A Reflective Security Architecture for Applications. PhD Thesis. Department of Computing, University of Newcastle upon Tyne (in preparation).

[W3C-RDF 2000] W3C. Resource Description Framework (RDF). RDF Specification Development. 2000. http://www.w3.org/RDF/

[W3C-SOAP] Simple Object Access Protocol (SOAP) 1.1. W3C Note May 2000. http://www.w3.org/TR/SOAP/.

[W3C-WSCL 2002] W3C. Web services conversation language (WSCL), version 1.0. The World Wide Web Consortium, 2002. http://www.w3.org/TR/wscl10/

[W3C-WSDL 2001] W3C. Web services description language (WSDL), version 1.1. The World Wide Web Consortium, 2001. http://www.w3.org/TR/wsdl

An Experience in Architectural Extensions: Active Objects in J2EE

Paola Inverardi, Fabio Mancinelli, Henry Muccini, and Patrizio Pelliccione

University of L'Aquila, Computer Science Department
Via Vetoio 1, 67010 L'Aquila, Italy
{inverard,mancinel,muccini,pellicci}@di.univaq.it

Abstract. In this paper we present an experience in architectural extension. The goal of our project was to provide *Active Objects* in the Java 2 Enterprise Edition (J2EE) reference architecture by suitable extensions that should not violate the architectural J2EE principles. Our approach to the problem was rather formal. We first formalized the notion of Active Object, the basic characteristics of the J2EE model and its component model Enterprise JavaBeans (EJB). Then, driven by the peculiar characteristics of an Active Object, we investigated several possible architectural extensions. The solutions were formalized as well and their consistency with the J2EE model was validated by using model checking techniques. In this way we discovered that only one of them was acceptable. The whole formalization and validation has been carried out by using the Charmy environment, where the architectural formalization makes use of diagrammatic notations, Scenarios and State Diagrams, and SPIN is the target model checking engine.

1 Introduction

In this paper we present an experience in architectural extension. A company asked us to evaluate the possibility to extend the Java 2 Enterprise Edition (J2EE) [13] reference architecture model, and therefore its component model Enterprise JavaBeans (EJB) [11], with Active Objects (AOs) in order to guarantee asynchronous method[1] invocation. The extension should not violate the architectural J2EE principles. Moreover we had some requirements to meet, i.e. the extension and the applications developed with it should be compatible with any J2EE implementation. This means that the extension has to be compatible with earlier versions of EJB and it could not use any implementation specific features. We approached the problem in a rather formal way. First, we formalized the notion of Active Object, the basic characteristics of the J2EE and EJB model. Then, driven by the peculiar characteristics of an Active Object, we investigated several possible architectural extensions. The solutions were formalized as well and their consistency with the J2EE model was validated by using model checking techniques. In this way we discovered the one that was acceptable.

---

[1] in the following, terms "method" and "service" will be used interchangeably.

N. Guelfi et al. (Eds.): FIDJI 2002, LNCS 2604, pp. 87–98, 2003.

The whole formalization and validation was carried out by using the Charmy [4] environment. In Charmy the architectural formalization makes use of diagrammatic notations, Scenarios and State Diagrams, and SPIN [14] is the target model checking engine. As a result of this work we realized that the approach we followed could actually be generalized and used to support evolutions (extensions/refinements) in software architecture. We have also applied the whole approach to EJB2.0 by proposing a new extension which uses its new features. This represented a way to validate the approach and a way to compare the two extensions. Summarizing, the contributions of the paper are the proposal of a J2EE architectural extension for Active Objects and an approach (together with a framework) to rigorously support architectural extensions. Our aim is to show that practical architectural extension problems can be rigorously treated with an acceptable degree of formality and state of the art tools. We agree that formal models may be successfully used for analysis and model checking. However, our approach tries to take a more liberal view in order to extend the support to rigorous reasoning beyond the classical bounds of strict formal reasoning on a model or on pairs of models. First, we do neither require to use a formal architectural language nor to completely specify the architectural descriptions. We try to exploit as much as possible the architectural artifacts, both static and dynamic, that exist in a standard development process. Second, we want to address evolution, that is we want to support extensions, and possibly refinements and thus consistency among different model abstractions. Third we want to show that rigorous reasoning can be supported on suitable portions of the specifications. We show how it is possible, in practice, to focus only on the properties and the specification portions relevant to the problem under consideration.

The paper is structured as follows. The next section outlines the approach to architectural extensions we followed. In Section 3 the relevant features of the Charmy environment are briefly summarized. Section 4 introduces J2EE, EJB1.1 and AO, and their formalization. Section 5 presents the architectural extensions to obtain AO in EJB1.1 and discusses their validation. In Section 6 EJB2.0 is considered and a different architectural extension is described and validated. Conclusions, related and future work are reported in Section 7.

2   The Approach: An Overview

The problem we are going to manage may be outlined as follows (Figure 1). Given a system, we describe its relevant properties using natural language, static diagrams (for static properties) and scenarios (for dynamic properties, like in other approaches [12,9]). Only relevant properties are considered. This corresponds to level 1 in Figure 1. Starting from this high level specification we can actually build a possible SA model encompassing both static (components and connectors) and dynamic (state-based models) information. This is represented in Figure 1 at the second level. The arrows linking backward the second level to the first represent a conformance checking between the SA specification and its reference architecture. We will use our framework to validate the SA con-

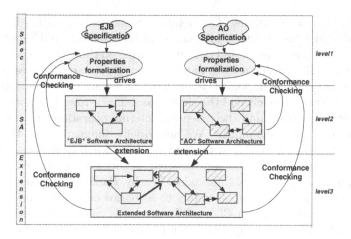

Fig. 1. The approach: an overview

formance with respect to the behavioral requirements. Often, for evolutionary purposes architectural models need to be extended or different aspects of the same system must be combined in order to get a more comprehensive model. The enhanced description still has to maintain the high level abstract properties. This situation is depicted in level 3 in Figure 1. The backward arrow, from level 3 to level 1, denotes that conformance checks must be done in order to guarantee the validity of the properties identified in the initial descriptions.

In the following we report our experience in extending J2EE with Active Objects. Following the approach outlined above we analyze the (informal) specifications of J2EE and AO, establishing the set of static and dynamic properties that constitute the high level architectural specifications. Then we provide actual architectural models for these high level descriptions and model-check their correctness with respect to the desired properties. Next step is to integrate the two models in a suitable way, so that both the high level properties of J2EE and AO are satisfied by the enhanced architecture. Its conformance is then proved.

3   The Charmy Framework

This section presents a brief overview of the Charmy (CHecking ARchitectural Model consistencY) framework [5,6,4]. The Charmy approach is based on the assumption that state diagrams and scenarios models provide distinct and complementary views of the system. They both represent dynamic aspects, they can be incomplete, in general they are not independent and can specify contradictory or inconsistent behaviors. To describe state diagrams and scenarios we refer to a notation general enough to encompass those generated by the architectural description languages used in the current practice and rich enough to allow for analysis. State diagrams are described using a State Transition Diagram notation close to the Promela syntax. This model is defined in [2] and used to represent

Promela-based state machines. The notation is shown in Fig. 3. where labels uniquely identifies the architectural communication channels and ? and ! operators denote respectively input and output operation on those channels. Scenarios (Fig. 2) are described using a UML notation, stereotyped so that i) each rectangular box represents a component, ii) each arrow defines a communication line (a channel) between the left and the right boxes. The arrows labels identify the communication channels and the τ denotes internal operations, i.e., something not visible from the environment. We now briefly summarize the three steps the approach is composed of: first the components state diagrams are translated into a Promela specification; then the system scenarios are expressed by Linear time Temporal Logic (LTL) [14] formulae. Finally, the SPIN [14] model checker verifies the LTL formulae corresponding to scenarios on the obtained Promela [14] model. This summary on Charmy framework is enough to understand the paper. Details about the mapping in Promela and LTL may be found in [5], practical examples are described in [5,4] and the tool supporting the approach is described in [4].

4   Specification and Formalization of J2EE, EJB, and AO

This section is dedicated to the specification and formalization of J2EE, its component model EJB and Active Objects. We go through the first two levels of the process pictured in Figure 1. The first subsection concerns J2EE-EJB, the second one AOs. In both subsections, we analyze the high level specifications trying to identify architectural components. We extract static and dynamic properties of interest, formalizing behavioral aspects through scenarios. These are architectural level scenarios, showing how architectural components interact. In the second step, driven by the informal specification and by the identified properties, we refine the SA providing a suitable description of components and connectors architectural behavior. The last step model checks these SA models with respect to the formalized scenarios.

4.1   The J2EE Software Architecture and the EJB Component Model

J2EE is the Sun Microsystems solution for enterprise application development. The J2EE architectural components are based on Java technology and provide all the middleware services needed by enterprise applications. The J2EE architectural style [13,8] is a three-tier style and its architecture components are the following: *Application components* (which implement the application logic, the presentation logic and the access logic to application services), *Container* (which gives the runtime support to application components, implicitly providing the available middleware services), *J2EE Standard Services* (a set of middleware services needed by enterprise applications) and a *Database*.

Since we are interested in extending the component behavior with active objects properties, we focus our attention on the J2EE component model: Enterprise JavaBeans (EJB). EJB is an architecture for component-based distributed computing. Enterprise beans are components of distributed transaction-oriented enterprise applications. They are J2EE application components and can be of several types [11]. However for our purposes we will focus only on Session Beans which implement the actual business logic for the application. All the component types are deployed in a container which acts as an implicit middleware which injects standard services to components. It is useful for our purposes to point out that EJB components are accessed through Remote Method Invocation (RMI) which allows only synchronous invocations (a client which requests a service must wait the computation to end before continuing). Moreover EJB components are non-reentrant, i.e. they cannot handle concurrent invocation from different clients.

EJB Properties formalization. In this paragraph we identify the relevant EJB dynamic properties and formalize them by means of architectural level scenarios.

EJB1. All instances of an EJB component are non-reentrant: clients are not able to concurrently call the same instance of a component. The scenario in Figure 2.a shows that an exception is raised, in case of concurrent calls to a stateful component.

EJB2. The invocation of an EJB component service is executed using RMI and it is, therefore, synchronous: a client that invokes a service is blocked waiting for the end of the required service computation. The scenario, in Figure 2.b, shows that the client and the EJB component can compute concurrently, but we prove that this scenario is never verified.

EJB Software Architecture. In this paragraph we refine the description and provide a more detailed SA for EJB. An EJB component is made of the following parts: *Enterprise Bean Class Instance* (the object which contains the actual implementation of the application logic), *EJB Remote Object (RO)* (the layer between the client and the actual component which enables the container to act as an implicit middleware before forwarding the call to the Enterprise Bean Class Instance) and the *Home Object (HO)* (the object which enables the client to acquire references to EJB Remote Objects)

The EJB static architecture and the components behavior are shown in Figure 3: the Client component has either internal operations ("τ") or makes requests to the RO component. RO invokes the EJB BeanClass and waits for the results. The EJB BeanClass computes the results and sends them back to RO. Finally, the Client receives the results ("?avail"). We can now prove that the EJB SA model conforms to the properties EJB1 and EJB2. This is enough for us to assess the conformance of this SA with respect to the high level specification.

4.2   Active and Passive Objects

There are many different definitions of Active Objects [7,10]. The typical definition says that *"an active object is an object or a component with its own thread*

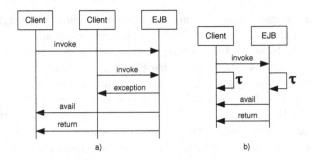

Fig. 2. EJB1 and EJB2 Scenarios

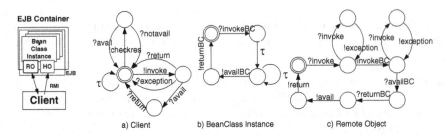

a) Client   b) BeanClass Instance   c) Remote Object

Fig. 3. EJB1.1 Software Architecture and Components Behavior

of control". This definition is too abstract and vague for our purposes. Thus we refined it in order to identify a well defined class of objects characterized by the abstract property of having a thread of control. Our analysis resulted in the following informal description of AO. It is the starting point to identify and formalize the high-level specification corresponding to the first level in Figure 1. In particular, an AO must be able to *concurrently run* with respect to other entities running in the system and, above all, with the client which requested its services; it must have a *well defined interface* that is exposed to other components and shows functionalities or services implementing the AO behavior; it may have a *per-client state* that is held during the computations.

From these properties we can argue that in order to be an AO, a component must support the *asynchronous method invocation*. Moreover, since Active Objects are a special class of components, we should consider that exported methods may get parameters as input values and may return some results. The second aspect is especially relevant since it introduces the issue of results handling. Typically a client asynchronously invokes a method, receives back the control and then runs in parallel with the called object. When the results have been computed by the called object, the client must be able to retrieve these values. This means that an AO model must provide a way to manage this situation.

AO Properties formalization. The relevant properties an object must exhibit in order to be an AO are the following:

AO1. An AO must be able to concurrently run with the client which requested its services. This property is needed to achieve the asynchronous method invocation. The scenario pictured Figure 4.a) shows the parallel computation between a Client and an Active Object.

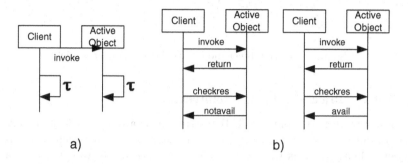

Fig. 4. Scenario AO1 and AO2

AO2. An AO must provide a mechanism to retrieve results. Since the computation is carried on independently of the client, there must be a way to check that the computation has finished and to retrieve the results. The scenario in Figure 4.b) shows the interaction between a Client and an Active Object. Notice the results requests ("checkres") and the availability of the results only when the computation is actually over.

AO and PO Software Architecture. The AO component that behaves as formalized in Figure 5.a): the client "invoke" the AO, the AO "return" the control to the client. The client may now send other invoke requests or ask to the AO results for previous computations. They will be available ("avail") only when the computation is finished ("τ"). Differently from AO, Passive Objects (PO) are components that do not allow asynchronous invocation. Figure 5.b) describes the PO behavior. Analogously to what we have done for EJB, we can now prove that the AO SA model correctly behaves with respect to properties AO1 and AO2. On the other hand, as expected, PO SA model does not.

5   Extending J2EE with Active Objects

In this section we propose solutions to the extension problem. We proceed in an incremental way. We first carry on a preliminary analysis which outlines the need of a serializer architecture and then we describe how this architecture can be suitably integrated in EJB in order to provide a correct SA model for Active Objects.

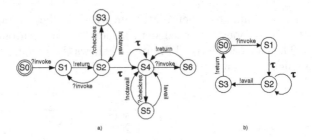

Fig. 5. a) Active Object model, b) Passive Object model

5.1   Active Object on J2EE Architecture

A preliminary idea to avoid the RMI restriction regarding synchronous invocation is to encapsulate each invocation in a separate thread which will carry it
on independently. In this way, the independent thread will wait the invocation
to complete while, the other components are free to continue their job. These
supplementary threads could be instantiated either on the component side or on
the client side. In both cases the specification is violated [11]: component side
threads are explicitly not allowed. Client side threads, on the other hand, potentially permitted, could lead to concurrent calls to the same component instance,
thus violating a previously cited property (Section 4.1). This first analysis suggests to refine this first approach concentrating on the client side and trying to
avoid the concurrent call to the same component instance problem. This can be
done by creating a *serializer* which filters all the invocations and executes them
one by one. The serializer will be composed of the following components: a *Buffer*
(which stores the invocation requests not yet executed), a *Scheduler* (which runs
in parallel with the other components, gets the requests and carries on the actual
invocations) and a *Passive Object* (which contains the application logic). This
serializer architecture is enough to achieve the AO concurrency property (AO1),
as described in Section 4.2, but is not enough to satisfy all of them. Since there
is not a direct link between Client and components, there is not a "well defined
interface" to the services and, more importantly, there is not a clear mechanism
to "recover the computation results" (i.e., property AO2 in Section 4.2 is violated). Thus we introduce two other components: the *Future* and the *Proxy*.
The former will contain the results of a particular method invocation and will
be used directly by the client in order to check il the requested computation is
over and, eventually to get the results. The latter exposes the AO interface (i.e.
the services implemented by the corresponding PO). We notice that both the
Future and the Proxy components fuctionalities could have been built into the
Client but this solution will limit the Client transparency.

The final architecture and the components behavior is in Figure 6. The
"Proxy" receives an invocation, enqueues the message (encoding the invocation),
and immediately returns the control. The "Scheduler" takes the request from the
"Queue" and invokes the actual implementation on the "PO". When the "PO"
computation finishes, it sends back the results to the "Scheduler" that stores

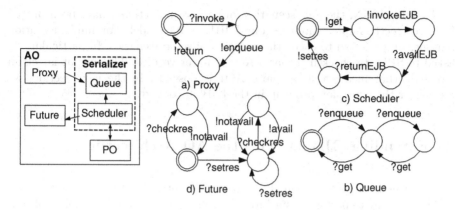

Fig. 6. The AO Software Architecture and components behavior

them into the "Future". This component can be queried for results availability. This model has been checked proving its conformance to the identified high-level properties. It makes us confident that this architecture is a valid implementation of the AO higher-level architecture defined in 4.2.

5.2   Extending EJB1.1 with the AO Architecture

We start from the AO architecture (Figure 6). In this architecture there is a Passive Object component. Since EJB1.1 components expose the same properties of a Passive Object [11], we replace the PO component in the AO architecture, with the EJB1.1 component. Figure 7 shows the integrated architecture topology, that will be denoted as EJB1.1+AO. From the dynamic point of view, its components behave similarly to components in the EJB1.1 (Figure 3) and AO (Figure 6) architectures. The new model only differs because, the Client sends the invocation to the Proxy (instead of the Remote Object) and the EJB component is directly used by the Scheduler, instead of the Client. Moreover, new behaviors may appear: the Scheduler in this new architecture has to manage also additional behaviors due to the EJB integration.

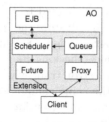

Fig. 7. EJB1.1 + AO Architecture

Running SPIN, the four scenarios formalized in Section 4 have been proved to be correctly implemented by our EJB1.1+AO model. For implementation reasons, we preferred to check the negation of some scenarios. In particular, we asked to SPIN to check if scenario AO1 is never verified. The output is "claim violated" that means that scenario AO1 is possible. In the next section, we reconsider the extension problem in the EJB2.0 context.

6   Extending EJB 2.0 with the AO Architecture

The current EJB specification (EJB2.0) [1] has introduced many new features, including a way to perform asynchronous method invocation. To accomplish this task a new component type has been added: the Message Driven Bean (MDB). MDBs act as message queue listeners implemented through the Java Messaging Service (JMS). MDBs do not have neither a Remote Object nor a Home Object. The only way for a client to interact with a MDB is to send a message to the JMS (Figure 8). MDBs behaves like Stateless Session Beans. The integration between the container and the JMS enables the notification to the MDB of the arrival of a message on the queue the MDB is listening on. A special method "onMessage" is called and the message sent by the client, is passed as a parameter. This solution enables the asynchronous invocation of a service implemented using an MDB. Once a client has sent a message, it can continue its activity independently from the notification process and from the execution of the service implemented with the "onMessage" method. Intuitively, we could argue that MDBs may provide a feasible solution to the asynchronous method invocation problem. However, MDB components present some limitations which violates the Active Object properties: *statelessness* (components do not have a per-client state), *lack of trasparency* (MDB services are invoked in a different way with respect to EJB components), *communication problems* (i.e. there is not a clear way to handle parameter passing and results recovery). Due to the enhanced EJB2.0 features, we will try to directly map the AO architecture components to the EJB2.0 architecture components: the JMS behaves as a Queue; the Scheduler functionalities are shared between the container-JMS integration (message retrieval) and the MDB component (actual service invocation); the Passive Object will be an EJB component; the Proxy is implemented by stateless EJB components which will expose the same interface of the Passive Object. It takes care of encoding the invocation to a message which is delivered to the JMS; the Future is replaced by entity bean components which will store the results for a later retrieval. The EJB2.0+AO architecture is shown in Figure 8. This extended architecture meets the Active Object properties but, checking its correctness with respect to the EJB properties, SPIN found an error trail: when a client makes two different asynchronous invocations (to the same component) and the second one is run before the ending of the first one, an exception is raised. The SPIN error trail puts in evidence that this unexpected behavior is due to Container which runs MDBs in parallel leading to the concurrent component invocations violating the

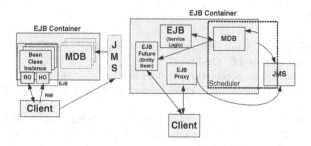

Fig. 8. EJB2.0 and EJB2.0+AO Architectures

property EJB1 in Section 4.1 (Figure 2.a). This result suggests that even in the enhanced EJB2.0 context the first solution we proposed still remains preferable.

7 Conclusions

We have presented the result of an experiment on architectural extension. The achieved results are two. The description of an extension which is a *correct realization* of its specification and the definition of an approach, and of a supporting framework, to carry out architectural extensions in a correct way. The approach rigorously defines what we mean for architectural specifications, at different levels of abstractions, and what we mean for *correct realization*. Moreover it shows that it can be supported by tools. We have experimented our ideas in the context of the Charmy environment but the approach we propose is obviously independent from the specification formalisms used and from the checking techniques. Future work will go in two directions. We are trying to experiment with different kind of high level properties or requirements; typically we would like to address non functional requirements like security. From the framework side we want to make the whole framework more integrable with standard development environments, notably UML based. Since the paper addresses several topics, many work may be related to it: architectural refinements, architecture evolutions on the SA side; model checking and view consistency on the conformance checking side. Other papers have been proposed to formally specify and analyze the EJB architecture. Since we do not have space here to discuss these related work, we direct interested readers to [3].

Acknowledgments. The authors would like to acknowledge the Italian M.I.U.R. national project SAHARA that partly supported this work.

References

1. L. G. DeMichiel, L. Ümit Yalçinalp, and S. Krishna. Enterprise JavaBeansTM Specification, Version 2.0. On-line at <http://java.sun.com/products/ejb/ docs.html>, year2001.
2. G. J. Holzmann. *Design and Validation of Computer Protocols.* Prentice Hall, 1991.
3. P. Inverardi, F. Mancinelli, H. Muccini, and P. Pelliccione. An Experience in Architectural Extensions: Active Objects in J2EE. In *Technical Report, University of L'Aquila, year 2002.* On-line at <http://www.henrymuccini.com/publications.htm>.
4. P. Inverardi, H. Muccini, and P. Pelliccione. Automated Check of Architectural Models Consistency using SPIN. In *the Automated Software Engineering Conference Proceedings (ASE 2001).* San Diego, California, November 2001.
5. P. Inverardi, H. Muccini, and P. Pelliccione. Checking Consistency Between Architectural Models Using SPIN. In *TR 02/01, University of L'Aquila.* On-line at <http://www.henrymuccini.com/publications.htm>, year 2001.
6. P. Inverardi, H. Muccini, and P. Pelliccione. Checking Consistency Between Architectural Models Using SPIN. In *Proc. the First Int. Workshop From Software Requirements to Architectures (STRAW'01),* year 2001.
7. T. Jenkinson. The Active Object Design Paradigm. On-line at <http://www.cs.ncl.ac.uk/people/t.j.jenkinson/home.formal/activeobjects.html>.
8. N. Kassem and the Enterprise Team. *Designing Enterprise Applications with the JavaTM 2 Platform, Enterprise Edition.* On-line at <http://java.sun.com/ j2ee/download.html>, year 2000.
9. R. Kazman, L. Bass, G. Abowd, and M. Web. Saam: A method for analyzing the properties of software architectures. *Proceedings of ICSE 16,* Sorrento, Italy:81–90, May 1994.
10. R. G. Lavender and D. C. Schmidt. Active Object - An Object Behavioral Pattern for Concurrent Programming. *Proceeding fo the Second Pattern Languages of Programming conference,* Monticello, Illinois, 1995.
11. V. Matena and M. Hapner. Enterprise JavaBeansTM Specification, v 1.1. On-line at <http://java.sun.com/products/ejb/docs.html>, year1999.
12. J. Ryser and M. Glinz. A Practical Approach to Validating and Testing Software Systems Using Scenarios. *QWE'99: Third International Software Quality Week Europe,* Brussels, Nov 1999.
13. B. Shannon. Java 2 Platform Enterprise Edition Specification, v1.3. On-line at <http://java.sun.com/ j2ee/>, year 2001.
14. SPIN. Home page on line at: <http://cm.bell-labs.com/cm/cs/what/spin/ index.html>.

Generating Pattern-Based Web Tutorials for Java Frameworks

Markku Hakala, Juha Hautamäki, Kai Koskimies, and Pekka Savolainen

Institute of Software Systems, Tampere University of Technology
P.O. Box 553, FIN- 33101 Tampere, Finland
{markku.hakala, csjuha, kk, sage}@cs.tut.fi

Abstract. Application frameworks are a popular technique to implement prod-uct-line architectures. The problem of communicating the relevant properties of a framework for application developers is studied. It is argued that a conven-tional API specification is not sufficient for a framework, but a pattern-based specification of the extension interface is required. A technique to generate a pattern-based tutorial for the extension interface of a framework is described, relying on an existing tool developed for the generation of a programming envi-ronment for a framework.

1 Introduction

A central problem in software development is the understanding of existing systems. This is particularly important in the case of software product-lines [1, 3]. A product-line is comprised of a set of reusable software assets that form the platform for a fam-ily of applications sharing similar structure and functionality. Such a platform is built around the common architecture of the application family, called the product-line architecture. The product-line approach is becoming increasingly popular in software industry as a systematic technique to achieve high level of reuse. In the product-line approach, you do not reuse only a collection of common services but the whole design of the applications as well. Today product-lines are the most important technological means for enterprises to gain shortened time-to-market, better quality of software products, and reduced costs.

In the case of product-lines, the underlying architecture and its implementation serve as an implementation platform for applications. In this type of application devel-opment, the central problem is how to map the requirements of the application to the concepts provided by the platform, rather than to the mechanisms of a general-purpose programming language. For example, the Enterprise JavaBeans architecture is based on the concepts of entity beans and session beans, and the central problem in EJB based application development is to map the appropriate parts of the domain model to these platform concepts. Hence it is of utmost importance for an application developer to understand thoroughly the platform architecture - in the same sense as it is impor-tant to understand the structures of the used programming language in conventional

N. Guelfi et al. (Eds.): FIDJI 2002, LNCS 2604, pp. 99–110, 2003.

programming. It is indeed justified to use the term *architecture-oriented programming* in the context of product-lines.

How to make the architecture and the conventions of the platform understandable for an application programmer, then? The traditional way is to document the application programming interface (API) of the platform in terms of interfaces and informal explanations, possibly supported by examples of the usage of the platform and hyperlinks helping to access related concepts. For example, JavaDoc can generate such an API documentation automatically directly on the basis of the source code, provided that certain commenting conventions have been followed. Indeed, the idea of automatically generated documentation is very desirable especially in the case of product-lines, because this guarantees that the documentation can be kept up to date. However, to understand the architecture of the platform and the principles of how the platform is supposed to be extended just by browsing through the API documentation becomes very difficult, if not impossible.

Frameworks have become a popular technique to implement product-line architectures within the object-oriented paradigm [4]. A framework is a collection of classes constituting the common structure and functionality of a family of OO systems. A framework differs from a conventional class library in that a framework is reused as a whole, rather than just using some of its services. A framework constitutes a skeleton for the applications, with holes for application-specific code that is called under the control of the framework using callback mechanisms.

Typically, a framework is extended by providing application-specific subclasses (implementations) for some of the framework's classes (interfaces), thus allowing application-specific code to be called by the framework. Hence such base classes in the framework can be regarded as a "specialization interface" of the framework. One could therefore expect that documenting this interface in an API-like fashion (for example, using JavaDoc or equivalent facilities) would be sufficient for the application developer to understand the relevant parts of the platform. Unfortunately, this is far from sufficient. The reason is that single extension points (like subclasses) are usually not independent of each other. Typically, the application developer has logical extension tasks that concern several extension points of the framework, and they have to be given in a consistent manner. As a concrete example, each introduction of an application-specific subclass for a framework class requires code in some other application class for instantiating that subclass. Hence these two extension points depend strongly on each other. Without understanding the relationships of individual extension points an application developer cannot hope to understand the platform as an implementation paradigm.

In this paper we will discuss a more general notion of an interface, based on the concept of a pattern. We will call it a *pattern interface*. We will show how the specialization interface of a framework can be documented using pattern interfaces instead of traditional API-like service interfaces. We will also demonstrate how such documentation can be generated automatically on the basis of existing knowledge about the specialization interface and previous applications of the framework.

The idea of documenting framework architecture through its design pattern instances has been presented before [10], even with tool support [11]. In this paper, however, we focus on documenting the specialization interface of a framework, rather than its architecture in general. In many cases these views are close, because the design pattern instances often appear in the borderline between a framework and its application. Another difference is that we investigate how the documentation could be produced automatically, based on some specification of the specialization interface.

A motivation for this work was the need for one of our industrial partners to establish a web site for the open source software available for all the units of the company. This web site should not only offer downloading, but also a systematic documentation of the available software systems so that the users can quickly obtain an understanding of the usage of the system. In the case of a software component this can be done with a conventional API specification, but in the case of an open source framework a more elaborated approach is required. Our vision is that a person interested in the framework could browse the documentation of the specialization interface in an intuitive manner through the web, and that such a facility could be produced automatically for the framework, using information that has been gathered from a sample application of the framework.

This work is part of a project investigating tool support for Java frameworks ([6, 7]). In that project, a tool prototype called Fred has been developed for assisting the specialization process of a framework. Fred makes use of so-called specialization patterns as a basis to generate an architecture-driven programming environment for the framework. Here we will interpret Fred's specialization patterns as a realization of pattern interfaces, and demonstrate how the automatic generation of pattern interface documentation can be accomplished using Fred. An advantage of Fred is that a sample specialization can be easily extracted from Fred after an application developer has accomplished her task. Otherwise the basic ideas presented in this paper are not dependent on Fred.

We proceed as follows. In the next section we will discuss the pattern interface concept and show how it can be used to specify the specialization interface of a framework. In Section 3 we will briefly introduce the Fred environment. In Section 4 we present a technique to generate documentation of the specialization interface of a framework based on the facilities provided by Fred. In Section 5 we present a practical example of the generated documentation for a small framework. Finally, we discuss some related work and present concluding remarks.

The tool set described in Section 4 is currently under implementation and will be freely available in the context of the next release of Fred (see http://practise.cs.tut.fi/Fred).

2   Patterns as Interfaces

Basically, an interface can be regarded as a contract between two software systems. A system defines (or refers to) a contract that specifies the requirements the system expects from another system. Any system that fulfills the contract can play the role of the latter system. This principle, sometimes called design-by-contract [12], has been well understood, but we argue that the conventional service-oriented interface concept can support this only in a limited way.

UML has introduced the notion of a collaboration as a "society of roles and other elements that work together to provide some co-operative behavior" [2]. We make use of a similar collaborative interface concept that we call a *pattern interface*, or simply a *pattern*. A pattern is a collection of *roles* for various language structures (classes, methods, attributes etc.), and a set of *constraints* on the roles. Each role is a slot that can be *bound* to an actual instance of a program element in a system: a class role is bound to a particular class, a method role is bound to a particular method, an attribute role is bound to a particular attribute etc. The constraints can specify the cardinality of the source structures bound to a role, or the relationships between the source structures bound to different roles. Similar notions of a pattern have been used and formalized elsewhere, too (e.g., see [15]). The structural relationships of classical design patterns [5] can be presented using such a pattern concept, but note that our pattern concept does not imply any particular run-time behavior for the source structures.

As an example of a pattern, consider a framework containing a base class that is assumed to be subclassed by the application. In the subclass, a particular method of the base class is assumed to be overridden. Further, the subclass is assumed to be instantiated in the "main" method of the root class of the application, taking care of the initialization of the application. These are closely related tasks that have to be reflected in the specification of the specialization interface of the framework. We can specify this part of the interface as a pattern consisting of the following roles: base class, method (in base class), derived class, method (in derived class), root class, method (in root class), and creation code (in method of root class). These roles have several constraints concerning the actual source elements bound to the roles. For example, certain source elements are required to be located within other elements, the derived class is required to inherit the base class, the method in the derived class is required to override the method in the base class etc.

In the context of frameworks, the strength of the pattern concept is that it allows various levels of binding. At the most abstract level, none of the roles in the pattern is bound to a concrete program element. This kind of pattern represents an abstract architectural solution without references to actual systems. For example, an abstract pattern might specify the idea of extending a framework by overwriting a method in an application-specific subclass, without referring to any particular framework. At the next level, a certain subset of the roles can be bound to concrete program elements. Such a pattern (instance) represents an interface a software system offers for other systems to hook up with it. In the case of a framework, a partially bound pattern specifies part of the specialization interface of the framework, fixing the roles that the elements of the framework play in the specialization but leaving the application-specific roles open. Finally, in some pattern (instance) all the roles of the pattern may be bound to actual program elements. In this case the pattern specifies either a fully implemented specialization, or an architectural solution occurring completely within the framework. For a more detailed description of a pattern, see [7].

We have investigated several real frameworks when extracting their specialization interface as patterns [6, 9, 17]. Even in middle-sized frameworks consisting of several hundreds of classes the number of patterns appears to be relatively small, typically 10-20. This is due to the fact that usually a pattern represents a major feature required for the application, and typically a framework is prepared for a fairly limited number of such features: it is the variance within the features that gives the frameworks their expressive power rather than the number of features. On the other hand, those patterns are fairly sizable, consisting of tens of roles.

3   Fred Environment

Fred (FRamework EDitor for Java) [6, 7] is a tool for generating an architecture-driven software development environment for a given framework, based on a specification of the framework's specialization interface as patterns. Fred supports the framework specialization process by guiding the application developer through a task list based on these pattern definitions. Fred keeps track of the progress of the tasks, verifying that the requirements of the framework architecture are followed as required in the patterns. Roughly speaking, Fred generates a task for any role binding that can be created at that point, given the bindings made so far.

Fred is unique in that the accompanying textual documentation is automatically adapted to the application context (e.g. application-specific names and terms), and that the integrated Java editor is "architecture-sensitive": it immediately notifies the user of an architectural conflict. In a sense, Fred can be compared to language-sensitive editors, but in Fred the rules to be checked are those of the architecture, not those of the underlying programming language.

In Fred, the pattern concept is called a *specialization pattern*. This is essentially a concrete realization and extension of the pattern concept discussed in the previous section. As a pattern, a specialization pattern is given in terms of roles, to be played by (or bound to) structural elements of a program, such as classes or methods. The same role can be played by a varying number of program elements. This is indicated by the *multiplicity* of the role; it defines the minimum and maximum number of bindings that may be created for the role. A single program element can participate in multiple patterns.

A role is always played by a particular kind of a program element. Consequently, we can speak of class roles, method roles, field roles etc. For each kind of a role, there is a set of *properties* that can be associated with the role. For instance, for a class role there is a property "inheritance" specifying the required inheritance relationship of each class associated with that role. Properties like this, specifying requirements for the concrete program elements playing the role are called *constraints*. For example, a simple inheritance pattern might consist of roles Base and Derived, with a constraint stating that the class bound to Derived must inherit the class bound to Base. Another constraint might state that the program element bound to a particular role must contain the element bound to another role; we call this a containment constraint. It is the duty of the tool to keep track of broken constraints and instruct the user to correct the situation. Other properties affect code generation or user instructions; for instance, most role kinds support a property "default name" for specifying the (default) name of the program element used when the tool generates a default implementation for the element.

The central part of the user interface of the Fred environment shows the current bindings of the roles for a selected pattern, structured according to the containment relationship of the roles. Since this relationship corresponds to the containment relationship of the program elements playing the roles, the given view looks very much like a conventional structural tree-view of a program. In this view, a red spot marks undone mandatory tasks, optional tasks are marked with a white spot. The actual to-do tasks are shown with respect to this view: for each bound role selected from the view, a separate task pane shows the tasks for binding the child roles, according to the containment relationship of the roles. The user interface of Fred is shown in Figure 1.

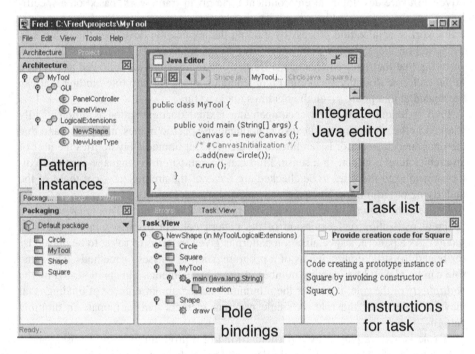

Fig. 1. Fred user interface

The application is built following the tasks generated by the tool. The tasks can be carried out by indicating the existing program element that plays the role, by asking the system to generate a default form for the bound element as specified by the pattern, or simply by typing the element using the Java editor and then binding it to the role. The system checks the bound element against the constraints of the pattern and generates remedial tasks if necessary. The task list evolves dynamically as new tasks become possible after completing others. The application programmer immediately sees the effect of the actions in the source code. Each individual task can be cancelled and redone. Hence the development process becomes highly interactive and incremental, giving the application programmer full control over the process.

An important feature of Fred is its support for adaptive user guidance: the task prompts and instructions are dynamically customized for the particular application at hand. This is achieved by giving generic task title and instruction templates in the pattern specifications, with parameters that are bound at pattern instantiation time. The actual parameters can be taken, for instance, from the names of the concrete program elements bound so far to the roles of the pattern.

4 Generating Specialization Tutorials Using Fred

Normally, Fred is used as a framework specialization tool. The framework developer describes the specialization interface of the framework in the form of patterns, and the application developer provides the application-specific parts under the guidance of the task lists implied by the patterns. The tasks carried out by the application developer eventually define one possible specialization path resulting in a structurally correct application.

It is widely accepted that framework documentation benefits from concrete specialization examples. Hence, it would be beneficial to store the actions made during a typical specialization process and let the future developers browse this information afterwards as part of framework documentation. Fred can be used to produce a technical solution for this. The basic idea is to record the steps taken by an "informed" application developer (possibly the framework developer herself) when using Fred, together with all the information associated with the patterns (like instructions, bindings of the roles, and code that is either generated or written by hand). The recording can be then replayed back and forth in a Fred-like user interface, illustrating the specialization process and showing the architectural context of the specialization steps. This leads to an interactive framework tutorial concept in which the application developer can follow the specialization steps in a representative case, see how the code gradually expands, learn the reasons for certain kinds of specialization actions and see how they are related to code. Hence, our idea is to turn Fred into a specialization recorder.

The amount of information that needs to be recorded is relatively small, because pattern instantiation in Fred is a non-destructive process. The hand-made changes to the source code may indeed be destructive, but the amount of destructive hand-written code for an example specialization tends to be small. Thus, it is not necessary to store the complete snapshots of the system after each specialization step. It will suffice to store only the hand-made changes and the bindings that result from the specialization process.

The information gathered this way allows the replay of the whole specialization process. The player program is able to show the execution of programming tasks, one by one. Associated with each task, the player can show the generated code, and how the developer modified it by hand to meet the needs of the particular example. The recorded textual tasks gives the rationale of each action just like they provided instructions for the developer when the specialization process was being recorded.

This form of framework documentation resembles the way the tutorials are conventionally written. New things are introduced gently one thing at a time in a logical order. This includes any exemplar code, which is typically provided in fragments instead of a revealing it all at once. Hence, using Fred to store the documentation process could be characterized as automatic generation of a tutorial for the framework. Using Fred for several specializations would result in tutorials for different kinds of example applications.

To support adoption of open-source frameworks, the documentation needs to be accessible on the web even prior to downloading the framework itself. This can be implemented using standard Java technologies. E.g., the documentation can be accessed by a Java applet contacting a Java servlet. The applet provides thus the user interface for the documentation player application, whereas the servlet would have access to the specialization data exported from Fred. We follow this scheme in the current implementation.

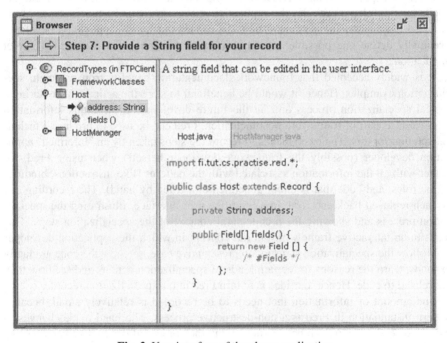

Fig. 2. User interface of the player application

The user interface of the player application is presented in Figure 2. It imitates the essential parts of the original Fred user interface, but allows only play and playback of the development process. Forward-button brings the user to the next specialization step. The selection is changed in the binding view to the binding that has been created in the step, or to the manual change that took place. Similarly, the description pane on the right is updated to show the documentation for the step, and the source code view highlights the piece of code that was generated or modified. Hence, it is possible to observe the specialization of an example application step by step. With each button click, the documentation grows incrementally, allowing the user to inspect all the previous steps. Similarly, the user is able to browse all the source code that has been produced at that point of specialization.

The steps are displayed as a tree that promotes the understanding of the recurring form that takes place in specialization of the particular framework. Our intention is that the user understands the framework specialization as an instantiation of a well-defined pattern, instead of an unrelated set of service method invocations. The tool does not explicitly teach the abstract form that takes place between the framework-application-boundary, but builds the big picture by using examples. This makes use of the developer's inherent ability to abstract − a way that has proven to be the easiest way to adopt complex structures.

5   Example: A Tutorial for a List-Box Framework

Framelets are small frameworks used as customisable building blocks for applications rather than application skeletons [14]. In contrast to application frameworks, framelets have very focussed functionality. The Red framework is a simple framelet used to demonstrate Fred [7]. Here we will use this framework to illustrate our ideas. Although this framework is so simple that it hardly needs extensive tutorials, it serves the purpose of making the discussion more concrete.

Red provides user interface facilities to maintain a list of Record-objects and to edit their fields. Typically, the Red framelet is used by deriving a new Record subclass with some application-specific fields. Once the application developer has created this new record type, the framelet provides facilities to automatically generate dialogs to set the values of the instantiated Record-objects.

The central concept of the Red framework is a record. A record is an arbitrary class with some member variables exposed to the framework as editable fields. In the example application, new Host records (we assume the application developer wants to create a list-box for ftp hosts) are created by the HostManager class that implements the RecordFactory interface. Each record object must implement the fields() method to create an adapter object for each field that it wants to expose to the framework. Although not assumed by the framework, the adapters are most conveniently implemented as anonymous inner classes, declared directly in the fields() method.

From the application developer's standpoint, one of the specialization problems is how to create a new record type that complies with the framework conventions. The framework expert, in turn, has identified this request as a specialization goal pursued by the application developer. We assume that the framework expert has used the Fred environment to create a specialization pattern called RecordTypes to guide the application developer through the specialization process for this goal.

Assume further that the ftp application has been chosen as the basis of the tutorial. The framework expert can then produce the ftp application using Fred in the recording mode. As a result, Fred generates a full trace of the specialization process. This trace can then be made available for future users of the Red framelet through the player application.

In Figure 2, a screenshot was presented for a situation where the application developer has reached a point where an address field has been added for a Host. The next step is to create an adapter object for the address field. When the developer clicks the forward button, the screen in Figure 3 is displayed. On the left, a small arrow indicates the associated Java element for each step while the role-specific documentation and source code are shown on the right. The documentation can contain links to more detailed Java documentation. It uses application-specific terms, like "address", which were obtained when the pattern was used and recorded. Also, the associated source code was given or generated during the original pattern usage.

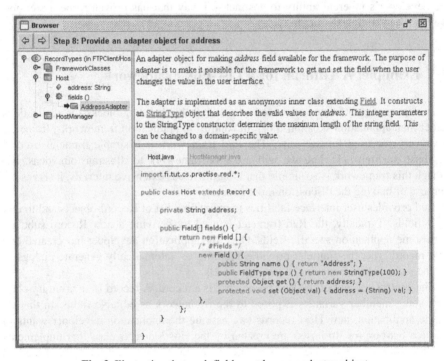

Fig. 3. Illustrating that each field must have an adapter-object

6   Related Work

We have discussed a technique to produce automatically the necessary programming interface documentation for application frameworks, based on the concept of a pattern. Our vision is to provide a facility which allows the potential user of an open source framework to browse through the essential parts of the system, imitating the actual use of the framework. This corresponds to a guided construction tour described by Kasper Østerbye et al. [13]. When available on a web site offering the downloading of the framework as well, this kind of facility can significantly support the distribution and acceptance of open source systems.

Thomas Vestdam suggests a system using elucidative programming, a variation of literate programming to provide program tutorials [16]. He describes a set of tools for creating and maintaining these tutorials. Created program tutorials can be viewed in a web browser and they provide hyperlink navigation between documentation, source code extracts and the actual program code. A special-purpose language called Source Code Extraction Language is used in describing source code fragments that should be included in the documentation. Whereas our approach provides dynamic visualization of actions recorded during the framework specialization process, Vestdam's system presents a technique to produce and maintain hyperlinked, static documentation.

7 Discussion

A possible weakness of our approach is that the pattern-based documentation easily becomes too implementation-oriented: the patterns relate the source structures nicely together, but they do not relate application requirements to code which would be more relevant for the application developer. To some extent this problem can be taken care of by associating patterns with textual explanations referring to the possible requirements of applications, but in general this approach gives no support for writing such explanations. We are currently investigating feature modeling techniques as a possible bridge between requirements and patterns, aiming at more systematic development of patterns from requirements.

To fully understand the strengths and weaknesses of our approach, we need more case studies. As one of the case studies, we are planning the generation of a web tutorial for J2EE. We feel that a platform like J2EE is particularly suitable for this type of documentation due to its rich pattern-oriented architectural conventions and need for web-based training. Since we have already produced a comprehensive collection of patterns for J2EE [8] in Fred, the tutorial can be achieved with fairly small effort.

Acknowledgements. This work is funded by the National Technology Agency of Finland (TEKES) and Nokia, Necsom, Sensor SC, and SysOpen.

References

[1] Bosch J.: Design and Use of Software Architectures - Adopting and evolving a product-line approach. Addsion-Wesley 2000.
[2] Booch G., Rumbaugh J., Jacobsen I.: The Unified Modeling Language User Guide. Addison-Wesley, 1999.
[3] Clements P., Northrop L.: Software Product Lines - Practices and Patterns. Addison-Wesley 2002.
[4] Fayad M.E., Schmidt D.C., Johnson R.E.: Building Application Frameworks — Object-Oriented Foundations of Framework Design. John Wiley & Sons, 2000.

[5] Gamma E., Helm R., Johnson R., Vlissides J.: Design Patterns — Elements of Reusable Object-Oriented Software. Addison-Wesley 1994.

[6] Hakala M., Hautamäki J., Koskimies K., Paakki J., Viljamaa A., Viljamaa J.: Annotating Reusable Software Architectures with Specialization Patterns. In: Proceedings of the Working IEEE/IFIP Conference on Software Architecture (WICSA'01), Amsterdam, August 2001, 171–180.

[7] Hakala M., Hautamäki J., Koskimies K., Paakki J., Viljamaa A., Viljamaa J.: Generating application development environments for Java frameworks. In: Proceedings of the 3rd International Conference on Generative and Component-Based Software Engineering (GCSE'01), Erfurt, Germany, September 2001, Springer, LNCS2186, 163–176.

[8] Hammouda I., Koskimies K.: Generating a Pattern-Based Application Development Environment for Enterprise JavaBeans. In: Proc. COMPSAC 2002, Oxford, England, August 2002.

[9] Hautamäki J.: Task-Driven Framework Specialization - Goal-Oriented Approach. Licentiate thesis, Report A-2002-9, Department of Computer and Information Sciences, University of Tampere, 2002.

[10] Johnson R.: Documenting Frameworks Using Patterns. In: Proc. of OOPSLA'92, Vancouver, Canada, October 1992, 63–76.

[11] Meusel M., Czarnecki K., Köpf W.: A Model for Structuring User Documentation of Object-Oriented Frameworks Using Patterns and Hypertext. In: Proc. of ECOOP '97, LNCS 1241, 496–510.

[12] Meyer B.: Object-Oriented Software Construction. Prentice-Hall 1988.

[13] Østerbye K., Madsen O.L., Sandvad. E., Bjerring C., Kanmeyer O., Skov S.H., Hansen F.O.: Hansen F., Documentation of Object-Oriented Systems and Frameworks, COT/2-42-V2.4, Centre for Object Technology, Danmark, 2000.

[14] Pree W., Koskimies K.: Framelets - Small is Beautiful. In: Fayad M., Schmidt D., Johnson R. (eds.): Building Application Frameworks - Object-Oriented Foundations of Framework Design. Wiley 1999, 411–414.

[15] Riehle R.: Framework Design — A Role Modeling Approach. Ph.D. thesis, ETH Zürich, Institute of Computer Systems, February 2000.

[16] Vestdam T.: Generating Consistent Program Tutorials, NWPER '02, Copenhagen, August 2002.

[17] Viljamaa A.: Pattern-Based Framework Annotation and Adaptation - A Systematic Approach. Licentiate thesis, Report C-2001-52, Department of Computer Science, University of Helsinki, 2001.

Massively Distributed Virtual Worlds: A Framework Approach

MaDViWorld: A Java Software Framework for Massively Distributed Virtual Worlds

Patrik Fuhrer and Jacques Pasquier-Rocha

University of Fribourg
Department of Informatics
Rue P.-A. de Faucigny 2
CH-1700 Fribourg
Switzerland
patrik.fuhrer@unifr.ch
http://diuf.unifr.ch/~fuhrer/

Abstract. The aim of this paper is to briefly present the general concept of virtual worlds and then to focus on distributed and decentralized ones. MaDViWorld is a Java framework for massively distributed virtual worlds. We first present its software architecture and then discuss some of its specialized features, namely: the object structure and the distributed event model. These are the main aspects that evolved since the first version of the framework. To conclude, some example objects and further potentialities of the framework are discussed.

1 Introduction

1.1 The Virtual World Paradigm

The document paradigm is well-known in today's Internet technology: documents are made available on one or several servers and client applications (e.g. Web browsers) are used in order to interact with them. The underlying metaphor is the one of a huge cross-referenced book where each user browses through the pages totally unaware of other users performing the same task at the same moment. All actions are asynchronous and, thus, there is no need for a central server to coordinate user interactions with the pages of the book or to take care of an event redistribution mechanism.

Within the *virtual world paradigm*, multiple users and active objects interact in the *same space*. Therefore they have a direct impact on each other. Within such systems, if a user interacts with an object, the other connected users can see her and start a dialog with her. Moreover, it is possible for a user to modify some properties of the world and all the other users present in the same subspace (e.g. the same room) must immediately be made aware of it. Examples of the virtual world paradigm range from simple graphical chat to sophisticated 3D virtual worlds used for military simulations.

N. Guelfi et al. (Eds.): FIDJI 2002, LNCS 2604, pp. 111–121, 2003.

For a good comprehension of the present paper, the following four terms need to be briefly explained (for more details the interested reader is refered to [6]):

1. *Avatars* are the virtual representation of the users. Concretely, an avatar is a tool that allows a given user to move through the world, to interact with its inhabitants and objects and that lets the other users know where she is and what she is doing.
2. In order to distinguish between near and distant elements it is essential to divide the world into subspaces where the users might or might not enter and in which all interactions take place. Otherwise, the world would not scale. We call such subspaces *rooms*.
3. Rooms are connected by *doors*, which an avatar can use for moving from one room to another.
4. *Objects* populate the rooms and they can be either passive, reactive or active. Furthermore, in a distributed world, it should be possible to "physically" transport a given object from one room to another.

The conceptual model, that emerges from these considerations, is shown in Figure 1. It represents a very simple world with four rooms, three avatars (James, Sylvia and Hans) and a single game object (TicTacToe). One can also see how the rooms are interconnected by three doors.

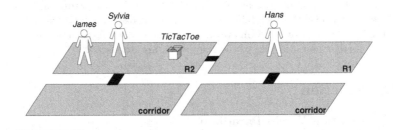

Fig. 1. The conceptual model of a simple world

1.2   MaDViWorld Goals

The main advantage of the document paradigm approach is that it allows a really distributed architecture with thousands of http servers interconnected all over the world. If a crash occurs, only the pages hosted by the failed or the no longer reachable servers become momentarily unavailable. The whole system is extremely robust and, since the connection of new decentralized servers is always possible, there is no limit to its growth.

At the software architecture level, systems based on the virtual world metaphor are clearly more complex. Indeed, the users directly interact with the original objects of the system and the resulting event must be correctly synchronized and forwarded in order to maintain the consistency of the world. This explains why most of them are based on a client-server model, for which a single server or more rarely a small cluster of servers contain all the world pertinent data and assume the world accessibility, consistency and persistence. On the client side, many of them enable interaction with the other users and the various objects of the world. This approach depends completely on the central server robustness and does not scale well. Some proposals for distributed environments can be found in the following projects: URBI ET ORBI [4], DIVE [5] and MASSIVE [10].

The goal of our research group is to define software solutions in order to support the virtual world paradigm presented above, without making concessions to the single server architecture. Actually, *MaDViWorld*, the acronym of the software framework presented in this paper, stands for Massively Distributed Virtual World, since its subspaces are distributed on an arbitrarily large amount of machines. The only requirement is that each machine containing a part of the world runs a small server application and is connected to other machines through the Internet. This obligation is exactly the same as the one required by the World Wide Web document paradigm approach, with all its advantages in terms of robustness and scalability.

2   MaDViWorld Software Architecture

First of all, it is important to notice that it is out of the scope of this paper to present the framework in all its details. This paper explains the concept of using a framework approach at a rather high level of abstraction and then concentrates on some critical points, that have been solved.

More detailed information is available in [6] and in [7], which describe the first version of the framework. Furthermore, an Object Programmer's Guide is reachable from the official MaDViWorld web site [3]. The guide includes a tutorial for developing new objects. The working framework can also be downloaded, with an installation guide and the Javadoc of the framework.

2.1   Massive Distribution Explained

In order to clarify what is meant by *massively distributed*, let us reconsider the conceptual model of the simple world presented in Figure 1. As already mentioned, there must be no central server but arbitrarily many of them and none of them has to know the whole world. Figure 2 shows a possible physical model, illustrating what concretely happens at runtime. Room R1, one of the two corridors and Sylvia's avatar run on Sylvia's machine, while Room R2, the other corridor and James' avatar run on James' machine. Finally Hans's avatar runs on Hans's own machine.

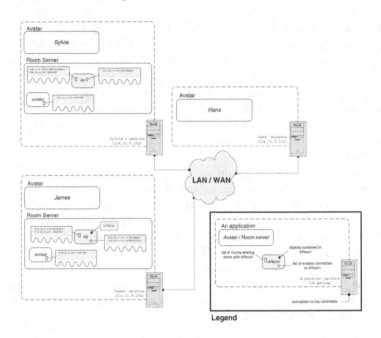

Fig. 2. One possible physical model for the conceptual model of Figure 1

2.2   The Framework Approach

There are a lot of available definitions for what a framework is. A complete and precise one is given in [12]. But let us take the following more concise one that can be found in [2]:

> A *framework* is a partially complete software (sub-) system that is intended to be instantiated. It defines the architecture for a family of (sub-) systems and provides the basic building blocks to create them. It also defines the places where adaptations for specific functionality should be made. In an object-oriented environment a framework consists of abstract and concrete classes. The instantiation of a framework involves composing and subclassing the existing classes. A framework for applications in a specific domain is called an *application framework.*

Keeping these definitions in mind, this section describes the MaDViWorld application framework. The different places where adaptations for specific functionality should be made will be identified and explained. These flexible points of the framework are commonly called *hot spots* and are opposed to the *frozen spots* (see [15]). An overview of the whole framework is shown in Figure 3. The root package for all the other MaDViWorld classes is `ch.unifr.diuf.madviworld`, and in the rest of the paper this will be omitted for evident convenience reasons.

First, let us consider an *horizontal* decomposition of Figure 3 building blocks:

- The communication between components is defined by a protocol. The upper layer of the framework fulfills this task. The framework user only has to understand this visible interface of the components. That's why MaDVi-World would rather be classified as a *black-box framework* (see [11]). The core package encloses all these interfaces.
- The middle layer contains the default implementation packages of the framework. It is composed of concrete and abstract classes.
- The lower layer, finally, is for the concrete implementation, where all the application specific classes are placed.

Second, let us decompose the blocks of Figure 3 *vertically*. From left to right one finds respectively all the packages and classes relative to the client applications (i.e. avatars), then those relative to the server applications (i.e. rooms) and those relative to the objects populating the rooms. Ultimately there are two utility packages, one containing packages and classes used by the framework and rightmost the event package. Obviously, the implementation or extension of the *Avatar*, *Room* and *Object* packages are the *hot spots* of the MaDViWorld framework. There are two types of activities for a framework user:

- The first one consists just in enriching the world with new types of active objects by providing the appropriate implementations of the wobject package. For this activity, users do not need to modify the standard avatar and room server application and they can resort to a little wizard application in order to install their new objects dynamically into a running (potentially remote) room.
- The second one consists in providing richer or better avatar and/or room server applications either by extending the default ones, or by both extending and implementing the appropriate framework extendable classes or by fully implementing the appropriate framework interfaces from scratch.

The current version of the framework consist of a total of approximatively 100 classes organized in 10 packages and counts 14'000 lines of code. If one counts all the already available objects, the total amount of classes is greater than 200 composed of 37'000 lines of code.

3   Objects and Events

This section focuses on the objects and particularly on the distributed event model of the framework, which is one of the aspects that was not yet present in the first version of MaDViWorld as presented in [6] and which plays a central role for objects.

3.1   Object Structure

The purpose of this section is to better understand the process of objects creation and use. Figure 4 illustrates how the wobject package has to be implemented

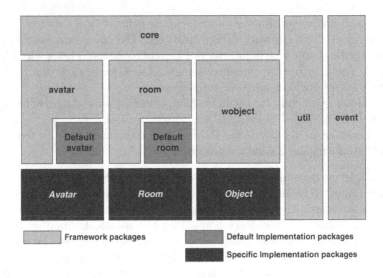

Fig. 3. Overview of the MaDViWorld framework

in order to develop new objects. For further comments about this package the reader is invited to consult the Object Programmer's Guide on [3].

In order to add a new object, the framework user has to create the corresponding `wobjects.newobj` package, which must contain two subpackages, one for the object's *implementation part* and one for its *graphical user interface* (GUI) *part*. This clean separation between the user interface and the object logic does not provide a two-way communication channel between these two parts. The client relationship between the `MyObjGUIImpl` class and the `MyObj` interface provides a one-way communication channel (from GUI to the implementation), but the implementation part cannot send information back to the GUI. The distributed event model designed to address this issue is presented below.

3.2   The Distributed Event Model

Events play a crucial role in the MaDViWorld framework. Schematically, each time the state of one of the world components changes, a corresponding event is fired by the altering subject and consumed by the registered listeners, which react appropriately. The management of all these events is a complex task:

- They are in reality remote events and several network problems can occur;
- Some of the events have to be fired to only a subset of all the listeners;
- Some listeners may not be interested in every type of event.

Thus the framework must offer a *distributed event model* that handles all these situations.

The two last points listed above, lead to the elaboration of an abstraction for creating unique identifiers. DUID is the acronym for Distributed Unique ID

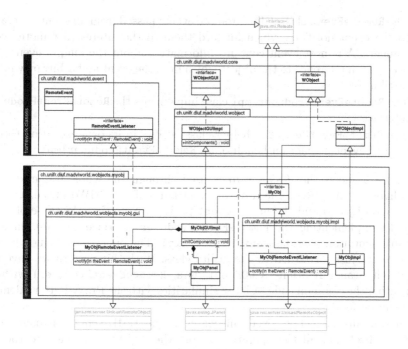

Fig. 4. Implementation of the `wobject` package

and is implemented in the `core.DUID` class[1]. Each room, object or avatar has an associated DUID that is generated by the framework, so that it can be identified without ambiguity. The use of such a DUID was inspired by [8].

It is now time to take a closer look at the content of the `event` package (see Figure 5) and how it solves the mentioned problems:

- The `RemoteEventListener` interface extends the `java.util.EventListener` interface and defines the single `notify()` method. Any object that wants to receive a notification of a remote event needs to implement it.
- The `RemoteEventProducer` interface defines the methods needed to register, unregister and notify event listeners used to communicate between different parts of the system. The register method takes as parameter the event type the listener is interested in. There are five possibilities: *all events, avatar* events, *room* events, *object* events and *"events for me"*. With the latter, the listener is only informed of events addressed explicitly to it (thanks to its DUID), without paying attention by whom.

---

[1] The DUID is the combination of a `java.rmi.server.UID` (an abstraction for creating identifiers that is unique with respect to the host on which it is generated) and an instance of `java.net.InetAddress` (a representation of the host's IP address where the object was created which makes the UID globally unique).

- The `RemoteEvent` class defines remote events passed from an event generator
  to the event notifiers, which forward them to the interested remote event
  listeners. A remote event contains information about the kind of event that
  occurred, a reference to the object which fired the event and arbitrarily many
  attributes.
- The `RemoteEventProducerImpl` class implements the `RemoteEventProducer`
  interface.
- The `RemoteEventNotifier` helper class notifies in its own execution thread
  a given event listener on behalf of an `RemoteEventProducerImpl`.

Figure 5 shows the *design pattern* used through the whole framework for
the collaboration between the three different parts of MaDViWorld (i.e. avatars,
rooms and objects) and the utility `event` package. Note that the three of them
are both implementing the `RemoteEventProducer` interface and are client of
its implementation, `RemoteEventProducerImpl`. The operations defined by the
interface are just forwarded to the utility class. With this pattern we have the
suited inheritance relation (a `WObject` 'is a' `RemoteEventProducer`) without
duplicating the common code. A lot of similarities with the Proxy Pattern defined
in [9] can be found.

To sum up the whole event mechanism, the UML sequence diagram of
Figure 6 dwells on all the operations, from the registration phase to the firing and notification of an event. First (a), the event consumer registers a
`RemoteEventListener` to a room, avatar or object whose events it is interested
in. Second (b), due to a state change an event is fired and all interested listeners
are notified, each by a `RemoteEventNotifier`. The informed listener can then
do the appropriate work with regard to the type of the event. On Figure 6,
one can also see the different methods invoked remotely across the LAN. This
pattern present some similarities with the *Jini distributed event programming
model*, which is specified in [1] and thoroughly explored in [14].

3.3   Some Examples of Objects

The MaDViWorld framework has been intensively used and tested in various
students projects. So, there is already a little collection of interesting objects
available. Here is a non exhaustive list of them:

- *Battleship*. This is a complete version of the legendary distracting two player
  board game. Its user interface includes graphics and sounds.
- *Minesweeper*. Analog to the battleship, but it is a single user object.
- *Tamagotchi*. These are little objects or virtual pets of which their owner has
  to take care of. They present the peculiarity that they are affected by what
  happens to their siblings. For instance, if another tamagotchi in the same
  room dies, they feel sad and their own health level will decrease. They are
  an example of "social" objects.
- *Whiteboard*. This simple version represents a basic collaborative editor.

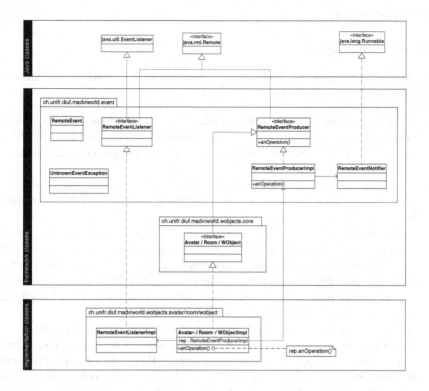

Fig. 5. Pattern used for integrating the event model in the framework

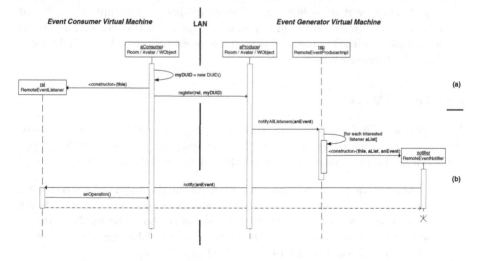

Fig. 6. (a) Setup of the event model (b) Notification of an event

4   Conclusion

4.1   Achievements

The actual version of the MaDViWorld framework has reached the following achievements:

- It is an *application framework* for highly distributed virtual worlds. It offers programmers the opportunity to transparently develop any kind of objects and test them in a virtual world, with all the advantages of mobility, remote execution, persistence, etc.
- As avatars, rooms and objects are distributed on several machines and are all interacting within the same world, an efficient *distributed event mechanism* is provided by the framework.
- In order to locate existing objects and services (room servers, rooms, avatars), the framework provides a *dual lookup mechanism*. On the one hand, it makes use of *rmiregistries* since its very first version. On the other hand, its latest release offers an important additional option. Indeed, it allows rooms and avatars to register themselves to remote Jini lookup services (*reggie*) and to act as well-behaved Jini services.
- Avatars can execute an object remotely, but the graphical user interface of the object always runs locally. As the avatars has no *a priori* knowledge of the kind of objects they will meet during their trip through the world, the framework provides a *graphical interface transport mechanism*. The core idea is that the graphical user interface and the implementation parts of an object are always clearly separated.
- The transport of *mobile objects* from one room to another is complex because it occurs in fact from one machine to another. So, when an avatar takes an object to carry it with her into a room running on a completely different machine, all the resources and class files relative to this object have to be moved along with it. This is all kept transparent for the end-user and hidden from the framework user.

4.2   Future Work

MaDViWorld is still evolving and some enhancements will be integrated in the coming versions and will improve the efficiency and the conviviality of the various applications. Future research will cover the following five main topics:

1. *Security.* On the one hand a security model inside the world (access to rooms, permissions,...) should be clearly defined and developed. On the other hand, security issues at the lower level of the framework should be resolved (downloading of classes, codebase verification, trusting of lookup services, etc.). An overview of existing solutions can be found in [13].
2. *Scripting.* The end-user should be able to change the behavior of objects at runtime.

3. *Static description.* Rooms and avatars with all their attributes should be described statically in a form of structured data such as XML and created "on the fly" by a parser tool. Persistence and state recovery mechanisms could then take advantage of this feature.
4. *Multimedia and 3D.* More complex space aspects of virtual worlds (rooms, avatars and objects) should be integrated.
5. *Real world example.* Developing concrete practical applications of the framework like educational worlds as virtual campus could be a possibility. Such a world is sketched in [6].

References

1. Arnold, K. et al.: The Jini Specification, Addison-Wesley:Reading, MA, 1999.
2. Buschmann, F. et al.:Pattern-Oriented Software Architecture - A System of Patterns, John Wiley and Sons:Chichester, 1996.
3. Department of Informatics, University of Fribourg (CH), Software Engineering Group. *MaDViWorld: a Software Framework for Massively Distributed Virtual Worlds* http://diuf.unifr.ch/softeng/projects/madviworld/ [10 September 2002].
4. Fabre, Y. et al.: A framework to dynamically manage distributed virtual environments. Virtual Worlds, Proceedings of the Second International Conference, VW 2000, Paris, France, 5–7 July. Springer: Berlin, 2000; 54–64.
5. Frécon E., Stenius M.: DIVE: A scaleable network architecture for distributed virtual environments (special issue on Distributed Virtual Environments). Distributed Systems Engineering Journal 1998; 5(3):91–100.
6. Fuhrer, P. et al.: MaDViWorld: a Software Framework for Massively Distributed Virtual Worlds. Software Practice and Experience, 2002, 32:645–668.
7. Fuhrer, P. et al.: The MaDViWorld Software Framework for Massively Distributed Virtual Worlds: Concepts, Examples and Implementation Solutions. Department of Informatics Internal Working Paper no 01–23, University of Fribourg (CH), Switzerland, July 2001.
8. Gachet, A.: A Software Framework for Developing Distributed Cooperative Decision Support Systems - Construction Phase, Department of Informatics Internal Working Paper no 02–02, University of Fribourg (CH), Switzerland, March 2002.
9. Gamma, E. et al.: Design Patterns: Elements of Reusable Object-Oriented Software, Addison-Wesley Professional Computing Series: Reading, MA, 1995.
10. Greenhalgh, C., Benford, S.: MASSIVE: A distributed virtual reality system incorporating spatial trading. Proceedings 15th International Conference on Distributed Computing Systems. IEEE Computer Society Press: Vancouver, Canada, 1995, 27–34.
11. Johnson, R. E., Foote B.: Designing Reusable Classes. Journal of Object-Oriented Programming 1(2), June/July 1988, pp. 22–35.
12. Larman, C.: Applying UML and Patterns, Prentice Hall PTR:Upper Saddle River, NJ, 2002.
13. Kouadri Mostéfaoui, G. et al: Security Models for the Jini Networking Technology: A Case Study, Department of Informatics Internal Working paper no 02–07, University of Fribourg (CH), Switzerland, May 2002.
14. Li, S.: Professional Jini, Wrox Press Ltd.:Birmingham, 2000.
15. Pree, W.: Design Patterns for Object-Oriented Software Development, Addison-Wesley: Reading, MA, 1995.

Distributed Java Platform with Programmable MIMD Capabilities

T. Keane[1], R. Allen[1], T.J. Naughton[1], J. McInerney[2], and J. Waldron[3]

[1] Department of Computer Science, National University of Ireland, Maynooth, Ireland
[2] Department of Biology, National University of Ireland, Maynooth, Ireland
[3] Department of Computer Science, Trinity College, Dublin 2, Ireland
Corresponding author: tom.naughton@may.ie

Abstract. A distributed Java platform has been designed and built for the simplified implementation of distributed Java applications. Its programmable nature means that code as well as data is distributed over a network. The platform is largely based on the Java Distributed Computation Library of Fritsche, Power, and Waldron. The generality of our system is demonstrated through the emulation of a MIMD (multiple instruction, multiple data) architecture. This is achieved by augmenting the server with a virtual pipeline processor. We explain the design of the system, its deployment over a university network, and its evaluation through a sample application.

1 Introduction

A class of distributed computation systems is based on the client-server model. This class is characterised by (i) clients that instigate all communication and have no knowledge of each other (no peer-to-peer communication), (ii) a server that has little information on, or control of, its clients, and (iii) computations that are insensitive to fluctuations in the number of clients or client failure. Well-known and successful systems in this class include the Great Internet Mersenne Prime Search (GIMPS) [1] and SETI@Home [2]. These systems are usually designed with a single application in mind, and are not generalisable or programmable. A Java distributed computation library (JDCL) [3] was designed to provide a simple general-purpose platform for developers who wish to quickly implement a distributed computation in the context of a SIMD (single instruction, multiple data) architecture. Its aims were to allow developers to abstract completely from networking details and to allow distributed computations to be reprogrammed without requiring any client-side administration. Its attractions included network and platform independence, simplicity of design, and ease of use for developers.

Our contribution has been to continue development of the system, bringing it to a level in terms of functionality and robustness that permits demonstration of a large-scale application. The JDCL was in an early stage of development and required a number of enhancements and modifications to bring it up to such a level. In addition to refining the functionality and efficiency of existing features of the JDCL [3] our system contains enhancements that are in line with the aspirations of its original developers. They include facilitating ease of distribution [the client consists of an initialisation file and a single jar (Java archive) file], and coping with client failure.

N. Guelfi et al. (Eds.): FIDJI 2002, LNCS 2604, pp. 122–131, 2003.
© Springer-Verlag Berlin Heidelberg 2003

The server is capable of both detecting client failure and redistributing the computational load.

Other enhancements (not aspirations of the original JDCL developers) include adding security to the clients, and expanding the range of applications that the JDCL can support. A security manager has been developed that limits the downloaded task's interaction with the client software and donor machine. The other major enhancement is the system's emulation of a MIMD (multiple instruction, multiple data) architecture. This is explained in Sect. 2. The design of the system is explained in Sect. 3. Section 4 gives a brief overview of how the system is programmed and in Sect. 5 the system is evaluated with an application from the field of bioinformatics.

Java proved to be an ideal language for the development of this system. It was possible to design a straightforward interface to the system: users are required to extend only two classes to completely reconfigure a distributed computation. Furthermore, identical clients (and identical downloaded tasks) could be run on a variety of platforms. Existing programmable distributed environments or libraries range from MPI [4] and PVM [5] to JavaSpaces [6] and the Java OO Neural Engine (Joone) [7].

2 Computational Theory for MIMD Emulation

A major enhancement of our system is its emulation of a MIMD architecture. In order to do this, the server simulates a pipeline processor capable of repackaging and redistributing partial results during a computation. In this section, we give the computational theory of MIMD emulation through client server processing.

Consider an input X, and a computation on that input $C(X)$ that returns some result r. We could say that $r = C(X)$. In client-server computing, the server partitions the input data into n segments

$$X = \sum_{i=0}^{n-1} x_i .$$

(1)

such that each transformation $x_i \rightarrow C(x_i) = r_i$ is performed by one of a set of clients. The server reconstructs the original result by combining these partial results

$$r = C(X) = \bigcup_{i=0}^{n-1} C(x_i) .$$

(2)

where $\bigcup$ denotes an appropriate combination operation. This is the starting assumption of work related to SPMD (single program, multiple data) computation through functional programming [8]. In pipeline processing, a computation is decomposed into m smaller transformations that each acts on the result of the previous transformation, $r = C(X) = c_{m-1}(c_{m-2}(\cdots c_1(c_0(X))\cdots))$, where X is the input. A recursive definition of this concept could be written as follows,

$$r_j = \begin{cases} c_0(X) & \text{if } j=0; \\ c_j(r_{j-1}) & \text{if } j>0. \end{cases} \tag{3}$$

where $r = r_{m-1}$ can be regarded as the seed to the recursion and defines the final result. The first clause in Eq. (3) is the terminating condition (passing the input to the first transformation) and the second clause describes how the result of any one transformation depends on the preceding transformation. We use the following compact notation to represent the recursive definition of Eq. (3),

$$r = C(X) = \prod_{j=0}^{m-1} c_j(X) . \tag{4}$$

where $\prod$ denotes the operation to appropriately pass the results of one transformation to another. Equation (4) describes passing the complete input X to transformation c_0, the result being passed to c_1, and so on. Staying within the pipeline processing paradigm, we could further partition the input into n segments, as described in Eq. (1), and pass each segment in turn through the complete sequence of m transformations. Appropriately combining the partial results at the end of the final transformation, as in Eq. (2), would allow us to write Eq. (4) as

$$r = C(X) = \bigcup_{i=0}^{n-1} \left(\prod_{j=0}^{m-1} c_j(x_i) \right) . \tag{5}$$

The advantages of the representation in Eq. (5) include the ability to arbitrarily change the granularity of the data throughput (some transformations may have restrictions on the size or format of their arguments) and to permit parallelisation of the computation. Pipeline computations could possibly be regarded as MISD (multiple instruction, single data).

It is possible to combine both the client-server (SIMD) and pipeline (MISD) models. This is important if we want to allow clients to effect arbitrary transforms rather than each one performing the same c_j. In this case, the server divides the computation as well as the data. It distributes to the clients a description of a transformation c_j as well as a data segment x_i. Since the partitioning shown in Eq. (1) is possible, there will not be any interdependencies between different parts of the data stream. Equations (4) and (2) could therefore be combined as

$$r = C(X) = \prod_{j=0}^{m-1} \bigcup_{i=0}^{n-1} c_j(x_i) . \tag{6}$$

which describes transforming all of the data segments with c_j before applying c_{j+1}, and so on. Since Eqs. (5) and (6) describe the same computation, this shows that the order in which each $c_j(x_i)$ is effected is unimportant, as long as one finds the appropriate $(\bigcup, \prod)$ pair. An out-of-order implementation of Eq. (6) is a MIMD computation. Consequently, an MIMD emulator is the by-product of a loosely coupled client-server simulation of a highly structured pipeline processor. This computational theory tells us nothing about how to find an appropriate $(\bigcup, \prod)$ pair, or how efficient the resulting MIMD emulation might be. Sanders [9] has proposed an efficient algorithm to emulate MIMD computations on a synchronous SIMD system. Our asynchronous system should admit emulation algorithms that are even more efficient because it completely avoids what Sanders calls SIMD overhead [9] (where the globally issued instruction is not required locally). Our system is still susceptible to load imbalance overhead but this problem-dependent issue is inherent to all parallel computing, including MIMD parallelism. Figure 1 shows an abstract model of the system.

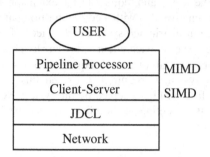

Fig. 1. System layers of abstraction

3 Design of the System

The design mirrors that of Sanders [9] with a number of enhancements inspired by our computational model. The user partitions the MIMD algorithm into multiple independent sequential stages, if possible. Each stage corresponds to a node in a theoretical 'pipeline.' The code corresponding to all stages (the Task) is sent to clients as a compiled Java class. Execution of each of the (one or more) stages then proceeds as a SIMD computation as in [9]. All stages of the pipeline could be 'processing' at the same time if the particular problem allowed. Our system is therefore most efficient at emulating MIMD computations that can be naturally expressed as a pipeline of SIMD computations. The overall system can be subdivided up into three main sections; common modules, server, and client.

3.1 Common Modules

We found that as with many distributed systems, there is a lot of overlap in terms of functionality between client and server. Each system (client and server) can keep two distinct logs: system logs and error logs. The system logs record system events as they happen. In the event of some catastrophic event (e.g. power loss), it may be possible to use these logs at the server to restart a particular problem at the point where it was halted. These logs are an optional feature on the client and are mainly used for debugging purposes.

Communications are performed on our system using Java sockets. We decided to produce one single module for use on the server and client to perform all socket communications. Its main functions are to open and close sockets, send and receive messages, and to terminate communications. The other shared communications module is the basic unit used for communication in the system called the Message class. It is be extendable so that a message can contain items such as data, algorithms, information on client status, and so on.

Each data unit that is sent out to be processed by our server has a user defined time limit associated with it. If the results for that unit have not returned to the server within the specified time, it is assumed that the unit has failed. This would normally happen through client failure, e.g. a donor machine being switched off. Additionally, if the client is not finished processing the unit when the time limit expires, it will contact the server and request a time extension. For these purposes, the server and client have been provided with a common timing module.

At the heart of our distributed system is the piece of compiled Java code that is downloaded from the server to each client – the `Task`. This Java class contains the algorithm that is executed over all of the subsequent data units that are received by the client. The user of the system is required to extend this common class. All tasks conforming to this interface will be accepted by the system. Any Java exceptions that occur in the task as it is executing at the client are fed back to the server via the communications protocol.

3.2 Server

The server can be divided up into three main sections (see Fig. 2). The `ServerEngine` is responsible for initialising the server at start-up. It reads in the user defined initialisation parameters via an external text file. After reading all of the initialisation options, it creates the log files, loads and checks the user defined classes (`DataHandler` and `Task`) and then creates the `ConnectionManager`. The `ServerEngine` also acts as the interface between the communications modules and the current running problem on the system. It also manages the lists of data units (pending and expired) that are currently out being processed by clients.

The `ConnectionManager` is responsible for listening on the server socket for new client connections and creating a new `ServerMessageHandler` thread to handle each connection. Each time a new client connection is received, a new Java thread is created that handles the communication on a separate port to the main port used by the server to listen for new connections.

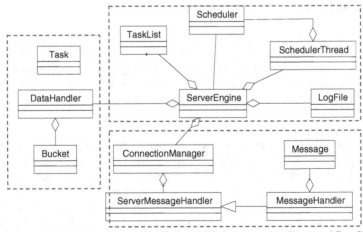

Fig. 2. Server design: the user extends Task (which is sent to the client) and DataHandler

3.3 Client

The client software can be divided up into two main sections (see Fig. 3). The ClientEngine is responsible for initialising the client software. Its first task is to read in the server details that are contained in the external text file that is included in the client installation. Once these details have been parsed correctly, the ClientEngine starts the security manager that remains in operation for the lifetime of the client. This strictly limits the client's interactions with the donor machine's resources. The final task of the ClientEngine is to start the communications section of the client.

The ClientMessageHandler is at the centre of the communications section of the system. It manages the communications protocol, receives and initialises the downloaded task and manages the execution of each data unit. Each downloaded algorithm is received by the client as a compiled Java class. By using Java's class loading facilities, the algorithm is subsequently dynamically loaded into the executing client. The ClientMessageHandler uses the shared timing module to monitor the time being taken to process each data unit. If a data unit is taking longer than its allotted time to process its data, the client can request a time extension. The client continues in an infinite loop requesting and processing data units from the server. When the server sends a new algorithm to the client, this new algorithm is loaded dynamically and all subsequent data units received are processed using the new algorithm. There are extensive exception handling mechanisms coded into the client so that the client should run continuously until explicitly shut down by the donor of the machine. Full details on the design of the JDCL and its extensions can be found in [3,9].

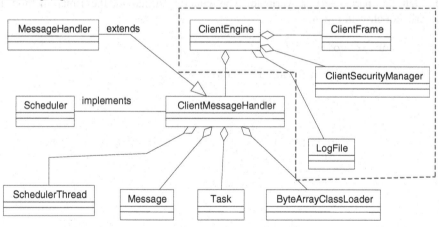

Fig. 3. Client design

4   Programming the System

To program the system with a given problem, there are two java classes that must be extended using the standard Java inheritance mechanisms. These are the DataHandler class and the Task class. The subclass of DataHandler specifies how to manage the data for the distributed computation. The subclass of Task is where the distributed algorithm is programmed. In order to program a MIMD computation, the user makes use of the Bucket class when designing their DataHandler.

4.1 DataHandler

The main purpose of the extended DataHandler is to manage all of the data relating to the current problem. The first section of the DataHandler is the init() method. The purpose of this method is to initialise whatever data structures are necessary for the overall computation. This can involve things such as setting up readers of files, initialising arrays, assigning variables values, etc. The next section is the getNextParameterSet() method. This is where the pre-processed data units are generated to be sent to the clients. This method is called every time a client requests a data unit to process. The return type is an Object array and since all Java classes inherit from the Object class, this method can return any data type supported by Java. The task running at the client receives this Object array as its data. Therefore, it is usual for the elements of this Object array to be explicitly typecasted at the client. The final section of the DataHandler is the resultsHandler() method.

4.2 Task

The subclass of the Task class describes how the data received by the clients is to be processed. There is only one method that must be extended in the task - the run() method. The pre-processed data that is sent by the server in each data unit is available through the parameterList variable. The general format of the run() method is described below in Fig. 4.

```
public void run(){
    try{
        Object[] array = parameterList;

        <actual algorithm here>

        returnList = new Object[];
        returnList[x] = // results of computation here
        endProcessing();
    }catch( Exception e ){
        exceptionInProcessing( e );
    }
}
```

Fig. 4. General form of run() method

The whole method is encompassed in one large try-catch statement. The purpose of this statement is to handle any exceptions the run() method can generate. All exceptions will be caught and are fed back to the server. The post-processed data is returned via the returnList Object array. At the bottom of the run() method is the endProcessing() which tells the client that the task has finished processing the data.

4.3 Bucket Class

The main purpose of this class is to effect the theoretical pipeline for MIMD computations. This allows the developer to set up the server to act like a pipeline processor (Fig. 5) with several different intermediary stages in the distributed computation.

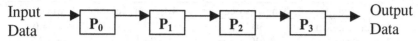

Input → P_0 → P_1 → P_2 → P_3 → Output
Data   Data

Fig. 5. Pipelined processes, where P_0 through P_4 are the processes

The pipeline is simulated by using the bucket class to represent the storage required at each stage of the pipeline. The information is stored in each bucket by using Java Vectors thus maintaining the type independence of the system. In a MIMD computation, the complete algorithm (including the code for all stages of the pipeline) is sent to each client with a flag being sent with each data unit to indicate which stage the data unit belongs to.

5   Application of System

Strands of DNA can be regarded as strings of base-4 symbols. The nucleotides adenine, guanine, cytosine, and thymine are represented by the symbols A, G, C, and T, respectively. Our application involved building up a picture of the repeated substrings within a DNA strand. We chose the DNA of the tuberculosis bacterium, which contained approximately 5M nucleotides. As well as exact-matched substrings, we also permitted insertions and deletions, up to a maximum in each case, to reflect the fact that slightly different DNA strings can code for the same functionality. In each case, we performed the search on the complete DNA strand and recorded the locations of all repeated substrings of length greater than 13 in a database. A more detailed account of our search algorithm and the results obtained is in preparation [10].

We ran the three distributed algorithms over the aforementioned laboratory of 90 clients and recorded the speedup data shown in Table 1. For these computations we did not have sole use of the laboratory. The number of processors varied over our computation but we noted that at all times at least 40 processors were working for the server. The disparity between speedups (i) and (ii) was due to choosing a work unit size for the former that was too small (thus not making efficient usage of the intra-laboratory network resources). The difference between speedups (ii) and (iii), we believe, simply reflects the uncertainty of resource-availability in a busy university laboratory environment. Taking only the results for insertions and deletions, our system has demonstrated an average speedup of 53 with (assuming a full complement of 90 processors) an efficiency of 59%. For a finer view of this speedup, we conducted an experiment in which the server distributed 100 equal work units among a number of dedicated clients. We varied the number of clients, recorded the computation time each time, and created the speedup plot shown in Fig. 6. This shows that with sole use of the laboratory resources, and for our specialised application, we could get very close to the theoretical speedup maximum. The theoretical speedup maximum was calculated from $S(p) = w/\lceil w/p \rceil$, where w denotes number of individual work units and where S, speedup, is parameterised by number of processors p.

Table 1. Speedup achieved for each of the three repeated substring search strategies

Search strategy	Single processor	40-90 processors	Speedup
(i) Exact matching	130 hours	28 hours	4.6
(ii) Insertions	1790 hours	31 hours	57.7
(iii) Deletions	1670 hours	35 hours	47.7

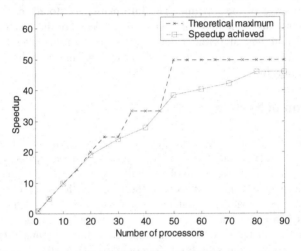

Fig. 6. Evaluation of speedup

6   Conclusion

We have refined the JDCL in terms of efficiency and functionality, including the successful extension of the system to emulate a MIMD architecture. This has allowed us to implement a large-scale bioinformatics application. The system is completely generalisable, and because it is written in Java, the developer interface is simplified to the extension of two classes. Work is ongoing on the next generation of this system. Several new features are to be incorporated into the new system including a multi-problem scheduler, compression, encryption and authentication of all communications, a remote server interface and the migration of all communications to Java RMI. Future work includes performing this type of DNA analysis on other similar size genomes with a view to eventually performing this type of analysis on the human genome.

We gratefully acknowledge assistance from the Department of Computer Science, NUI Maynooth, and technicians M. Monaghan, P. Marshall, and J. Cotter.

The continuation of this research has recently been funded by the Irish Research Council for Science, Engineering and Technology: funded by the National Development Plan.

References

[1] G. Woltman, "Great Internet Mersenne Prime Search," 1996. <http://www.mersenne.org>
[2] SETI@Home - Search for Extraterrestial Intelligence at Home, 1999. <http:// setiathome.ssl.berkeley.edu>
[3] K. Fritsche, J. Power, J. Waldron, "A Java distributed computation library," *Proc. 2nd International Conference on Parallel and Distributed Computing, Applications and Technologies* (PDCAT2001), pp. 236–243, Taipei, Taiwan, July 2001.
[4] Message Passing Interface Forum, "MPI: A message-passing interface standard," *International Journal of Supercomputer Applications and High Performance Computing* 8(3/4), 159–416, 1994.
[5] V. S. Sunderam, "PVM: a framework for parallel distributed computing," *Concurrency: Practice and Experience* 2(4), 315–340, 1990.
[6] Sun Microsystems, "JavaSpaces Technology," 2001. <http://java.sun.com/products/javaspaces>
[7] VA Linux Systems, Inc, "Joone - Java object oriented neural engine," 2001. <http://joone.sourceforge.net/>
[8] F. Loulergue, G. Hains, C. Foisy, "A calculus of functional BSP programs," Science of Computer Programming, 37, 253–277, 2000.
[9] P. Sanders, "Emulating MIMD behaviour on SIMD machines," *International Conference on Massively Parallel Processing Applications and Development*, pp. 313–321, Delft, 1994. Elsevier. (Extended version in "Efficient emulation of MIMD behavior on SIMD machines," Technical Report IB 29/95, Universität Karlsruhe, Fakultät für Informatik, 1995.)
[10] R. Allen, T. Keane, T.J. Naughton, J. McInerney, J. Waldron, "Segmental duplication in Tuberculosis genome," submitted October 2002.

JGrid: Exploiting Jini for the Development of Grid Applications

Alastair Hampshire[1] and Gordon S. Blair[2]

[1] School of Computer Science and Information Technology, University of Nottingham,
Jubilee Campus, Wollaton Road, Nottingham, NG8 1BB
axh@cs.nott.ac.uk

[2] Department of Computing, Lancaster University, Lancaster, LA1 4YR
gordon@comp.lancs.ac.uk

Abstract. Grid Computing is a concept that focuses on transparent resource sharing in a dynamic distributed environment, which allows several distributed resources to be combined and used to achieve a single task. This is useful because it has the potential to provide users with resources that would otherwise be unavailable to them. This project aims to show that object oriented techniques and more specifically Java/ Jini can be used to develop a grid computing environment, JGrid, which simplifies the task of developing grid applications by providing a high level interface to GRID resources. This document presents an analysis of JGrid based upon an environmental modelling algorithm used to test the system, which demonstrates some significant advantages over more low-level grid environments such as Globus.

1 Introduction

Grid Computing [Grid01, Ian99] is a concept that focuses on transparent resource sharing in a dynamic distributed environment, where sharing refers to direct access to remote computers and their associated resources, as opposed to conventional file sharing as seen in the Internet. Resources are shared by attaching them to a grid-enabled network, allowing clients to communicate with resources without knowing their location.

Scientists and Engineers have developed Grid Computing applications because of their ability to provide large quantities of processing power without the expense of using traditional high performance computing methods such as massively parallel processors, supercomputers etc. A number of middleware platforms have been developed to support the development of such applications. Many of these platforms are low level in nature and are consequently difficult to use. In contrast, a number of advancements have recently been made in the middleware community that, we believe, can usefully be exploited in a GRID environment; examples of such trends include distributed object computing, component-based software development, resource discovery platforms, etc. The aim of this paper is to investigate the potential role of advanced middleware concepts in the GRID. In particular, we examine the contribution of Jini together with Java in this area.

N. Guelfi et al. (Eds.): FIDJI 2002, LNCS 2604, pp. 132–142, 2003.
© Springer-Verlag Berlin Heidelberg 2003

The features of Jini/ Java we are particularly interested in are as follows:

- The use of Jini's discovery/ lookup/ join protocol to support dynamic discovery of GRID resources, including processing resources and data resources;
- The use of leasing to allow soft-state allocation of available GRID resources;
- The use of Jini's event service to keep track of changes in available GRID resources;
- The use of Java for cross platform compatibility;
- The more general applicability of object-oriented techniques to ease the development of, often complex, GRID applications.

Note that Java is not traditionally thought of as a good language for developing high-performance applications. However techniques are being uncovered, such as exception free code, which may improve its suitability [Moreira01]. Therefore, another aim of this project is to demonstrate that Java and Jini are suitable tools for the development of high performance Grid computing environments.

To accomplish these aims, an object oriented high performance grid computing environment, JGrid, has been developed using Java and Jini. The remainder of this paper presents JGrid in some detail, evaluates the contributions of JGrid, and compares this platform to other middleware services for Grid Computing.

2   Background

2.1   Existing Grid Computing Environments

A number of middleware platforms have been developed for the GRID. As mentioned above, most of these platforms are quite low level with their roots in work on parallel programming environments, the most notable example being Globus. A number of more high-level platforms have also been developed. We briefly examine a selection of low level and higher-level platforms below.

The two low level platforms we examine are Globus and Gridware. Globus [Globus01] is currently the most widely used approach for the construction of Grid environments. It provides a set of services, the Globus toolkit, which implement features such as resource discovery, resource management, communication, security etc. These services are distinct, which allows them to be incorporated into applications incrementally. This allows the application programmer to decide which grid services he wishes to provide.

Gridware [Gridware01] is a grid computing engine designed by Sun Microsystems to locate and harness idle resources on a network. A central holding area queues all jobs for execution along with the requirements of the job, which may consist of available memory, execution speed and available software licences. Gridware matches the available resources to the job requirements. When a resource becomes available the Sun Grid Engine software will dispatch a suitable job to that resource.

Both the above are interesting platforms, however they are low-level in nature and thus make it a difficult and error prone task to write GRID applications.

The two high level platforms we examine are Legion and GriT. Legion [Legion01] is an object oriented grid environment in which everything, whether hardware or software, is represented by an object. It is designed for large scale resource sharing, involving millions of hosts. The idea is to allow a user to work at a single workstation, making use of multiple distributed objects, but with the impression that all the work is being done on the local machine.

GRID TAO (or GriT) [Gokhale03] is a CORBA based platform building on the TAO real-time CORBA implementation from Washington University. The aim of this work is to raise the level of abstraction for GRID programming and also to provide support for quality of service, building on the underlying features of TAO. More specifically, the project exploits the recent implementation of the CORBA Component Model in TAO and also its noteworthy architecture based on the Meta Resource Broker, adding flexibility in terms of resource management.

This is an interesting project, which shares our vision of higher level programming environments for the GRID. It is however at a fairly early stage of development and also does not address the issue of resource discovery in dynamic environments.

2.2   Jini

Jini [Jini01] was developed by Sun Microsystems to allow dynamic (I.e. services can be created and removed at any time) distributed environments to be created, which allow clients and services to communicate with each other whilst possessing only a minimal knowledge about each other. Any service wanting to participate in a Jini organisation must find and join a Jini lookup service. For redundancy, more than one lookup service may be available, in this case the service may choose to join some or all of the available lookup services. A client wishing to make use of a service finds all lookup services and retrieves a list of available services. The client can then choose and make use of whichever service he wants to use.

Jini has been chosen because it provides several features that may be particularly useful for the development of grid environments, such as automatic discovery of new resources and eventual clean up of crashed resources (See section 1 for more details). In addition, because Jini is based on Java, it makes use of Java's cross platform compatibility, which is particularly useful for grid environments.

3   Design

This section outlines the design of an object oriented grid environment, JGrid, implemented using Jini & Java. JGrid allows a client machine to make seamless and transparent use of multiple distributed computational resources, referred to as a *processor service* (PS). The following design principles were defined:

- **The system should be as dynamic as possible,** allowing it to cope with PSs being created and destroyed sporadically. Further, the system should be able to recover, with no loss of data, should a PS crash.
- **The system must be reusable.** The user must be able to solve any problem they want by simply "plugging in" a new algorithm at the client. This simplifies the task of writing applications that can make use of grid resources.

3.1   JGrid System Architecture

Fig. 1 shows how the various components of the system interact. For a machine to make its processor available within a grid environment it must start a *PS*, which locates and joins a Jini lookup service. The Jini lookup service is used to store a list of references to available services and their associated attributes.

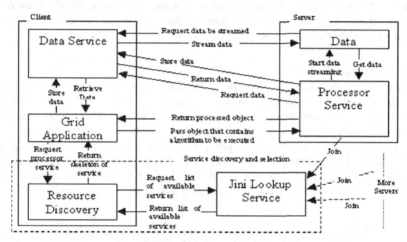

Fig. 1. JGrid system architecture

Resource discovery and selection is achieved by finding all available lookup services to obtain a list of potential services. To find the most appropriate service, the attributes for the desired service are compared to the attributes of available services.

The client first writes the algorithm for the real world problem to be solved. Next the client passes the attributes of the required services to the *resource discovery and selection mechanism*, which returns the appropriate service(s). It then passes the object containing the algorithm to be executed to the remote *PS*. The remote *PS* processes the object and returns a result to the client. A client is able to make use of as many *PSs* as required/available.

The rest of this section will look at each component of the system in more detail.

3.2   Processor Service Design

The PS is the software used to represent and control a processor. For a computer to be included in the Grid it must install and run this software which, when executed, registers itself with any Jini lookup services on the network. This allows clients to discover and pass objects to the PS, which will process the object and return it.

The PS requires the following attributes: Name (String) – The name "processor service" identifies the PS, CPU Speed (constant Integer), Spare_capacity (Integer), Over_use_flag (Boolean), Minimum_spare_capacity (constant Integer).

3.2.1   Passing Objects

Any object that is to be passed to and processed by a remote PS must implement an interface that guarantees it is "executable" by the service. This is achieved by including an **execute** method, which contains the algorithm to be processed. All PSs implement an interface that ensures they are able to process executable objects, by implementing a **process** method that takes an "executable" object and calls its execute method. A client wishing to make use of a remote processor simply uses its PS interface to call the process method, passing the "executable" object. The service then processes and returns the object to the client.

3.2.2   Limiting Usage

Because several clients may wish to use a PS simultaneously, there must be a way to limit the number of clients that can use the service at once. The simplest method would be a flag to denote that the service is in use and so stop other clients using it.

This method however is not ideal because in some cases (e.g. on fast cluster machines) it may be advantageous to process multiple client requests simultaneously. Another method makes use of the overuse flag; a Jini lookup service will only return a list of services that are not being overused. Whenever the *spare_capacity* is less than the *minimum_spare_capacity* the *over_use_flag* is set.

3.2.3   Leasing

To make use of a PS, a client must first request a lease for that service. To keep hold of the PS, the client must periodically renew its lease. When the client passes an object to the PS for processing, the PS first checks to see if the client has a valid lease before proceeding. If the client does not hold a valid lease then an exception is thrown. When a client has finished using a service, it must return the lease. If a lease times out, the PS assumes the client has crashed or ungracefully terminated its connection. This ensures that a client cannot indefinitely hold a service without regular renewal messages and thus helps to provide a more robust architecture.

3.3   Service Discovery and Selection Design

The service discovery and selection mechanism is a reusable component that keeps track of available services and handles requests from a client for a service. However, the client does not use this mechanism to communicate with the service, instead the client downloads a stub of the service from the computer that is running the service. This stub then allows the client to directly communicate with the service.

This key component will be initialised with the name "processor service" and the attributes of the service required. The class will then retrieve information from a Jini lookup service about available services that match the specified criteria. The information retrieved will be stored within the class. When a client makes a request, the PS with the highest *spare_capacity* is selected. *Spare_capacity* represents the amount of spare processing power within the processor and is calculated as follows:

$$spare\_capacity = \frac{CPU\_Speed}{Num\_of\_clients + 1}$$

This algorithm is designed only to be functional. Potential future work involves looking into more advanced service selection mechanisms.

In order to make the system as dynamic as possible, the information stored in the service discovery class must be kept informed of changes to the Grid. It therefore monitors for the addition/removal of further Jini lookup services. The service discovery class will also be informed when a PS has joined or left the Jini lookup service as well as when the attributes of a PS have changed such that they were desirable and have become undesirable or visa versa.

3.4   Passing Data

Data can be passed to the PS stored inside the algorithm object. However this is not efficient, especially when transferring large amounts of data. Therefore, the following data passing mechanisms have been defined.

The data service is designed to improve the performance of the system by storing the data at the client, allowing the service to access the data on demand. The data service contains a hashtable into which data can be placed alongside a tag that will identify it. Various methods have been implemented to allow different types of data to be entered into and removed from the data service. This allows a single hashtable to store multiple sets of data of differing types. The client can enter all the data required into the data service and then pass an interface of the data service to the PS alongside the executable object. Because the user who programmed the executable is aware of how the data were placed into the data service, the algorithm is able to retrieve those data from the data service on demand.

In some situations, e.g. with large data sets, it would be advantageous to fetch the data from the data service just before it is required, so the processor does not have to wait for the data to be copied across the network. The data streamer achieves this by streaming the data across the network into a buffer on the PS machine. The data can then be extracted from the buffer when they are needed, instead of being dragged across the networks. The data streamer is designed to be as flexible as possible, allowing the user to specify the streaming parameters: how often data are copied across the network as well as the number of data items in each copy.

3.5   Client Design

The client makes use of the service discovery and selection mechanism, by initialising it with the attributes for the required service and then requesting as many services as it needs. It is the job of the client to make the best use of available resources by splitting the problem into separate sections. Each section can then make use of a different computational resource thus improving the performance of the system. The sections must be carefully selected, because they must be sufficiently heavyweight to outweigh the costs of shipping code around the network, but there must be enough sections to make use of several processors. The environment can be used by simply 'plugging in' the algorithm for a problem, which greatly simplifies the task of writing applications that make use of grid resources.

3.6 Summary

The most important objective of JGrid is to be as dynamic and robust as possible, i.e. it must be able to cope with continual changes in the grid environment. To achieve this, the service discovery and selection mechanism has been carefully designed to keep track of the changing grid environment.

The most important aspect of the design is the method by which objects are passed to and processed by remote services, because it is this object passing and processing that is fundamental to the functioning of the system. Other important aspects include the use of Leasing to improve the robustness of the architecture, the use of processor attributes in service selection and the advanced data passing mechanisms such as the data service and data streamer. Finally, the system is designed to be reusable, by allowing users to 'plug in' new algorithms to solve new problems.

4 Evaluation

Typical problems that could be solved using a grid environment such as JGrid, must be sufficiently complex to require large computational resources. In addition the problem must be separable into many coarse grained and loosely coupled subtasks, which can be processed separately and then amalgamated to produce a final solution.

Several different algorithms were used to test the functionality and performance of the system in operation. The most important algorithm used was the flow prediction problem [Young94], which involves running several simulations of the same algorithm with varied parameters. Each simulation predicts a river flow data set based on a collected rainfall data set. Each calculated flow data set is then compared to a collected flow data set, to see which statistically fits the best. The parameters of the best fitting simulation can then be used in the future to predict river flows from rainfall data. This problem has formed the basis of both the quantitative and qualitative evaluation.

4.1 Quantitative Evaluation

The test, as outlined above, was conducted by varying both the number of processors used in the grid and the workload placed upon the grid. The results where then compared to similar tests carried out on a standalone machine. The results demonstrated that for a light workload, a standalone environment is more efficient. This is because the time taken to discover available services and ship objects around the network outweighs the performance increase of using multiple processors. However, once the workload is sufficiently weighty, the cost of the initial service discovery and object shipping become negligible compared to the overall processing time and the grid environment is able to offer significantly better performance than a standalone machine.

Further results were also taken that demonstrated a significant performance increase when using a grid environment containing more available PSs. This shows that multiple resources can be effectively combined to reduce the overall computation time for a given algorithm.

4.2   Qualitative Evaluation

4.2.1   Java & Jini's Suitability for High Performance Grid Environments

Grid computing environments will generally consist of a heterogeneous collection of resources. Because of Java's *platform independence* Jini is clearly well suited to a heterogeneous environment, being able to ship code to any machine that supports the Java virtual machine without having to recompile.

Java provides a *serialisation mechanism* that allows objects to be converted into a flat byte array, for transporting over a network. When the serialised object reaches its destination it can be de-serialised into its previous form. This clearly makes it easy to ship code around a network, something that is very important for the development of Grid environments.

Jini's resource discovery techniques are extremely easy to use; all a service must do is discover a lookup service and join it. Clients can then simply perform a lookup to discover available services. Jini is also very dynamic to changes in available services, with remote events being used to notify interested parties of changes to the available resources. Jini makes use of leasing to provide an architecture that is robust to unexpected changes in available resources. Clearly these techniques are ideally suited to the development of grid computing environments.

However there are reservations about the use of Java and Jini for the development of grid computing environments. Jini has primarily been designed for use within small communities and it is debatable whether the lookup service will scale well in large systems. In addition, Java is not traditionally thought of as the natural choice for high performance computing. However some current research suggests Java's performance characteristic may be significantly better than previously assumed [Moreira01, Pancake01, Kielmann01].

In summary, Java and Jini provide exactly the sort of platform independent, dynamic and robust resource discovery protocol that is required for a grid computing environment. However it is debatable whether Jini scales well to large grids and whether Java is fast enough to support high performance computing.

4.2.2   A Comparison of JGrid to Globus

Globus is currently the most widely used Grid development toolkit. This section compares aspects of Globus to JGrid in an attempt to show some of the benefits and weaknesses derived from using object oriented programming techniques, specifically Java & Jini, for the development of high performance grid computing environments.

One of the most immediately obvious advantages of using Java is its platform independence, as discussed earlier. Because Java code is interpreted, it can be easily submitted to any platform that supports the Java virtual machine. By contrast, Globus is platform specific and would require a range of binaries compiled for various platforms. Before shipping code, Globus has to query the operating system of the target machine to ascertain the platform being used and thus select the appropriate binary file. Because distributed systems are very often heterogeneous JGrid has a clear advantage over Globus because of its portable nature.

JGrid is able to react to changes in the grid environment in a very high level and effective way. Remote events are used to keep clients informed of addition and removal of services, whilst leasing is used to ensure a robust architecture that can cope with unexpected or unintended changes to the grid.

Results in Globus are returned as textual outputs. JGrid provides more powerful features for returning results, because of its object-oriented architecture. The client may define a specific 'results' object or set of 'results' objects to store the output and include methods to allow the results to be easily retrieved.

Globus is essentially a set of tools that can be utilised in C/C++, which are widely accepted to be efficient and fast programming languages. JGrid, by contrast uses Java. Whether Java is suitable for high performance computing applications is open to debate, however it is clear and widely accepted that C and C++ offer better performance than Java.

In summary, it is clear that JGrid provides or has the potential to provide several features that are not supported by Globus, most notably platform independence. Globus however has a clear performance advantage over JGrid. JGrid provides the user with a higher level interface to the grid and therefore simplifies the task of creating applications that can make use of the grid.

5   Future Work

There is a great deal of potential future work that could be carried out in this area, however due to space requirements, only the major issues are mentioned here. One possible extension to this project is that of dynamic reconfiguration. If, while a remote object is being processed by a PS, another more powerful/ suitable PS becomes available, dynamic reconfiguration would allow the object to be migrated to the new processor. This is a desirable characteristic of a Grid environment, as it would allow a client to make better use of available resources.

More advanced fault tolerance techniques could be included that periodically save the state of the computation. Should a PS crash, the computation would not need to be restarted from the beginning.

A more complex service selection mechanism could be used, for example an attribute specifying available memory might be useful for data intensive computations. Also the system could take into account the fact that some processor architectures are more effective at processing some tasks than others.

As mentioned earlier, inter-object communication allows two objects being remotely processed on separate machines to communicate with each other. It would be worthwhile investigating how effectively Jini could support this functionality, using features such as the Java Messaging Service and JavaSpaces. In a similar area, further work could be done to exploit the protocol independence inherent in Jini to interface to other more lightweight protocols such as MPI

6   Related Work

There are numerous other projects similar to the one described in this document, some of which are outlined below. Many other projects can be found in the grid forum at the following address: http://www-unix.mcs.anl.gov/gridforum/jini/

Clifford [Clifford00] has developed JiniGrid, which uses Jini to create a grid environment, which shares computational servers using the task farm paradigm. A task farm consists of a number of worker processes, each typically running on their own processor and all co-ordinated by a master process. The master module, known as the TaskFarmService, must join the Jini lookup service to allow it to be located by a client. Any problem to be solved is broken down into several component problems (tasks) to be processed separately by different worker processes. The results are all returned to the master process, which combines them to produce the overall result.

ICENI [Furmento02] exploits Java and Jini in a similar fashion to JGrid by providing a grid middleware that builds on top of current grid services to provide a more high level interface for applications. The 'added value' allows for the matching of applications with underlying resources and services, to maximise the usage of available resources. ICENI uses the notion of a *Computational Community,* to which a group of individuals or organisations with a common goal can contribute their resources. A resource manager manages resources within a private domain and a policy manager controls access to these resources by users in the public computational community. A domain manager is used to publish available resources within one or more public computational community. Users interact with the public computational community using tools such as a resource browser.

The main contribution of the JGrid work is to present both the design of a Jini based Grid computing environment and a detailed evaluation based on environmental sciences modelling algorithms used to test the system.

7   Conclusion

This paper has described the design and implementation of JGrid, a high level middleware for GRID computing building on Jini and Java. The work has been evaluated both quantitatively and qualitatively, based on experiences of developing an environmental modelling simulation for river flow forecasting.

The major results from this work are:

- The *integration* of Jini's discovery/ lookup/ join, leasing and the event service do help considerably in the development of GRID applications by managing the dynamics of the underlying GRID environment;
- The JGrid platform, through its use of object-oriented techniques, maintains a clean *separation of concerns* between the application and the underlying middleware infrastructure in terms of data sharing and resource discovery services.

As well as the above, JGrid benefits from the cross platform compatibility inherent in Java. The approach also lends itself strongly to dynamic re-configuration (although at the time of writing this has not yet been implemented). Other areas of future work include more advanced fault tolerance, enhanced service selection and inter-object communication. Finally, the simulation work demonstrates that realistic GRID applications can be constructed using the Java language and that through the use of Jini, a reusable architecture can be created which simplifies the development of applications that make use of a GRID environment.

References

[Grid01]	The Grid Forum http://www.gridforum.org/
[Globus01]	Globus http://www.globus.org/
[Gridware01]	SunTM Grid Engine Software http://www.sun.com/software/gridware/
[Legion01]	LEGION – Worldwide virtual computer http://legion.virginia.edu/
[Jini01]	Jini technology community resource http://www.jini.org/
[Ian99]	Ian Foster and Carl Kesselman, "The Grid, Blueprint for a new Computing Infrastructure", Morgan Kaufmann Publishers 1999
[Moreira01]	José E. Moreira, Samuel P. Midkiff, Manish Gupta, Pedro V. Artigas, Peng Wu and George Almasi, "The Ninja Project", Communications of the ACM, Vol. 44, No. 10, pp 102–109, October 2001
[Pancake01]	Cherri M. Pancake and Christian Lengauer, "High-performance Java", Communications of the ACM, Vol. 44, No. 10, pp 99–101, October 2001
[Kielmann01]	Thilo Kielmann, Philip Hatcher, Luc Bougé and Henri E. Bal, "Enabling Java for High-Performance computing", Communications of the ACM, Vol. 44, No. 10, pp 110–117, October 2001
[Clifford00]	Benjamin Clifford, "JiniGrid: Specification and Implementation of a task farm service for Jini", Edinburgh Parallel Computer Centre SSP Report, EPCC-SS-2000-02, September 2000
[Furmento02]	Nathalie Furmento, Anthony Mayer, Stephen McGough, Steven Newhouse, Tony Field and John Darlington, "ICENI: Optimisation of Component Applications within a Grid Environment", submitted to Journal of Parallel Computing, February 2002
[Gokhale03]	Aniruddha Gokhale, Douglas C. Schmidt, Balachandran Natarajan, Nanbor Wang, "Applying Model-Integrated Synthesis and Provisioning of GRID Applications", Submitted to Hawaii International Conference on System Sciences, HICSS-36, Hawaii, January 2003.
[Young94]	Peter C. Young and Keith J. Beven, "Data-based mechanistic modelling and the rainfall-flow non-linearity", Environmetrics, Vol. 5, pp 335–3

Managing Dependencies in Component-Based Distributed Applications

Sascha Alda, Markus Won, and Armin B. Cremers

Department of Applied Computer Science, University of Bonn,
Römerstrasse 164, 53117 Bonn, Germany.
{alda, won, abc}@cs.uni-bonn.de
http://www.cs.uni-bonn.de/III

Abstract. The drift away from monolithic towards distributed, service-oriented application scenarios results in a couple of new challenges concerning the management of these systems. One particular area is the management of dependencies between services. Dependencies can have different appearances, for instance, functional dependencies, semantic integrity conditions, or even dependencies to hardware resources. In this paper we consider services which are provided by software components. The usage of software components promises to allow for flexible and highly tailorable software systems. In the context of our research we consider dependencies in order to enhance the tailorability of component-based, distributed applications. We explain different occurrences of dependencies as well as the necessity of dependency management for adaptations in component-based applications. The paper focuses on a component architecture which allows the deployment of components as well as the management of dependencies between components.

1 Introduction

Software applications are nowadays composed of distributed services rather than of building blocks residing on a local machine. Novel technologies such as Web Services, distributed component architectures, or peer-to-peer frameworks such as JXTA [17] have recently pushed this trend. All these services are conceptualized on top of middleware technologies to accomplish remote interaction across machine boundaries. Apparently, these distributed and service-oriented applications result in a plethora of new challenges concerning the management of these applications. Besides service composition management (intending to yield an optimal service composition for a specific application) another essential field is the *management of dependencies* among services. Simply speaking, one can consider a dependency as a kind of relationship between two (distributed) services. As we will see later, a dependency can necessarily have different occurrences.

Dependency management is essential for a couple of reasons. Services can become unavailable for a time, are subject to changes, or become unreliable. Applications (or

N. Guelfi et al. (Eds.): FIDJI 2002, LNCS 2604, pp. 143–154, 2003.

other services) depending on such services must be notified accordingly, so that they can adapt to the new situation. Dependency management also can facilitate other management activities such as fault management [8], accounting management [6], or tailorability management [1].

In this paper, we consider services, which are supplied by *software components* [18]. The usage of software components grants to have highly adaptable software application since components can be deployed during runtime of an application. In the context of our research work, we analyze to what extend dependencies between distributed components influence the tailorability of component-based applications. We examine strategies to enhancing the decision making whether or not it is feasible to adapt a component on which other components depend. Particularly in the area of distributed applications where the constituting components interact in a peer-to-peer [14] fashion, it is by all means expensive to detect all *direct and transitive* dependencies between components.

The paper is organized as follows: section 2 elaborates different occurrences of dependencies especially in the field of component technology. Section 3 presents our component architecture FREEVOLVE. This architecture allows to deploy distributed component-based Java applications, which can be structured either in a client-server fashion or according to the peer-to-peer paradigm. Furthermore, the architecture supports tailorability as well as the management of dependencies between components. Section 4 finally concludes this paper.

2   Dependencies

Dependencies between different components within a system exist in the way that the whole application becomes unstable if those dependencies are broken or violated. Normally, there is no reason why this should happen during work with an application (whether it is designed component-based or not). However, this can necessarily occur in the case that (distributed) applications change during runtime. Such changes can appear in many ways. In the following we will concentrate on two fields of applications where those changes (and therefore possibly violated dependencies) are not only normal but also intended in a special way.

Tailorability of Components. Most of the software sold nowadays are off-the-shelf products designed to meet the requirements of very different types of users. One way to meet these requirements is to design software that is flexible in such a way that it can be used in very different contexts [7, 12]. This flexibility can be achieved by tailorable design architectures. The idea behind this concept is that every user can tailor his software in the way that it meets his personal working contexts best. In this way the parts of specification and design can be done during the use. According to the ideas of participatory design [7] users then have more possibilities to form the software in the way they want to.

Component-based architectures were basically developed with the idea of higher reusability of parts of software. Components can be used to build those highly flexible software. The same operations that are used when composing software during development (i.e. choosing components, parameterizing them, binding them together) are then the basis for a tailoring language. Especially if the components have a GUI representation it is quite easy to design appropriate tailoring languages including a visual representation. Although both – the idea of adapting an application seen as a composition of components and the use of visual tailoring language which supports only very few tailoring mechanisms – are well understood by users, there is a need for further support during tailoring time.

Here doing errors during tailoring can violate dependencies between components that work together. Frese et al. [5] discuss the amount of errors (that take about 12% of working time) that users do during their work. They present empirical studies that show that not only beginners but also experienced users do errors (as part of their "working style"). Furthermore, they distinguish between different types of errors i.e. those, which can be corrected easily, or those that cannot even be located directly. What can be learned from this study is that doing errors during use and especially during tailoring of software is normal or even an intended using behavior. Therefore, supporting mechanisms which can help finding failures (broken dependencies), understanding the composition, or testing the current composition in an exploring environment seem to be very useful.

Failures in Peer-to-Peer Applications. In the dynamic nature of peer-to-peer applications it is founded that one peer can not know all the other peers. Especially the information concerning the up-to-date network composition it gets is time-shifted. So violated dependencies (seen from the perspective of one special peer) stem from broken connections to some other peers which services are needed or inconsistencies between several services that work together. Apparently, observing dependencies between services can not solve the time-shift problem. The fact that, mostly, independent peers cooperate together and have to be adapted in the way that they do so can actually be described by dependencies. Peer-to-peer networks are highly dynamic; therefore a single peer has to continuously adapt itself according to a changed environment. These adaptations can either be tackled manually (*tailorability*) or by means of automatisms which change the configuration of the peer stand-alone (*adaptivity*). In the second way there have to be descriptions how a peer should be connected to other peers, which services it needs, and how parameters can be changed to allow for a better fitting into the environment.

2.1.   Classification of Dependencies

In the following we present a classification of dependencies between components. Basically, we distinguish among three different types of dependencies. The first group comprehends syntactical dependencies, where a communication between two components actually takes place (Event Flow, Data Flow, and Functional Dependency). The second group is also based on a syntactical level but without direct communication between the dependent components (Implicit Dependencies). The latter group of dependencies finally describes semantic properties between components.

Event Flow. The event flow between two components is one of the most common dependencies, which is integrated in nearly all prevalent component models. An event flow typically consists of an event source and an event sink. An event source produces an event (e.g. if a component changes its state), which is eventually passed to one or more event sinks. In order to be notified an event sink must subscribe to the source (observer pattern). An event flow is uni-directional, that is, an event sink does not send back an (confirmation) event to the source. In addition to these properties, various other are conceivable: the FLEXIBEAN Model [15] for example provides a remote event flow across machine boundaries through the incorporation of the RMI technology. With respect to the CORBA COMPONENT MODEL (CCM) 3.0 [11] event notification is asynchronous, i.e. time-shifted. In both models, providing two components with an event flow is performed by using *ports*, the connecting points of components. In doing so, the port of the sink must compulsory be compatible to the port of the source.

Data Flow. The data flow represents the flow of information between two components. In contrast to an event flow, where only little information about an event is transmitted, data flow rather illustrates a continuous flow between two components. This flow of data is typically not instantiated by a state change but requested and started through an interaction with a user. Furthermore, data flow is mostly synchronous (not time-shifted) and bi-directional, that is, the direction of the flow between two components can be alternating. In the FLEXIBEAN Component Model a bi-directional channel is modeled by means of a *shared object*. Here, two components have equal access to a shared object, which can be used to exchange arbitrary objects.

Functional Dependency. By a functional dependent component we understand a component, which depends on certain methods or interfaces provided by another component. This connection between two components is obviously synchronous and uni-directional. In the CORBA COMPONENT MODEL 3.0, a subset of the overall set of interfaces a component does provide is termed *facet*. A facet provides a special view a component can have on an other component. In other words, a facet represents the role a component can adopt during its life-cycle. Additionally, a component can navigate between the facets of an other component and is thus able to change the view during runtime. A violation occurs, if some facets are removed or become unavailable after the adaptation of the component.

Implicit Dependencies. In contrast to the first dependency types, implicit dependencies [9] impose no direct communication (e.g. method call, or information flow) between components. These dependencies exist between services supplied by components and services stemming from basic underlying services such as memory, or scheduling, which may have an indirect influence on the performance of a component.

Semantic Constraints and Integrity Conditions. Normally, state-of-the-art development tools and platforms do syntactically checks on the code or – in case of component-based architectures – composition. Nonetheless, there are cases in which syntactic correct compositions do not work properly. Or they do work properly but not in the intended way (seen from the perspective of a composer or a tailoring user). In many cases "integrity information" added to a component by its developer might help avoiding failures. Another idea is to design "application templates" where conditions according to a group of applications like the group of word processors or a group of different database query front ends. Both approaches are based on the assumption that special meta information on the components and about domains or groups of applications can be given or added to the component set. The approach described in the following is based on the tailoring techniques mentioned above, but the concept can be used to support adaptive strategies within a peer-to-peer network as well. In both cases it seems to be useful to try to match the resulting integrity conditions to the basic design or tailoring operations, that is:

Parameterization of components: There can be mutual dependencies between different parameters within one component. They can be checked within the component's functionality. The idea is very similar to constraints or triggers in the world of databases. Here dependencies between data records can be described. Updating, deleting, or adding actions are checked according to those conditions. In the case of component-based software explicit descriptions of dependencies between parameters not only ensure the correct parameterization but also explain parts of the functionality. This helps understanding the component's semantics. External dependencies between parameters of different components also have to be described explicitly.

Changing the connections: As shown above in component-based architectures syntactical dependencies such as event flows can be checked. Compilers usually master these checks. Furthermore, additional semantic information can be given about what a component needs from its environment or which services it provides. This idea is similar to the Parameterized Contracts [13]. The slightly different approach which we call Event Flow Integrity (EFI) (for more detail see [20, 21]) takes into account where data are produced, transformed into other data, and consumed. Our approach here deals with the idea that not only two interacting components are to be investigated (according to the integrity of an application) but the whole composition can be seen as a network. Thus as well as workflows (in WFMS) they can be seen as directed graphs and therefore analyzed in a similar way (c.f. next section about dependencies in peer-to-peer applications). Those graphs can be analyzed in the way that every essentially needed event is produced and the producer is connected transitively to the consumer. Events that have to be consumed can be treated in the same way.

Adding/removing components: The third basic operation set – adding and removing components – has also impact on integrity conditions described above. Event Flow Integrity can be violated if components are removed from a composition. On the other hand, if one adds a component to an existing application this new component may have certain conditions that describe which of its provided data have to be consumed or which input is necessary. Furthermore, we could define conditions that describe a set of applications. Thus, similar to the conditions on parameters, we could demand that a component of type X has to be part of the composition. More subtle rules can be designed by using propositional logic terms (if component a is part of application X then there must be a component b or a component c). Birngruber [3] describe application templates in CoPL (Component Plan Language). This plan describes a composition and parameterization possibilities. Using this plan an interactive agent builds up a composition. This approach is very helpful for designing new applications but does not support any concepts of flexible or tailorable applications.

The sum of the integrity concepts described above then allows for easier tailoring (less failures), a better understanding of the application, if detailed descriptions are added to the integrity conditions, or better adaptivity strategies of dynamic peer-to-peer applications, if integrity conditions are taken into account. It is an obvious fact that the more semantical information about dependencies are available, the higher the degree of adaptivity of a peer application.

2.2   Characteristics of Dependencies in Peer-to-Peer Networks

In distributed applications, in particular in peer-to-peer applications, components can have either *direct* or *transitive* dependencies on other components. Transitive dependencies can occur, if a component (re-)provides data, events or services to components, which are based on services consumed by third-party (remote) components. Apparently, these dependencies between distributed services can result in a complex and unmanageable network, mostly not transparent to the owner of a component or a peer. However, the exposure of all dependent components is necessary for some management activities, for instance for tailoring a certain component. In a trivial way, one can think of one of the two following proceedings:

- No tailoring is allowed until all dependencies have been released (which normally precedes a notification to all (known) dependent components)
- Instant tailoring without taking care of any dependencies

Apparently, both proceedings appear rather sub-optimal: the first may lead to a deadlock, while the latter may obviously lead to a system failure.

In order to tackle this problem, a couple of alternatives, more sophisticated strategies have been evolved [1, 4, 6]. All approaches propose the computation of a dependency graph. In such a graphical representation, nodes represent components while edges denote the dependencies between these nodes or components, respectively. The information of the components and their dependencies is not explicitly incorporated in the respective component models, but extracted from the underlying architecture, which keeps track of all necessary information. A graph-based approach serves as a visualization of a dependency network but may also be the foundation for a network analysis, which could enhance management activities.

3   Component Architecture FREEVOLVE

In the last years, component-based architectures [18] have become quite fashionable in the field of software engineering. A very important property of a component is its reusability and the independent development of components. Thus, components can be seen as small programs which can exist and run alone but may also be combined with other components. Thus, an application normally consists of several components that are connected with each other.

Tailorable software can be designed if an underlying platform provides for tailoring operations, so that users can change the composition easily. Those tailoring operations are mainly the same as used in composition tools which developers use except that they are much easier to handle and hide most of the complexity [15]. This idea was implemented in the FREEVOLVE (former: EVOLVE) platform [15] [16] which will be described as follows. Additionally, we describe our current efforts to incorporate an adequate dependency management in the platform, which serves as a necessary prerequisite for the tailorability of components belonging to distributed applications.

3.1   FREEVOLVE as Client Server Platform

The FREEVOLVE platform is based on the FLEXIBEAN component model, which has already been depicted in section 2.1. FREEVOLVE is a client-server architecture where all components initially reside on the server. Compositions of these components (constituting concrete applications) are described in a language called CAT. There are CAT files for both server-sided as well as client-sided compositions and another CAT-file (DCAT) to describe the remote interaction between client and server components (see figure 1). When starting a FREEVOLVE client (currently realized as an Applet and as a stand-alone implementation) descriptions for the client's compositions are transferred to the respective client. After choosing an application the components needed to build up the application are also transferred and instantiated. These applications can then be tailored by the users according to their likes and dislikes. During runtime, applications are executed according to the client-server paradigm.

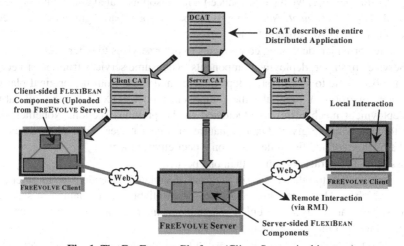

Fig. 1. The FREEVOLVE Platform (Client-Server Architecture)

According to ease the learning of a tailoring language and environment it is due to the designer of a component set to choose the right granularity. Thus, beginners start to compose their own applications by using few components which provide for a great amount of functionality whereas more experienced users can combine more components which are smaller.[1] Evaluating tests have shown that this design seems to be very promising. A second step to ease the learning therefore is to allow for a layered architectures [19] which means that several components can be stick together and saved as one larger.

One of the remaining problems is that it is not clear to the users in which situation which component to choose or how the components have to be bound together. Seen from the perspective of the developers the semantics of the components as well as their parameters and interfaces have to become more transparent. There are some other concepts [10] to create a better understanding of tailoring languages as well as of the resulting applications. In the following (see 3.4) we will describe in more detail the possibilities that can be provided by an integrity checking system that is not intended to auto-correct tailoring errors but shows and explains them. These hints are given visually or in help texts which allow for more detailed explanations.

3.2   Extending FREEVOLVE to a Peer-to-Peer Platform

As already mentioned, FREEVOLVE has originally been conceived as a client-server platform. Although the imposed client-server paradigm fits for a couple of conventional applications, increasingly new application scenarios with multiple equal servers can not be considered [2, 9]. In order to be able to support such decentral peer-to-peer applications, we are about to extend FREEVOLVE towards to a peer-to-peer platform [1, 2]. For this purpose, we have introduced a more sophisticated client environment, a so-called *peer environment*. According to the peer-to-peer paradigm, a peer is accomplished to take over two different roles:

- Service provider, deploying components to offer services to other peers
- Service consumer, deploying components to consume services from other peer

We have been able to seamlessly adopt fundamental ideas from the original platform to the new platform, in particular the component model FLEXIBEAN, the tailorability and deployment mechanisms as elucidated in the previous section. Nonetheless, in order to cope with the given dynamic nature of a peer-to-peer network, we have exposed a plethora of additional demands on a peer environment:

- Possibility to interact with more than one peer
- Dynamic switch to other peers (in the case of violated dependencies to other services, which e.g. have gotten unavailable, or unreliable. As explained in section 2, this switch can be executed either manually in interaction with the user or semi-autonomously (adaptively) by the platform)
- Definition of inner-dependencies between provided and consumed services (a peer is thus able to provide data or events it has consumed by other third-party peers)
- Advertisement of services (which may incorporate a semantic description or quality of service aspects of the respective service)

---

[1] FREEVOLVE allows for hierarchical construction of components. Thus an – so called – abstract component can contain several other components. So, the usage of components can be eased without restrictions to the flexibility.

- Accountability and billing of services (relevant, if a peer provides service liable to charges, which must be invoiced to the respective consumers)

In the current version, the peer-to-peer platform is still compatible to the conventional client-server platform, yielding to a *hybrid architecture*. Consequently, a conventional client can still interact with a peer (server role) on the one hand and, on the other hand, can act as client to interact with a FREEVOLVE server.

For our intentions we have used the JXTA [17] platform from Sun as the fundamental framework for the peer environment. JXTA is an open network generic platform for peer-to-peer computing, providing a common set of open protocols for developing peer-to-peer applications. Developers can revert to an open source reference implementation also provided by Sun. This one has also been taken for our work. Particularly, JXTA defines how peers can discover each other and how a single peer can advertise and discover network services within a peer-to-peer network. However, JXTA does not prescribe in what way a concrete service is to be invoked nor which remote technology is to be used. Hence, the remote interaction between components is still handled by RMI, which is required by the FLEXIBEAN component model, anyway.

3.3   Handling Dependencies in the Peer-to-Peer Platform

In the new version of FREEVOLVE we are also engaged to integrate concepts for the management of dependencies between distributed components belonging to peer-to-peer applications. We propose a *pre-analysis* of the given peer network, which reveals all direct and transitive dependencies between components[1]. The resulting dependency graph supports the decision process, whether or not it is feasible or even economically to execute the tailoring process for a certain component. Besides, an overview is provided, if some services or peers have become unavailable or unreliable.

Due to the nature of our FLEXIBEAN component model we are yet able to handle two different dependencies, event and data flow, respectively. These dependencies are defined in the corresponding CAT files of a composition. All dependencies starting from a single component, that is, all inner dependencies among provided and consumed services and all remote dependencies to other components can be explored through the so-called DEPENDENCY API of a peer. To compute the dependency graph, the necessary data of all affected peers is thereby collected by an agent which successively migrates to all peers. Dependencies themselves are described in a XML-based notation. Each dependency is annotated with additional parameters. These parameters are based on the classification catalogue as introduced in [8]. From this collection we have basically adopted the parameters DEPENDENCY STRENGTH (denotes how strongly the dependent component depends on the respective components) and DEPENDENCY CRITICALITY (to indicate how a certain dependency must be satisfied in terms of the resource this component depends on). By means of these additional parameters we obtain a weighted graph. All parameters are edited manually, but we are working on mechanisms for an automated fixing.

3.4   FREEVOLVE Platform and Integrity Checking

Both the standard FREEVOLVE platform as well as the extended peer-to-peer version have to be supported by an integrity checking module. So far this has only been done for the classical tailoring environment. In case of the standard FREEVOLVE client there is now an additional client that is called *Tailoring Client*. This special client was developed for experienced users that want to change a composition. The look and feel was taken from integrated development environments (see figure 2). In the upper left side (1) one can see the complete component net of an application. All components and their provided and used ports are displayed. The small green icons indicate if a port is an input or an output. Additionally one can see, if the port is optional or has to be used (according to the idea of event flow integrity). The upper right window shows the same component net in a tree view. Here the details of a component are listed and parameters can be set. The third window shows messages that are generated by the integrity check. Furthermore, icons (circled) mark components, parameters or ports of components which may be the source of a failure according to the integrity strategy.

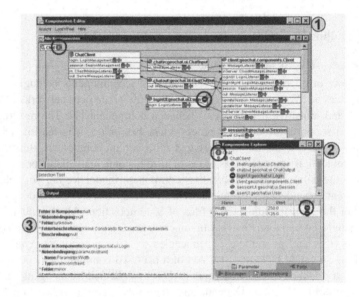

Fig. 2. The Tailoring Client

The integrity check is integrated loosely according to the strategy pattern. Therefore, FREEVOLVE allows for extensions or refinements of the integrity strategy. The integrity conditions or dependencies are explicitly saved in XML. They are loaded by the strategy when analyzing a distinct composition. The explicit description of integrity conditions that are not coded into the components themselves allows for more flexibility, in the way that they can be changed or added according to a special domain. However, only very experienced users should do this.

4   Conclusions

In this paper we have presented a component architecture, which allows one to deploy distributed client-server as well as peer-to-peer applications. We provide mechanisms for tailorability and explained fundamental ideas for the adaptivity of applications. The later mechanism is somewhat essential in a peer-to-peer environment, where services are not known à priori or become unavailable after a time. Further, we explained our approach to handle dependencies between components, that is, the constituting building blocks of an application. Besides a graph-based approach to master dependencies especially in peer-to-peer applications, we have incorporated the possibility to define semantic conditions between components.

References

1. Alda, S., "Adaptability in Component-Based Peer-to-Peer Applications", in Proc. of the IEEE Int'l Conf. on Peer-to-Peer Computing. Linköpings, Schweden, September 2002.
2. Alda, S., Radetzki, U., Bergmann, A., Cremers, A.B., "A component-based and adaptable Platform for networked Cooperations in Civil and Building Engineering", in Proc. of the 9th Int'l Conf. on Computing in Civil and Building Engineering. Taipei, Taiwan, 2002.
3. Birngruber, D., "A Software Composition Language and Its Implementation", in Perspectives of System Informatics (PSI 2001), vol. LNCS 2244, D. B. Bjorner, M.; Zamulin, A. V., Ed. Novosibirsk, Russland: Springer, 2001, S. 519–529.
4. Ensel, C., Keller, A., "Managing Application Service Dependencies with XML and the Resource Description Framework", in Proc. of the 7th Int'l IFIP/IEEE Symposium on Integrated Management (IM 2001), IEEE Publishing. May 2001.
5. Frese, M., Irmer, C., and Prümper, J., "Das Konzept Fehlermanagement: Eine Strategie des Umgangs mit Handlungsfehlern in der Mensch-Computer-Interaktion", in "Software für die Arbeit von morgen", M. Frese et. al., Ed. Berlin: Springer Verlag, 1991, pp. 241–252.
6. Hasselmayer, P., "Managing Dynamic Service Dependencies", in Proc. of the 12th Int'l Workshop on Distributed Systems: Operations and Management DSOM 2001. Nancy, France, October 2001. pp. 141–150.
7. Henderson, A. and Kyng M., "There's No Place Like Home. Continuing Design in Use", in Design at Work, Lawrence Erlbaum Associates, Publishers, 1991, 219–240.
8. Keller, A., Kar, G., "Dynamic Dependencies in Application Service Management", in Proc. of the Int'l Conf. on Parallel and Distributed Processing Techniques and Applications, Las Vegas, 2002.
9. Kon, F., Campbell, R.H., "Dependence Management in Component-Based Distributed Systems", in IEEE Concurrency January-March 2000, No. 1, Vol. 8.
10. Mackay, W. E., "Users and customizable Software: A Co-Adaptive Phenomenon", Boston (MA): MIT, 1990.
11. OMG, "Corba Component Model 3.0", http://www.omg.org, 2002
12. Oppermann, R. and Simm, H., "Adaptability: User-Initiated Individualization", in Adaptive User Support – Ergonomic Design of Manually and Automatically Adaptable Software, R. Oppermann, Ed. Hillsdale, New Jersey: Lawrence Erlbaum Ass, 1994.

13. Reussner, R. H., "The use of parameterised contracts for architecting systems with software components", in Proc. of 6th Int'l Workshop on Component-Oriented Programming (WCOP'01), 2001.
14. Shirky, C., What is P2P.. and what isn't. The O'Reilly Network, 2000. http://openP2P.com
15. Stiemerling, O., Hinken, R., Cremers, A. B., "The EVOLVE Tailoring Platform: Supporting the Evolution of Component-Based Groupware", in: Proc. of EDOC'99, IEEE Press, Mannheim, 1999, pp. 106–115.
16. Stiemerling, O., Cremers, A.B., "The EVOLVE Project: Component-Based Tailorability for CSCW Applications", AI & Society, 14, Springer-Verlag London, 2000, pp. 120–141.
17. Sun Microsystems, JXTA v1.0 Protocols Specification. http://spec.jxta.org/v1.0/, 2001
18. Szyperski, C., "Component Software – Beyond object-oriented programming", Addison-Wesley, 1997.
19. Won, M., "Komponentenbasierte Anpassbarkeit – Anwendung auf ein Suchtool für Groupware", Master Thesis, Institute for Computer Science III, University of Bonn, 1998.
20. Won, M., "Checking integrity of component-based architectures", in Proc. of CSCW 2000, Workshop on Component-Based Groupware, Philadelphia, 2000.
21. Won, M., Cremers, A. B., "Supporting End-User Tailoring of Component-Based Software – Checking integrity of compositions", in Proc. of CoLogNet 2002 Workshop affiliated with LOPSTR 2002, Madrid, Spain.

A Notation for Component-Based Design of Java Applications*

Catalin Amza and Gianna Reggio

DISI – Università di Genova, Italy
{amza,reggio}@disi.unige.it

Abstract. In this paper we present JTN2 (Java Targeted Notation 2) a notation for component-based design of Java applications. JTN2 defines a component model based on the fundamental object-oriented principles: abstraction, encapsulation, modularization and typing. Indeed, JTN2 is an extension of JTN, an object-oriented, formal, visual notation for designing concurrent Java applications. JTN2 component model aims to deal with three issues of Java based component development: component definition, component interconnection and component implementation in Java. JTN2 allows a component to be described, understood and analyzed independently from other components. Pre-designed components are interconnected to form complete systems. JTN2 provides a static type system that checks if two components can be interconnected. Java code can be, then, generated automatically by taking advantage of multiple Java technologies, e.g., JavaBeans, Enterprise JavaBeans and JINI.

1 Introduction

In this paper we present JTN2 [1] (Java Targeted Notation 2) a notation for component-based design of Java applications. JTN2 focuses on two major issues of component-based development at the design level: component definition and component interconnection.

In JTN2 we define a component model based on fundamental object-oriented principles: abstraction, encapsulation, modularization and typing [2]. JTN2 is an extension of JTN [4], an object-oriented, formal, visual notation, developed by our group in Genova for designing concurrent Java applications. JTN supports the core object oriented concepts: class, object, information hiding and specialization. JTN differentiates between active and passive objects and between objects and the interaction between them in order to support concurrency. The interactions between objects are modeled by means of connectors. JTN2 adds support for components that can be described, understood and analyzed independently from other components. A component has to come with a clear specification of the services it provides [11].

---

* This work is supported by the Luxembourg Ministry of Higher Education and Research under the title | project n° BFR00/040 and by the Italian National Project SAHARA (Software Architecture for Heterogeneous Access Networks infrastructure) funded by MIUR.

N. Guelfi et al. (Eds.): FIDJI 2002, LNCS 2604, pp. 155–164, 2003.

Because a component cannot make any assumption about the environment in which it will be used, its definition should specify the services required, such that the component can work. Furthermore, the implementation of the services provided by the component should be separated from its specification and encapsulated. Pre-designed components can be interconnected to form the complete system or a larger-grained component. In JTN2 we extend the connectors introduced in JTN to describe how components are connected.

As for JTN, we aim to provide JTN2 with a well-defined syntax and a formal semantic, leading to precise and analyzable design. For instance, one of the requirements for the components to work together is that they must be compatible. [13] identifies at least two levels of compatibility between components: type and dynamic behavior. The former one refers to the type of messages exchanged between two cooperating components. The later focus on the dynamic interaction behavior, such as the communication protocol the components use to exchange data. For the moment, JTN2 is concerned with component compatibility only at the type level.

The specification of a well-defined syntax and the formal background, combined with the mapping of the JTN concepts to Java, allows tools to automatically generate Java code from the JTN diagrams. Java code can be generated from a JTN2 component. For the same JTN2 model, the generated code may vary depending by the targeted Java component related technologies, e.g., JavaBeans [7], Enterprise Java Beans [8], and JINI [9,10].

JTN2 is appropriate for modeling large scale Java applications, that run in a single address space. It does not support adequate concepts to describe applications that run on different address spaces on the same machine or on different machines. We intend to extend the notation to support the development of distributed and mobile system.

1.1 Related Work

The UML (Unified Modeling Language)[12] general purpose modeling language that has emerged as a widely used, standardized notation for describing visual, object-oriented models. JTN2 aims to be UML compatible where appropriate, enhancing its acceptance but introduces new concepts when required.

However, UML does not provide constructs related to component-based design. For instance, the "UML components" are used to describe the physical, deployable pieces of the system, unlike the more abstract notion of components needed by the component-oriented design.

In [6] UML is extended to include additional concepts for component based design by defining a profile that supports components (called capsules), connectors and ports. UML 2.0 (available by 2004) is intended to be more suited for component-based development then the previous versions, but its approach will remain object-oriented. We think that object-oriented concepts are necessary but not enough for building component software. Indeed, in JTN and JTN2 we introduce concepts that are not necessarily object-oriented: component, connector and service.

In addition to expressiveness, the object-oriented notations based on UML lack formal semantics. This makes more complex the formal verification of design and automatic code generation.

Moreover, UML is not concerned (so much of the current notations) about the programming language that will be used for coding the application. Instead, any concept supported by the JTN2 notation is mapped to Java. This will help the developer to take in account the features and the limitations of the Java programming language during the design phase and will ease to automate the generation of Java code.

In this paper we focus on component notation. The definition of the formal semantics and the mapping to Java associated with the JTN2 notation are part of our future work. In section 2 we present the main concepts supported by JTN2: object, class, relationship, connector and component. In section 3 we describe the visual notation using a case study. Finally, in section 4 we sketch some conclusions and future work.

2   JTN2 Underlying Concepts

Object-Oriented Concepts

In [2] an *object* is defined as an "entity with a well-defined boundary and identity that encapsulates state and behavior". *Data values* are static data used by other entities. In contrast with objects, data values are "atemporal, unchanged and non-instantiated" [2]. Furthermore, data values have no identity, so it is not possible to differentiate between two instances of the same data value. An *active object* is one that owns a thread and can initiate an independent activity. On the other hand, a *passive object* is one that cannot initiate an independent activity and, in consequence, can change its state only when explicitly acted upon. JTN2 differentiates between the values, the passive and the active objects.

An object consists of a collection of *attributes* representing its state and a collection of *services* representing means of interaction with other objects. There are two kinds of services: *methods*, provided by the passive objects, and *communication channels* provided by the active objects.

An object can interact with a passive object by calling a method provided by the passive object. If multiple active objects can call simultaneous a method provided by a passive object, then the access to the passive object is synchronized. In this situation, the use of synchronization is necessary to ensure that the access of active objects to passive objects never creates data races. Active objects do not provide methods outside; instead they interact with other active objects or with external entities using I/O operations through communication channels. A communication channel is an abstraction for an unidirectional point-to-point communication between two entities with I/O capabilities.

A *class* is a description of a set of entities with the same properties. In JTN2 there are three kinds of classes: datatype, passive and active class whose instances are values, passive and active objects respectively. A class definition is split in two parts: an interface and a body. The *class interface* defines the services provided by the instances of the class, whereas the *class body* provides an implementation for them. The class body is separated from the class interface and completely encapsulated.

JTN2 requires to assign a *type* to each entity used in the model. The most common data types, either primitive (int, char) or structural (array, list), are predefined. In addition, each user defined class introduces a new type.

In an OO perspective, stand-alone classes are not meaningful; most of them are related to accomplish more complex functionality. Thus, we complete the class descriptions with relevant relationships between them: dependency and generalization/specialization. A dependency relationship denotes a client/server relationship between two classes: the client uses the functionality provided by the server class.

A generalization/specialization relationship denotes a relationship that supports:

- Subclassing, that is inheritance of the class body
- Subtyping, that is inheritance of the class interface
- Substitutability, that is object of the specialized element (the child) are substitutable for objects of the generalized element (the parent).

Conventional design modeling notations, as the UML, focuses on the static structure of the system, leaving the description of the architecture and of the interaction among objects implicit, distributed and difficult to identify. In JTN2 we explicitly model the run-time architecture of the system by describing the objects and the interactions among them in the architecture diagram. The architecture diagram is essentially a graph whose nodes correspond to the entities building the application and whose arcs, named connectors, correspond to the interactions among them. There are two kinds of connectors:

- Method call connectors. A method call connector is an architectural abstraction corresponding to a standard method call in the Java programming language.
- Channel connectors. A channel connector is an architectural abstraction corresponding to a message exchange mechanism through abstract communication channels (streams in Java).

Component

A *component* is an entity that denotes a collection of cooperating objects and/or components relevant to a particular concept, goal or purpose.

A component has three distinct parts: an interface, a body and a context. The *component interface* defines the services that the component provides to its clients and those that it requires from other components in the system. We extend the notion of service defined in the previous section to denote a named set of related methods and communication channels. The *component context* defines all the classes used by the services defined in the component interface and makes them visible for all external entities using the component. This is a novel approach that allows other components to use introspection mechanisms in order to discover the services that a component requires/provides. The *component body* describes how the services provided by the component are implemented, using the required ones, if is the case.

A *component class* is a description of a set of components with the same interface, body and context.

The components are interconnected through the means of *service connectors*. A service connector links a service required by a component with a service provided by another component by mapping the methods/channels of the required service to the methods/channels of the provided service. A required service can be connected to a provided service if the methods/channels of the required service can be mapped to the methods/channels of the provided service. A method/channel can be mapped to another method/channel if they have the same type.

3   JTN2 Notation

In this section we use a simplified version of the LuxDeal [5] case study to exemplify the JTN2 notation. LuxDeal is a free online barter service that brings together people that want to exchange goods and services. The simplified application provides only the following functionality: when a new user connects to the application, she/he will have the possibility to create a new account by providing some useful information. The application is decomposed as follows:

- Account component. This component manages the user accounts. The Account component allows the user to create a new account and access account information. The account information is saved to a database, so it can be retrieved latter.
- Dbhelper component. This component provides database access services.

The two components are connected together to provide the overall functionality of the application. Here, for simplicity, the concurrent and distributed aspects of the application are ignored. We focus on component definition and integration, without concern about the internal realization of the services.

Component Definition

A component class is described in JTN2 by the following diagrams:

- An interface diagram that presents the component interface together with the component context.
- A body class diagram that shows the class structure of the component body.
- A body architecture diagram that shows the internal structure of the component.

Figure 1 gives the interface diagram of the Account component class. The component interface is shown as a rectangle with heavy border, divided in two compartments. The top compartment shows the name of the component. The bottom compartment shows the services provided and required by the component, separated by dashed lines. For instance, the Account interface defines two provided services: Account and Access and one required service, DBAccess. The service Access consists of three methods: getLogin, getPassword and getName; the services Account and DBAccess consist only of one method each: register and getConnection respectively. The passive class [1] Connection is defined in the component context, together with PreparedStatement, which is required by the class Connection.

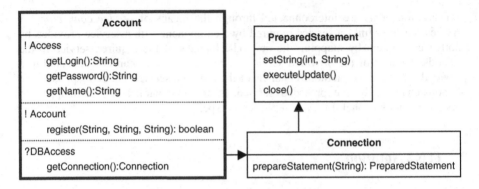

Fig. 1. Account component class – interface diagram

Figures 2 and 3 give the body of the Account component. The Account component body is defined using three classes (figure 2): AccountModel that encapsulates the component state and the access services, the AccountController that implements the registration service and the AccountDAO that implements the persistence functionality and requires a database access service.

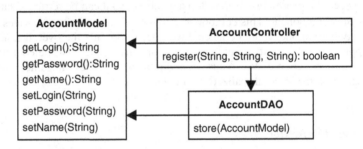

Fig. 2. Account component class – body class diagram

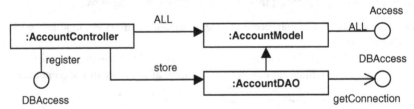

Fig. 3. Account component class – body architecture diagram

The body diagrams associated with all the classes can be found in [1].

Figure 3 shows that an object of the type AccountController interacts with an object of the type AccountModel to modify the state of the account and with an object of the type AccountDAO to store the state of the account. The object of the type AccountModel implements the service Access. The object of the type AccountDAO is a helper object that contributes to the implementation of the service Account by accessing the component state and stores it in a database. It requires a service that provides access to a database. The interactions between the constituents of the component are described by means of method call connectors. The connectors are labeled with the names of the methods they model or with the keyword ALL if all the methods defined by an object/service are called.

The Account component requires database access to store all information provided by a user during the registration process. Figure 4 gives the interface diagram of the Dbhelper component class that implements the database access service. The body diagram is given in [1].

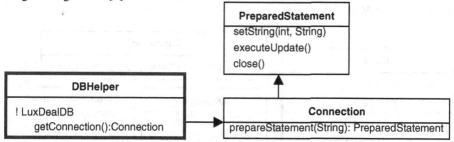

Fig. 4. Dbhelper component class – interface diagram

Component Integration

One or more pre-designed components can be integrated to form a complete application, or a larger-grained component. The resulting application is described by the following diagrams:

- A class diagram that shows the interfaces of the used component classes (with their context) and of additional (datatype, active, passive) classes required by the application (e.g., glue classes) together with their mutual relationships
- The body diagrams of all additional classes appearing on the class diagram
- An architecture diagram that shows the instances composing the system and the interactions among them.

In our example we do not have additional classes, but only components, so the class diagram consists only of the components defined in figure 1 and figure 4.

Fig. 5. Example application - the architecture diagram

Figure 5 shows how two components are composed together.

Two components Account and Dbhelper are composed together by connecting the service DBAccess required by the component Account with the service LuxDealDB provided by the component Dbhelper. The two services can be connected because they match, that is the method getConnection defined by the service DBAccess matches the method getConnection defined by the service LuxDealDB. The service matching is checked by using the component context.

However, if a service provided by a component does not match with a service required by another component, they can be connected using a glue object. For instance, let us consider that every time a new user is registered, we want a message to be sent to the system administrator. To do that we want to reuse a component Message that allows a registered member to send a message to another member. The sent message is stored in the database, so it can be retrieved later. Figure 6 shows the interface diagram for the Message component. The Account component requires a new service, Message that defines the method sendMessage. Figure 7 shows the interface diagram for the Account component class.

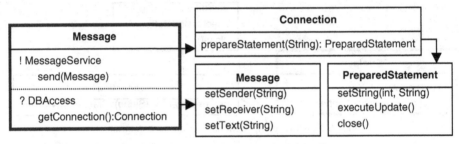

Fig. 6. Message component class - interface diagram

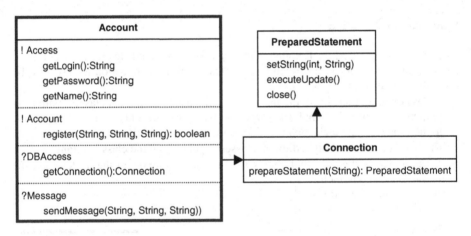

Fig. 7. Account component class – interface diagram

Because the service Message required by the component Account is not compatible with the service MessageService provided by the component Message, we need to add a glue object. In our example, the role of the glue object is to convert the service required by the component Account to the service provided by the component Message, so they can match. In JTN2 we allow an object to be connected to a service (provided or required) through a method call connector. Figure 8 shows the application class diagram and figure 9 shows the new application architecture.

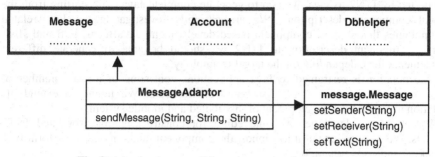

Fig. 8. Adapting incompatible components – the class diagram

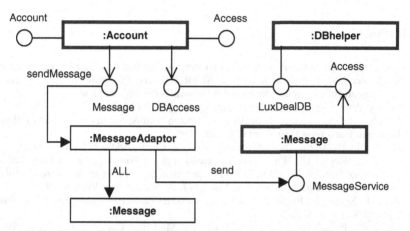

Fig. 9. Adapting incompatible components – the architecture diagram

4   Conclusion and Future Work

In this paper, we have proposed a component model, at the basis of a visual design notation JTN2, that allows complex systems to be built from independently understandable, reusable building blocks. Our model is based on the principles of the object-oriented modeling: abstraction, encapsulation, modularity, typing and hierarchy. In addition to well-known object-oriented concepts it supports the concepts of connector and component as first-class model abstractions.

JTN2 aims to answer to two fundamental issues of component-oriented modeling: component definition and component composition. A component can be described, understand and analyzed independently. By defining the services required by a component to function correctly, we allow a component to be compiled and deployed independently. Then, more complex components and applications can be built by wiring pre-designed components. If two components are incompatible, they can be adapted by adding supplementary glue components.

In future, we intend to provide JTN2 with a well-defined syntax and a formal semantic, so we can check the models for inconsistencies. By mapping the concepts supported by JTN2 to Java, we aim to generate complete Java code starting from the visual component descriptions. We are currently investigating the Java related technologies that support component-based development: JavaBeans, EJB and JINI. For a component description in JTN2 we should be able to generate different implementations, depending on the target technology.

The notation is restrained to Java applications consisting of a static number of components that run in a non-distributed environment. We intend to extend the notation to support the development of distributed and mobile system.

We also have developed a visual editor for constructing object-oriented JNT2 models. We want to extend it to support the component notation and to perform type checking and code generation.

References

1. Amza, C., Reggio, G.: A Notation For Component-Based Design of Java Applications. Long Version. Technical Report. DISI-TR-2002-20. Dipartimento di Informatica e Scienze dell'Informatione. Universita di Genova. Available online at: ftp://ftp.disi.unige.it/person/AmzaC/papers/jtn2_02.pdf (2002)
2. Booch, G.: Object-Oriented Analysis and Design with Applications. Second Edition. The Benjamin/Cummings Publishing Company (1994)
3. Booch, G.: The Unified Modeling Language User Guide. Addison-Wesley (2000)
4. Coscia, E., Reggio,G.: JTN:A Java-Targeted Graphical Formal Notations for Reactive and Concurrent Systems. In: FASE 99 – Fundamental Approaches on Software Engineering. Lecture Notes in Computer Science. Vol. 1577. Berlin, Springer Verlag (1999)
5. Ries, B., Sterges,P.: Requirements for the LuxDeal Prototype. Luxembourg University of Applied Sceineces (2002)
6. Selic, B., Raumbaugh, J.: Using UML for Modeling Complex Real-Time Systems. Rational Software. Available online at http://www.rational.com/products/whitepapers/UML-rt.pdf (1999)
7. Sun Microsystems : JavaBeans Specification. Version 1.01. Available online at http://java.sun.com/products/javabeans/docs/spec.html (1997)
8. Sun Microsystems : Enterprise Java Beans Specification. Version 2.1. .Available online at http://java.sun.com/products/ejb/docs.html (2002)
9. Sun Microsystems : JINI Architecture Specification. Available online at http:// sun.com/jini/jini1.1html/jini-title.html (2000)
10. Sun Microsystems. JINI Technology Core Platform Specification. Version 1.1. Available online at http://sun.com/jini/specs/jini1.1html/core-tilte.html (2000)
11. Szypersky, C.: Component Software – Beyond Object Oriented Programming. Addison-Wesley and ACM Press (1998)
12. UML Revision Task Force: OMG UML v.1.3 specification. Available at http://www.rational.com/media/uml/post.pdf (1999)
13. Xiong, Y.: An Extensible Type System for Component-Based Design. Ph.D. Thesis. University of California at Berkeley (2002)

WCT: A Wrapper for Component Testing

Antonia Bertolino and Andrea Polini*

ISTI-CNR, Area della Ricerca CNR di Pisa, Via Moruzzi, 1
56124 Pisa, Italy
{bertolino, a.polini}@iei.pi.cnr.it

Abstract. Within component based (CB) software development, testing becomes a crucial activity for interoperability validation, but enabling test execution over an externally acquired component is difficult and labor-intensive. To address such problem, we propose the WCT component, a generic test wrapper that dynamically adapts the component interfaces, making the test execution independent from any specific component implementation. The wrapper does not require that the component implements any specific interface for testing purposes, it permits to easily reconfigure the subsystem under test after the introduction/removal/substitution of a component, and helps optimize test reuse, by keeping trace of the test cases that directly affect the wrapped component.

1 Introduction

Component based (CB) methodologies are today largely used in all the classical engineering branches. Their adoption is mainly motivated by the need to get more predictable timing and costs of the development phase. Although the introduction of a CB paradigm also in the software engineering branch has been advocated for long time [1], it is only in the last years that we can observe significant advances towards the real applicability of this methodology to software production. Proof of this progress is the advent of the first successful component models such as COM+/.Net, EJB, Java-Beans, CCM. However, in spite of these advances, we can certainly say that CB production is not Software Engineering state of practice yet. What is still lacking for the real take-up of the CB paradigm is a major revision of the software process, to address the peculiarity of a CB production. In [2] a list of important challenges in the CBSE is discussed.

A first and basic difference between the traditional production methodology and a CB one is in the non-deterministic distribution, in time and in space, of the CB development process. In fact in CB production the "pieces" that will constitute the final assembled system can be acquired from many other organizations, that do not necessarily communicate or synchronize with each other. Moreover the acquired elements are not in general developed as a consequence of a specific requirements specification, instead are retrieved from the market as pre-built elements.

---

* Andrea Polini's PhD grant is supported by Ericsson Lab Italy in the framework of the Pisatel initiative (http://www.iei.pi.cnr.it/ERI).

In this scenario we can distinguish, at least, two different stakeholders. The first is the **component developer**, who is engaged in the construction of the components that will be released to third parties. The second kind of stakeholder is represented by the **system constructor**; this is himself/herself a software developer, who builds a system by assembling together some components, either internally developed or externally acquired. Certainly the CB paradigm mainly affects the process of the system constructor. In [3] we have outlined a possible iterative process that tries to address the new requirements of a CB production; another process is shown in [4]. Within the process of the system constructor, we can note the presence of two new related phases, referred to as the *searching phase* and the *selection phase*.

Aim of the searching phase is to find one or more components that can be assembled in the system to address some specific functional requirements. This search is not an easy job and requires specific tools; in particular, one active research direction tries to identify what kind of information (and how) can be attached to the component by the component developer, so to automate, as much as possible, the task.

Aim of the selection phase is to choose the component, among those identified by the previous phase, which is the most suitable for the system under construction. It is obvious that in the general case the result of the searching phase cannot be a single component for which the full conformity with the searched one can be guaranteed; therefore a validation phase is necessary to evaluate the components and to select the most promising one.

In practice these two phases are particularly hard, since it is generally the rule to provide the component without the source code (black-box); moreover, the attached documentation is often incomplete or only limited to the explanation of how to use the provided API.

A direct consequence of this lack of information is generally referred to as the "component trust problem", to indicate that the system constructor, who acquires a component from the component developer, needs some means to get a better understanding of what the component does and how it behaves. In this context, our perspective is in studying **how to use testing techniques for the validation and selection of the components**, so contributing to the mitigation of the component trust problem. In particular we are studying how the testing activities and tools must be reviewed and augmented to take in account the peculiarities of a CB development.

So far we have used the term "component" in a complete general form. A reference definition for the concept of component is still debated and in the literature there is not yet a universal agreement. An often reported definition is that provided in [5]: "*A software component is a unit of composition with contractually specified interfaces and explicit context dependencies only. A software component can be deployed independently and is subject to composition by third parties*". With respect to this definition we take a more simplified view, and, as in [6], we identify a component with a system or subsystem developed by one organization, deployed by one or more different organizations, and possibly provided without the source code. According to this definition, we will consider also a class or a set of classes as a particular example of a component.

Regarding the technical aspects of the methodology, we require that the used component model foresees basic introspection mechanisms, because we need to retrieve at run-time information mostly referring to the component interfaces. As a consequence, we have adopted the Java language.

2 Related Work

As recognized in [7], several techniques can be usefully combined to reduce the component trust problem (formal specification, Design by Contract, testing and others), and further research is still necessary. Different approaches are under study to address the problem; in particular some authors suggest to add supplementary information to the component, in the form of metadata, with the objective to increase the analysis capability of the system constructor [6][8]. Another approach proposes to establish independent agencies that act as software certification laboratories. The main duty of this agencies would be the certification of the components (as done in many other engineering disciplines) so to increase guarantee of adequate behavior [9].

Regarding testing, in our knowledge there is not much work addressing the problem: we list three different proposals. A first approach proposes to embed test cases in the component itself (Built-In Tests) in the form of methods externally visible [10]. A disadvantage of this approach is the size growth of components that have to contain also code specific for the testing phase. To overcome this problem, another approach introduced the concept of a testable architecture. This architecture foresees that the components implement a particular interface for testing purposes, that permits to execute pre-built tests without the necessity to include them in the component code [11]. Finally in another approach [12], the authors propose to provide the component user with the test cases that the component has undergone in the form of a XML file. In this case the authors also provide, attached to the component, a tool for the re-execution of the test cases.

It is worth noting that, differently from the listed approaches, we do not impose that a component implements any particular interface, so to make this task less costly and more generally applicable. Moreover our aim is to provide the component user with tools to simplify the execution of test cases developed on the base of the specification for the searched components, permitting at the same time the re-execution of the test cases provided by the component developer.

3 The Testing Phase in CB Development

It is our belief that a revision of the development process is a necessary precondition for the effective success of a CB production, and this revision must also concern in particular the testing stage. In [3] we have outlined a possible direction for the revision of the testing process. In particular we have highlighted that the traditional three phases of the testing process (unit, integration and system test) can be revisited in terms of three corresponding new phases, respectively referred to as *component*, *deployment* and *system* test.

Briefly, in the component test phase, the component is tested in the component developer environment, to ascertain the conformance of the component to the developer specifications. However, as many authors recognized [13], the tests performed by the developer are clearly inadequate to guarantee the dependable use of the component in the final application environment (that of the system constructor). The testing should be repeated also in the final environment, both for the component as a single element and when integrated with the other interacting components. Therefore the deployment test phase performed by the component user results composed of two sub-phases: in the first phase a selected component is evaluated directly invoking the provided API; in the second phase, the component is inserted in a subsystem and then integration-tested as an element of the subsystem. The last stage of system test does not show notable differences with respect to the traditional one.

From the above discussion, the system constructor process must involve at least two kinds of independents teams. The first is the searching team, who on the base of precise specifications looks for components that, in their understanding, correspond to the searched ones. The second team instead, on the base of the specification, develops test cases that can be used to ascertain the conformance of the found selected components to the searched ones.

Probably the major costs induced in CB development can be ascribed to the two illustrated phases, and then any little improvement, thanks to suitable techniques and tools, can bring great benefits. In particular it is worth noting that a lot of the work made by the two kinds of teams can be in principle carried on in parallel, and therefore it is important to adopt a methodology that permits the effective exploitation of this possibility.

4   WCT, a Wrapper for Testing Purposes

In this section we introduce the structure of the WCT, a wrapper to be integrated in a CB testing platform, to permit the easy reconfiguration of the subsystem under test when components are introduced or removed. A WCT basic feature is flexibility, in that we do not require that the component to be wrapped within a WCT component implements any particular interface.

As we have said, the testing stage is probably the most expensive phase in component based production. Hence, means for reducing its cost and "gaining time" are extremely important. We can identify two major costs in the testing stage. The first can be identified in the effort to set up the system into a configuration suitable for executing the tests, the second is the controlled execution of the test cases on the subsystem.

To reduce these two sources of costs we have thought to intervene at the level of the component to be integrated, providing a wrapper model that can be used to bind the component, thus saving time and effort in two important respects:

1.   it is easier to set up the test configuration, e.g., to reconfigure the component/subsystem under test adding components, in the place of stubs, or to substitute components with new candidates
2.   it is easier to identify the "indispensable" test case to be rerun when a candidate component is substituted with a more promising one.

In the following of this section we present in detail the proposed approach.

4.1   WCT: The Constituent Elements

The WCT wrapper has a fixed structure that is independent from the connected components. It can be removed, e.g., for performance purposes, when a final configuration is identified, to be substituted with a static wrapper: clearly the test wrapper can be very useful to develop the permanent wrapper, because it can be taken as a reference model, like a prototype.

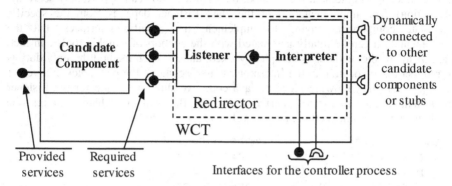

Fig. 1. Schema of the WCT illustrating the constituent elements and the various connections.

The approach forecasts to connect all the required interfaces of a candidate component to a "standard" component named the **Redirector**. As we will see this consists of two parts: one depending on the candidate component, and the second fixed for each instance of the Redirector. As illustrated in Figure 1, the composition of a candidate component and of the Redirector forms a new component, named **WCT**, that provides to the external world the same services of the candidate component but does not statically requires any particular service. Only at run-time, to realize the subsystem under test, the binding between the various components is established as the result of the appropriate interpretation of a XML document. Therefore a subsystem under test, at each time, results from the composition of more WCTs. The configuration of the subsystem can be modified also at run-time, e.g., by inserting a candidate component in the place of a stub or by substituting a component with a more promising one.

To clarify the approach and how it works, it can be useful to describe in detail the structure of the WCT and in particular of the Redirector. The duty of the Redirector is exactly to *redirect* (then its name) at run-time the invocations made by the candidate component towards other candidate components (or otherwise stubs) that opportunely provide the required services. To put in place the redirection, it uses three main elements (see also Fig. 1):

1. the Listener class
2. the Interpreter class
3. a XML file named "XMLAdapter"

In the following, we describe in detail these elements. We refer to the **associate component** to indicate the component that is contained in the same WCT of the Redirector, and to the **attached components** to indicate the components that provide the required services to the associate component.

The Listener Class. Main target of the class Listener is to isolate the associate component from the attached components. In other words, this class act as a proxy, postponing to a subsequent moment the instantiation of one or more real attached components, which will be able to manage the invocations made by the associate component. To do this, the Listener class has to implement all the interfaces that the associate component requires, but instead of giving, for each method, a real implementation, it delegates this task to the Interpreter class (as we will see the latter, in turn, does not implement the method, but "knows who" can opportunely serve the invocation). The implementation of the class Listener depends from the specific candidate component, having to implement the specific interfaces, but the implementation can be totally automated with the support of suitable tools[1]. In fact, the scheme of the methods is completely fixed, and for each method the only duty is to redirect the invocation to the Interpreter class packaging the parameter in a vector of objects. In the following piece of Java code, we show a scheme for the Listener class that implements two interfaces A and B, each of which requires the implementation of one method, respectively named "a" and "b".

```
public class Listener implements A,B{
    private Interpreter interpreter;
    public Listener(Interpreter interpreter) {
        this.interpreter = interpreter;}
    public t1 a(tA1 p1,…,tAn pn) {
        Object[] parameters = new Object[] {p1,…,pn}²;
        return (t1)interpreter.execMethod("a",parameters);}
    public t2 b(tB1 p1,…,tBn pm) {
        Object[] parameters = new Object[] {p1,…,pm};
        return (t2)interpreter.execMethod("b",parameters);}
}
```

The Interpreter Class. If the duty of the Listener classes is to "deceive" the candidate component simulating the presence of the attached components, the main duty of the Interpreter class is to redirect, at run-time, the invocations towards an implementation that can really give suitable answers. The redirection is based on the information retrieved from the XMLAdapter, that contains the rules based on which the redirection will be based (in the next section we explain in major detail how to draw up this file).

To identify the method, or methods, that must be invoked, as a consequence of a request made by the associate component, the instance of the Interpreter class uses the introspection mechanisms provided by the component model, trying to retrieve information from the attached components. In particular to apply the model we exploit the Java introspection mechanism which permits to retrieve information from all the public methods and to invoke, on the base of these information, a selected method. The use of reflection permits the easy reconfiguration of the system, allowing for the introduction of new candidate components taking the place of a stub or substituting a candidate component with a more promising one.

The class Interpreter presents two main public methods. The first method is invoked by the controller of the testing process that provides the name of the XMLAdapter. Obtained the name, the method reacts by parsing the file (to do this the interpreter contains an instance of a suitable XML parser) and storing the retrieved in-

---

[1] It is worth noting that in the specific case of a clash in one or more of the method names enclosed in the required interfaces, it will be necessary to use more then one Listener class.

[2] In Java we need also to use a wrapper type when the parameter is of a basic type.

formation in appropriate data structures. Through the invocation of this method, the controller of the testing process can reconfigure the subsystem under test.

The second method, instead, is invoked by the associated listener and is appointed to redirect the invocations, made by the associate component, to the opportune method (methods) of the attached components. To perform this task the method uses the information stored in the data structures by the XML parser, and uses the reflection mechanisms on the attached components.

We think that this method, that has the control over the methods invocations of the associate component, can be augmented to perform other useful tasks. A first task that comes to mind is the recording of method invocations to keep trace of each test case execution. This tracing facility may result particularly useful when we consider the replacing of a stub with a real component or the substitution of a candidate component with a more promising one. In fact, having recorded the test cases that stimulate a particular method, in the case of a replacement we can re-execute only the test sequences exercising the methods affected by the substitution.

The XMLAdapter file. Aim of the XMLAdapter is to provide a means by which the searching teams can explicitly formulate the correspondences between a client component (the component that needs a service) and a server component (the component that provides the services). Several levels of mismatches can exist between a searched component and a found one. These are immediate consequences of the selection process. In fact, we suppose that the selection of a candidate component has to follow some "semantic" principles, in the sense that the choice is mainly based on the understanding of what a component does, understanding that the searching teams must derive from the documentation associated to the component. This "choice" obviously implies the necessity of suitable wrappers to actually permit the "syntactic" interaction among components. Our approach is to codify the rules that establish the correspondence in the XMLAdapter, a XML file with definite tags, that can be parsed by the Interpreter to redirect the invocations made by the associated component. We have identified several levels of mismatch between the client and the server components, that can be overcome with the use of the XMLAdapter:

1. differences in the methods names and signatures:
   a. the methods have different names
   b. the methods have the same number and types of parameters, but they are declared in different order
   c. the parameters have different types, but we can make them compatible, through suitable transformations. It can be also necessary to set some default parameters.
2. one method in the client component corresponds to the execution of more than one method, in one or more server components.

Regarding the structure of the XMLAdapter, it can be divided in two parts. The first part specifies the component instances (that can also be remote) that must be used and manages the invocations of the associated component. In the second part, for each invocation of the associated component, the corresponding sequence of methods and transformations, that must be invoked in the attached components, are specified.

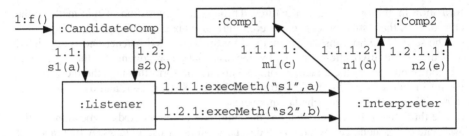

Fig. 2. Collaboration diagram that illustrates the interaction between the WCT elements and two attached components. In particular to provide service f the associated component requires two services, s1 and s2. To provide this services the Interpreter instance opportunely transforms the invocations of s1 and s2 into sequences of invocations of the services provided by the two attached components Comp1 and Comp2.

5 Discussion and Future Work

In this section we explain how the WCT component can be used in CB development. In particular we outline the scheme of a general platform for component deployment testing, within which the WCT component can be employed for assembling and testing the components.

The general structure of the platform is shown in Figure 3. The main target of this platform is to provide the capability to exploit the potential parallelism in the activities of the searching and testing teams. In fact, following the approach proposed in [14], we suppose that the test cases are defined by the system constructor, before the component is acquired, on the basis of a virtual component specification. The structure of this virtual component can be derived from the system specifications, which are also used as a reference by the searching teams.

For the purposes of presentation, we have spoken so far of the acquisition of a single component. Indeed, when we have to assembly a "piece of software" within a CB system, in our approach there is no difference between a "monolithic" component or instead a "composite" component, made by more opportunely connected components. Since a subsystem can be externally viewed as a single component, the testing teams can use the same platform to codify the test cases for exercising either a component, or a composite subsystem (such as the gray box in Figure 3). To do that the subsystem under test is viewed itself as a component with a specified virtual interface that expresses the functionality that a real instance of the subsystem has to provide. On the basis of the virtual interface the test cases are codified and stored in a suitable repository to be later used when the subsystem will be instantiated. It follows that the derivation of the test cases and the searching activity can largely proceed in parallel, since the codification of the test cases in this way is not dependent from any particular implementation.

As we can see, the platform shown in Figure 3 is composed of three main elements. The first is the Tester Component, widely described in [14], that permit the application of the test cases established by the testing teams on the subsystem. The second element of the approach is the Controller, which is a distributed interface that permit to control the testing process, in particular giving to the testing teams a means to add developed test cases, and to the searching teams a means to modify the subsystem structure. The use of the WCT components, as constituent elements of a subsystem under test (that constitute the third element in the figure), is particularly useful at this stage. In fact, each time a searching team identifies a potential candidate component, to be able to insert the latter in the subsystem it is only necessary to modify the XMLAdapter associated with those components that need to invoke the new inserted one. However, when the introduction/removal/substitution of a component has also effect on the external interface of the subsystem, it is necessary that the set of test cases used by the Tester Component is accordingly modified.

The WCT can also be fruitfully employed to reduce the number of test cases to be re-executed when a new component is introduced. To do that, the Interpreter in the WCT can keep trace of the methods that are invoked by the associated component during the execution of a test case, and communicate them to the Controller. This information can be opportunely stored by the Controller and then used to establish the set of regression test cases, when a new component is inserted and an invocation is redirected. Concluding, in this paper we have briefly revisited the testing process in CB development and we have highlighted how the testing activity can result particularly useful in the component selection phase. We have then presented the notion of a test wrapper that can be usefully employed by a system constructor to test sets of integrated components (subsystem) within his/her environment.

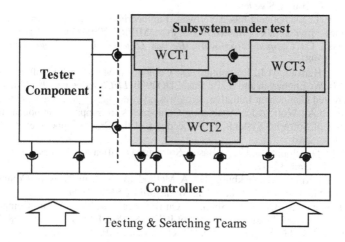

Fig. 3. The whole logical structure of a possible subsystem under test composed of three components. The figure shows the Tester Component and the Controller, that constitutes the interface towards the Testing and Searching teams.

Favorable features of the proposed approach are that: it does not require that the component implements any specific interface for testing purpose; it permits an easy and fast reconfiguration of a subsystem after the introduction/removal/substitution of a component within the subsystem; and finally it is possible to introduce in the WCT useful features for regression testing purposes: in particular, we have outlined how it is possible to reduce the number of test cases to re-execute at each reconfiguration.

The WCT wrapper is part of a long term research project addressing CB testing. Our aim is to employ the WCT component within a more general platform for CB testing currently under development.

In the next future we will work at the implementation of the mentioned testing platform. In particular we intend to formalize as much as possible the drawing up of the XMLAdapter by means of suitable graphical interfaces that partially automate the process. It is also our objective to reuse as much as possible existing tools, as for instance Junit [15], a framework developed for the early testing of OO code but that can be partially revisited in the CB testing field. Lastly, we also plan to validate the approach within industrial CB production using real case studies.

References

1. McIllroy, D.: Mass Produced Software Components. In P. Naur and B. Randall Eds, Software Eng.: Report on a Conf. by the NATO Science Committee, pp 138–155, Brussels, 1968.
2. Crnkovic, I.: Component-based Software Engineering – New Challenges in Software Development. Software Focus, John Wiley & Sons Eds, December2001
3. Bertolino, A., Polini, A.: Re-thinking the Development Process of Component-Based Software. ECBS02 Workshop on CBSE, Composing Systems From Components, April 10–11, 2002, Lund, Sweden.
4. Crnkovic, I.: Component-based Software Engineering – New Paradigm of Software Development. Invited talk & Invited report, Proc. MIPRO 2001, Opatija, Croatia , May 2001.
5. Szyperski, C.: *Component Software: Beyond Object Oriented Programming*, Addison-Wesley, 1998.
6. Orso, A., Harrold, M.J., Rosenblum, D.: Component Metadata for Software Engineering Tasks. In W. Emmerich and S. Tai Eds. EDO2000, *LNCS 1999*, pp.129–144.
7. The Trusted Component Initiative: http://trusted-components.org, Access date 2002-09-21
8. Stafford, J.A., Wolf, A.L.: Annotating Components to Support Component-Based Static Analyses of Software Systems. In Proceedings of the Grace Hopper Celeb. of Women in Computing 2001.
9. Voas, J.: Developing a Usage-Based Software Certification Process. *IEEE Computer*, August 2000, pp. 32–37.
10. Wang, Y., King, G., Wickburg, H.: A Method for Built-in Tests in Component-based Software Maintenance. In Proceedings of the 3rd ECSMR, 1999.
11. Gao, J., Gupta, K., Gupta, S., Shim, S.: On Building Testable Software Components. In J. Dean, and A. Gravel Eds, Proceedings of ICCBSS 2002, LNCS 2255, pp.108–121.
12. Morris, J., Lee, G., Parker, K., Bundell, G.A., Lam, C.P.: Software Component Certification. *IEEE Computer*, September 2001, pp.30–36.
13. Weyuker, E.: Testing Component-Based Software: A Cautionary Tale. *IEEE Software*, Sept./Oct. 1998, pp. 54–59.
14. Bertolino, A., Polini, A.: A Framework for Component Deployment Testing. Proceedings of the ACM/IEEE International Conference on Software Engineering ICSE 2003 (to appear), Portland, USA, May 3–10, 2003
15. JUnit: http://www.junit.org.

A Java Middleware for Guaranteeing Privacy of Distributed Tuple Spaces*

Lorenzo Bettini and Rocco De Nicola

Dipartimento di Sistemi e Informatica, Università di Firenze
Via Lombroso 6/17, 50134 Firenze, Italy
{bettini,denicola}@dsi.unifi.it

Abstract. The tuple space communication model, such as the one used in *Linda*, provides great flexibility for modeling concurrent, distributed and mobile processes. In a distributed setting with mobile agents, particular attention is needed for protecting sites and information. We have designed and developed a Java middleware, KLAVA, for implementing distributed tuple spaces and operations to support agent interaction and mobility. In this paper, we extend the KLAVA middleware with cryptographic primitives that enable encryption and decryption of tuple fields. We describe the actual implementation of the new primitives and provide a few examples. The proposed extension is general enough to be applied to similar Java frameworks using multiple distributed tuples spaces possibly dealing with mobility.

1   Introduction

A successful approach to concurrent programming is the one relying on the Linda coordination model [11]. Processes communicate by reading and writing *tuples* in a shared memory called *tuple space*. Control of accesses is guaranteed by requiring that tuples selection be *associative*, by means of pattern matching. The communication model is *asynchronous*, *anonymous*, and *generative*, i.e., tuple's life-time is independent of producer's life time.

The Linda model has been adopted in many communication frameworks such as, e.g., *JavaSpaces* [1] and *T Spaces* [10], and for adding the tuple space communication model to existing programming languages. More recently, distributed variants of tuple spaces have been proposed to exploit the Linda model for programming distributed applications over wide area networks [7,2], possibly exploiting code mobility [8,12]. As shown in [9], where several messaging models for mobile agents are examined, the *blackboard* approach, of which the tuple space model is a variant, is one of the most favorable and flexible.

Sharing data over a wide area network such as Internet, calls for very strong security mechanisms. Computers and data are exposed to eavesdropping and

* This work has been partially supported by EU within the FET – Global Computing initiative project *MIKADO* IST-2001-32222, by MIUR project *NAPOLI* and by Microsoft project *NAPI*. The funding bodies are not responsible for any use that might be made of the results presented here.

N. Guelfi et al. (Eds.): FIDJI 2002, LNCS 2604, pp. 175–184, 2003.

manipulations. Dealing with these issues is even more important in the context of code mobility, where code or agents can be moved over the different sites of a net. Malicious agents could seriously damage hosts and compromise their integrity, and may tamper and brainwash other agents. On the other hand, malicious hosts may extract sensible data from agents, change their execution or modify their text [17,13].

The flexibility of the shared tuple space model opens possible security holes; it basically provides no access protection to the shared data. Indeed there is no way to determine the issuer of an operation to the tuple space and there is no way to protect data: a process may (even not intentionally) retrieve/erase data that do not belong to it and shared data can be easily modified and corrupted. In spite of this, within the Linda based approaches, very little attention has been devoted to protection and access control.

In this paper we present a Java middleware for building distributed and mobile code applications interacting through tuple spaces, by means of cryptography. In this middleware, classical Linda operations are extended for handling encrypted data. Primitives are also supplied for encrypting and decrypting tuple contents. This finer granularity allows mobile agents (that are not supposed to carry private keys with them when migrating) to collect encrypted data, while executing on remote sites, and decrypt them safely when back at the home site.

The proposed extension, while targeted to our middleware for mobile agents interacting through distributed tuple spaces, KLAVA [4], is still general enough to be applied to similar Java frameworks using multiple distributed tuples spaces possibly dealing with mobility, such, e.g., [12,1,7]. Indeed, this extension represents a compromise between the flexibility and open nature of Linda and of mobile code, and the privacy of data in a distributed context.

2   Distributed Private Generative Communications

The Linda communication model [11] is based on the notion of *tuple space* that is a multiset of *tuples*. These are just sequences of items, called *fields* that are of two kinds: *actual fields*, i.e., values and identifiers, and *formal fields*, i.e., variables. Syntactically, a formal field is denoted with !*ide*, where *ide* is an identifier. Tuples can be inserted in a tuple space with the operation **out** and retrieved from a tuple space with the operations **in** and **read** (**read** does not withdraw the tuple from the tuple space). If no matching tuple is found, both **in** and **read** block the process that execute them, until a matching tuple becomes available. *Pattern-matching* is used to select tuples from the tuple space; two tuples match if they have the same number of fields and corresponding fields do match: a formal field matches any value of the same type, and two actual fields match only if they are identical (but two formals never match). For instance, if *Val* is an integer variable, then tuples ("foo", "bar", !*Val*) and ("foo", "bar", 300) do match. After matching, the variable of a formal field gets the value of the matched field; in the previous example, after matching, *Val* will contain the integer value 300.

The middleware we are presenting is based on KLAVA [4], a Java framework implementing KLAIM (*Kernel Language for Agent Interaction and Mobility*) [8] that provides features for programming distributed applications with mobile code and mobile agents, relying on communication via multiple distributed tuple spaces. KLAIM extends Linda by handling multiple distributed tuple spaces: tuple spaces are placed on *nodes* (or *sites*), which are part of a *net*. Each node contains a tuple space and a set of processes, and can be accessed through its *locality*. Thus, classical Linda operations are indexed with the locality of the node they have to be performed at. A reserved locality, `self`, can be used to access the current execution site. Moreover in KLAIM processes are first class data, in that they can be transmitted and exchanged among sites, so that mobile code and mobile agent applications can be easily programmed.

For guaranteing privacy of data stored in tuple spaces we have extended KLAVA with some cryptographic primitives. In our view, this extension is a good tradeoff between the open nature of Linda (and of mobile code) and data privacy. In particular we aim at having this extension as smooth as possible, so that the original model is not perverted.

The basic idea is that a tuple may contain both clear text fields and encrypted fields. All the encrypted fields of a specific tuple are encrypted with a single key. This choice simplifies the overall design and does not harm usability of the system; it would be unusual that different fields of the same tuple are encrypted with different keys. Encrypted fields completely hide the encrypted contents that they embody: they even hide the type of the contents. This strengthens the secrecy of data (it is not even possible to know the type of sensible information).

In line with the open nature of the Linda model, our main intention is not to prohibit processes to retrieve data belonging to other processes, but to guarantee that these data be read and modified only by entitled processes. A shared tuple space is basically a shared communication channel: in such a channel information can be freely read and modified.

At the same time one of our aims is avoiding that wrong data be retrieved by mistake. Clear text fields of a tuple can be used as identifiers for filtering tuples (as in the Linda philosophy), but if a matching tuple contains encrypted fields, which a process is not able to decrypt, it is also sensible that the tuple is put back in the tuple space if it was withdrawn with an **in**. Moreover, in such cases, a process may want to try to retrieve another matching tuple, possibly until the right one is retrieved (i.e., a tuple for which it has the appropriate decryption key), and to be blocked until one is available, in case no such tuple is found.

Within our framework it is possible to

- use tuple fields with encrypted data;
- encrypt tuple fields with specific keys;
- decrypt a tuple with encrypted fields;
- use variants of the operations **in** and **read** (**ink** and **readk**) to atomically retrieve a tuple and decrypt its contents.

The modified versions of the retrieving operations, **ink** and **readk**, are based on the following procedure:

1. look for and possibly retrieve a matching tuple,
2. attempt a decryption of the encrypted fields of the retrieved tuple
3. if the decryption fails:
   a) if the operation was an **ink** then put the retrieved tuple back in the tuple space,
   b) look for alternative matching tuples,
4. if all these attempts fail, then block until another matching tuple is available.

Thus the programmer is relieved from the burden of executing all these internal tasks, and when a **readk** or an **ink** operation succeeds it is guaranteed that the retrieved tuple has been correctly decrypted. Basically the original Linda pattern matching mechanism is not modified: encrypted fields are seen as ordinary fields that have type `KCipher` (as shown in Section 3). It can be seen as an extended pattern matching mechanism that, after the structural matching, also attempts to decrypt encrypted fields.

In case mobile code is used, the above approach may be unsafe. Indeed, symmetric and asymmetric key encryption techniques rely on the secrecy of the key (in asymmetric encryption the private key must be kept secret). Thus, a fundamental requirement is that *mobile code and mobile agents must not carry private keys when migrating to a remote site* ("Software agents have no hopes of keeping cryptographic keys secret in a realistic, efficient setting" [17]). This implies that the above introduced operations **ink** and **readk** cannot be used by a mobile agent executing on a remote site, because they would require carrying over a key for decryption.

For mobile agents it is then necessary to supply a finer grain retrieval mechanism. For this reason we introduced also operations for the explicit decryption of tuples: a tuple, containing encrypted fields, will be retrieved by a mobile agent by means of standard **in** and **read** operations and no automatic decryption will be attempted. The actual decryption of the retrieved tuples can take place when the agent is executing at the home site, where the key for decryption is available and can be safely used. Typically a mobile agent system consists of stationary agents, that do not migrate, and mobile agents that visit other sites in the network, and, upon arrival at the home site, can communicate with the stationary agents.

Thus the basic idea is that mobile agents collect encrypted data at remote sites and communicate these data to the stationary agents, which can safely decrypt their contents. Obviously, if some data are retrieved by mistake, it is up to the agents to put it back on the site from where they were withdrawn. This restriction of the protocol for fetching tuples is necessary if one wants to avoid running the risk of leaking private keys. On the contrary, public keys can be safely transported and communicated. By using public keys mobile agents are able to encrypt the data collected along their itinerary.

Notice that there is no guarantee that a "wrong" tuple is put back: our framework addresses privacy, not security, i.e., even if data can be stolen, still it cannot be read. Should this be not acceptable, one should resort to a secure channel-based communication model, and give up the Linda shared tuple space model. Indeed the functionalities of our framework are similar to the one provided, e.g., by *PGP* [18] that does not avoid e-mails be eavesdropped and stolen, but their contents are still private since they are unreadable for those that do not own the right decryption key.

An alternative approach could be that of physically removing an encrypted tuple, retrieved with an **in**, only when the home site of the agent that performed the **in**, notifies that the decryption has taken place successfully. Such a tuple would be restored if the decryption is acknowledged to have failed or after a specific timeout expired. However, this approach makes a tuple's life time dependent on that of a mobile agent, which, by its own nature, is independent and autonomous: agents would be expected to accomplish their task within a specific amount of time. Moreover, inconsistencies could arise in case successful decryption acknowledgments arrive after the timeout has expired.

3 Implementation

KLAVA [4] is deployed as an extensible Java package, Klava, that defines the classes and the run-time system for developing distributed and mobile code applications according to the programming model of KLAIM. In KLAVA processes are instances of subclasses of class KlavaProcess and can use methods for accessing a tuple space of a node: out(t,1), for inserting the tuple t into the tuple space of the node at locality 1, read(t,1) and in(t,1), for, respectively, reading and withdrawing a tuple matching with t from the tuple space of the node at locality 1. Moreover the method eval(P,1) can be used for spawning a KlavaProcess P for remote execution on site 1. Some wrapper classes are supplied for tuple fields such as KString, KInteger, etc.

The extension of this package, CRYPTOKLAVA, provides the cryptography features described in the previous section. We have used the *Java Cryptography Extension (JCE)* [14], a set of packages that provide a framework and implementations for encryption, key generation and key agreement, and Message Authentication Code (MAC) algorithms. JCE defines a set of standard API, so that different cryptography algorithms can be plugged into a system or an application, without modifying the existing code. Keys and certificates can be safely stored in a *Keystore*, an encrypted archive.

CRYPTOKLAVA is implemented as a subpackage of the package Klava, namely Klava.crypto, so that it is self-contained and does not affect the main package. In the rest of this section we will describe the main classes of the package Klava.crypto, implementing cryptographic features.

The class KCipher is introduced in order to handle formal and actual fields containing encrypted data (it follows the KLAVA convention that wrapper classes for tuple items start with a K). Basically it can be seen as a wrapper for standard KLAVA tuple fields. This class includes the following fields:

```
protected byte[] encItem; // encrypted data
protected Object ref; // reference to the real tuple item
protected String alg; // enc−dec algorithm type
```

The reference **ref** will be **null** when the field is a formal field, or the field has not yet been decrypted. After retrieving a matching tuple, **encItem** will contain the encrypted data (that is always stored and manipulated as an array of bytes). After the decryption, **ref** will refer to the decrypted data. Conversely, upon creation of an actual field, **ref** will contain the data to be encrypted; after encryption, **encItem** will contain the encrypted data, while **ref** will be set to **null** (so that the garbage collector can eventually erase such clear data also from the memory). **alg** stores information about the algorithm used for encryption and decryption.

An actual encrypted tuple field can be created by firstly creating a standard KLAVA tuple field (in the example a string) and then by passing such field to an instance of class **KCipher**:

```
KString s = new KString("foo");
KCipher ks = new KCipher(s);
```

Similarly the following code creates an encrypted string formal tuple field (In KLAVA a formal field is created by instantiating an object from a KLAVA class for tuple fields – such as **KString**, **KInteger**, etc. – through the default constructor):

```
KString s = new KString();
KCipher ks = new KCipher(s);
```

KCipher supplies methods **enc** and **dec** for respectively encrypting and decrypting data represented by the tuple field. These methods receive, as parameter, the **Key** that has to be used for encryption and decryption, and **enc** also accepts the specification of the algorithm. These methods can be invoked only by the classes of the package.

The class **Tuplex** extends the standard KLAVA class **Tuple**, in order to contain fields of class **KCipher**, besides standard tuple fields; apart from providing methods for cryptographic primitives, it also serves as a first filter during matching: it will avoid that ordinary tuples (containing only clear text data) be matched with encrypted tuples. Once tuple fields are inserted into a **Tuplex** object, the **KCipher** fields can be encrypted by means of the method **encode**. For instance, the following code

```
KString ps = new KString("clear");
KCipher ks = new KCipher(new KString("secret"));
Tuplex t = new Tuplex();
t.add(ps); t.add(ks);
t.encode();
```

creates a tuple where the first field is a clear text string, and the second is a field to be encrypted, and then actually encrypts the **KCipher** field by calling **encode**. Also **encode** can receive parameters specifying the key and the algorithm for the encryption; otherwise the default values are used. **encode** basically calls the previously described method **enc** on every **KCipher** tuple field, thus ensuring that all encrypted fields within a tuple rely on the same key and algorithm.

As for the retrieval operation, this can be performed either with the new introduced operations, **ink** and **readk**, if they are executed on the local site

```
KString s = new KString();
KString sec = new KString();
KCipher ks = new KCipher(sec);
Tuplex t = new Tuplex();
t.add(s); t.add(ks);
ink(t, l);
Print("encrypted data is: " + sec);
```

or by first retrieving the tuple and then manually decoding encrypted fields:

```
... // as above
in(t, l);
...
t.decode();
Print("encrypted data is: " + sec);
```

Notice that in both cases references contained in an encrypted field (such as **sec**) are automatically updated during the decryption. The **ink** in the former example is performed at a remote site but this does not mean that the key travels in the net: as explained in the previous section, the matching mechanism is implicitly split into a retrieve phase (which takes place remotely) and a decryption phase (which takes place locally).

Operations **ink** and **readk** are provided as methods in the class `Klava-Processx`, which extends the class `KlavaProcess` for standard processes. `Klava-Processx` also keeps information about the `KeyStore` of the process and the default keys to be used for encryption and decryption. Obviously these fields are `transient` so that they are not delivered together with the process, should it migrate to a remote site. All these extended classes make the extension of KLAVA completely modular: no modification was made to the original KLAVA classes.

Finally, let us observe that, thanks to abstractions provided by the JCE, all the introduced operations are independent of the specific cryptography mechanism, so both symmetric and asymmetric encryption schemes can be employed.

In the next section we will present a programming example of use of these new cryptographic primitives; further examples, also dealing with a mobile agent scenario, can be found in [3].

4   An Encrypted Chat System

The chat system we present in this section is simplified, but it implements the basic features that are common to several real chat systems. The system consists of a `ChatServer` and many `ChatClients` and it is a variant of the one presented in [4] with the new cryptographic primitives. When a client sends a message, the server has to deliver the message to all connected clients. If a message is "private", it will be delivered only to the clients specified in the list sent along with the message.

Messages are normally delivered through the network as clear text, so they can be read by everyone:

– an eavesdropper can intercept the messages and read their contents;
– a misbehaving chat server can examine clients' messages.

Moreover, the messages might also be modified so that a client believes he is receiving messages from another client, while it would be reading messages forged by a "man in the middle".

While this is normally acceptable, due to the open nature of a chat system, nonetheless there could be situations when the privacy and integrity of messages is a major concern; for instance if two clients want to engage a private communication. This is a typical scenario where cryptography can solve the problem of privacy (through encryption).

In this example we implement a chat server and a chat client, capable of handling private encrypted messages:

– when the client wants to send a private message to a specific receiver, it encrypts the body of the message with a key;
– the server receives the message and simply forwards it to the receiver;
– the receiver will receive the message with the encrypted body and it can decrypt it with the appropriate key.

Notice that clients that want to communicate privately must have agreed about the specific key to be used during the private message exchange; this is definitely the case with symmetric keys. As for public and private key encryption the receiver can simply use its private key, to decrypt a message encrypted with its own public key.

A private message is represented by a tuple of shape ("PERSONAL", $<body>$, $<recipient>$, $<sender>$), where $<recipient>$ and $<sender>$ are, respectively, the locality of the client the message is destined to and the locality of the issuer of the message. Basically, when a client wants to send a message with an encrypted body, it will have to perform the following steps:

```
Tuplex t = new Tuplex() ;
KCipher cryptMessage = new KCipher( message ) ;
t.add( new KString( "PERSONAL" ) );
t.add( cryptMessage ) ;
t.add( selectedUser ) ;
t.add( self ) ;
t.encode();
out( t, server ) ;
```

where **message** is the actual message body.

The server handles encrypted messages by retrieving them through the following actions (it will deliver the tuple without the field $<recipient>$, which is useless at this time):

```
KString message = new KString() ;
KCipher cryptMessage = new KCipher( message ) ;
Locality to = new PhysicalLocality() ;
Locality from = new PhysicalLocality() ;
```

```
Tuplex t = new Tuplex() ;
t.add( new KString( "PERSONAL" ) );
t.add( cryptMessage ) ;
t.add( to ) ;
t.add( from ) ;
in( t, self ) ;
```

and it delivers the message to the recipient as follows:

```
out( new Tuplex(new KString ("PERSONAL"), cryptMessage, from), to );
```

On the other hand, the receiver, which is always waiting for incoming messages, will read and decrypt a message (in one atomic step), by means of the operation **ink**:

```
KString message = new KString() ;
KCipher cryptMessage = new KCipher( message ) ;
KString from = new KString() ;
Tuplex t = new Tuplex() ;
t.add( new KString( "PERSONAL" ) ) ;
t.add( cryptMessage ) ;
t.add( from ) ;
ink( t, self ) ;
Print("Received message: " + message);
```

Both the server and the clients execute these operations within the loop for handling incoming messages.

5   Conclusions and Related Work

Since tuple space operations can be used both by local processes and by mobile agents, the extended operations, presented in this paper, address both the privacy of hosts and of mobile agents. We did not deal with key distribution explicitly that can be seen as an orthogonal problem. Digital signatures can be smoothly integrated in our framework and the pattern matching extended accordingly.

The work that is closer to ours is [5], which introduces the *Secure Object Space* (SECOS) model. This model is intended to extend Linda with fine-grained access control semantics. In SECOS all tuple fields are locked with a key, and each field must be locked with a different key. The basic idea is that a process, upon retrieving a tuple, can see only the fields for which he owns the corresponding key. The structure of a tuple does not influence pattern matching: due to an introduced *subsumption* rule, a template can match also a bigger tuple, and fields can be reordered during the matching. [6] proposes a similar, but richer framework, SecSpaces, where also resource access control and tuple space partitioning facilities are provided (orthogonal and complementary to our approach).

All these features tend to alter the original Linda model, while our principal aim is to provide an extension of the Linda communication model that can be smoothly integrated into the existing features, without significantly changing the original model. Moreover, neither SECOS nor SecSpaces handle code mobility, which is one of our main concerns.

Mobility imposes additional restrictions on the underlying model, e.g., requiring that agents do not carry private keys during migrations, and calls for alternatives such as explicit encryption and decryption mechanisms and a two-stage pattern matching. Indeed the problem of protecting an agent against a malicious host is even more complicated than that of protecting a host from a malicious agent (we refer to the papers in [15,16]).

References

1. K. Arnold, E. Freeman, and S. Hupfer. *JavaSpaces Principles, Patterns and Practice*. Addison-Wesley, 1999.
2. K. Arnold, B. O'Sullivan, R. Scheifler, J. Waldo, and A. Wollrath. *The Jini Specification*. Addison-Wesley, 1999.
3. L. Bettini. *Linguistic Constructs for Object-Oriented Mobile Code Programming & their Implementations*. PhD thesis, Dip. di Matematica, Università di Siena, 2003. forthcoming.
4. L. Bettini, R. De Nicola, and R. Pugliese. KLAVA: a Java package for distributed and mobile applications. *Software – Practice and Experience*, 32(14):1365–1394, 2002.
5. C. Bryce, M. Oriol, and J. Vitek. A Coordination Model for Agents Based on Secure Spaces. In P. Ciancarini and A. Wolf, editors, *Proc. 3rd Int. Conf. on Coordination Models and Languages*, number 1594 in LNCS, pages 4–20. Springer-Verlag, 1999.
6. N. Busi, R. Gorrieri, R. Lucchi, and G. Zavattaro. SecSpaces: a Data-driven Coordination Model for Environments Open to Untrusted Agents. In *Proc. of FOCLASA'02*, ENTCS. Elsevier, 2002.
7. P. Ciancarini and D. Rossi. Jada - Coordination and Communication for Java Agents. In J. Vitek and C. Tschudin, editors, *Mobile Object Systems - Towards the Programmable Internet*, number 1222 in LNCS, pages 213–228. Springer, 1997.
8. R. De Nicola, G. Ferrari, and R. Pugliese. KLAIM: a Kernel Language for Agents Interaction and Mobility. *IEEE Transactions on Software Engineering*, 24(5):315–330, 1998.
9. D. Deugo. Choosing a Mobile Agent Messaging Model. In *Proc. of ISADS 2001*, pages 278–286. IEEE, 2001.
10. D. Ford, T. Lehman, S. McLaughry, and P. Wyckoff. T Spaces. *IBM Systems Journal*, pages 454–474, August 1998.
11. D. Gelernter. Generative Communication in Linda. *ACM Transactions on Programming Languages and Systems*, 7(1):80–112, 1985.
12. G. Picco, A. Murphy, and G.-C. Roman. LIME: Linda Meets Mobility. In D. Garlan, editor, *Proc. ICSE'99*, pages 368–377. ACM Press, 1999.
13. T. Sander and C. Tschudin. Protecting Mobile Agents Against Malicious Hosts. In Vigna [15].
14. Sun Microsystems. *Java Cryptography Extension (JCE), Refence Guide*, 2001.
15. G. Vigna, editor. *Mobile Agents and Security*. Number 1419 in LNCS. Springer, 1998.
16. J. Vitek and C. Jensen, editors. *Secure Internet Programming: Security Issues for Mobile and Distributed Objects*, number 1603 in LNCS. Springer-Verlag, 1999.
17. B. Yee. A Sanctuary For Mobile Agents. In Vitek and Jensen [16], pages 261–273.
18. P. Zimmermann. *The Official PGP User's Guide*. MIT Press, 1995.

Designing Fault-Tolerant Mobile Systems

Giovanna Di Marzo Serugendo[1] and Alexander Romanovsky[2]

[1] Centre Universitatire d'Informatique, University of Geneva,
CH-1211 Geneva 4, Switzerland
Giovanna.Dimarzo@cui.unige.ch

[2] School of Computing Science, University of Newcastle,
NE1 7RU Newcastle upon Tyne, UK
Alexander.Romanovsky@newcastle.ac.uk

Abstract. The purpose of this paper is to investigate how several innovative techniques, not all initially intended for fault-tolerance, can be applied in providing fault tolerance of complex mobile agent systems. Due to their roaming nature, mobile agents usually run on Java-based platforms, which ensures full portability of mobile code. The first part of the paper discusses specific characteristics of mobile systems, outlines the application areas benefiting from code mobility, and shows why the existing error recovery techniques are not suitable for mobile systems. In the next part of the paper we present evaluation criteria for fault tolerance techniques, and propose several possible solutions for error recovery at the application level: meta-agent, Coordinated Atomic actions, asynchronous resolution, self-repair, and proof carrying code. The intention is to allow system developers to choose the approach which is suited best to the characteristics of the mobile agent application to be designed. To this end we discuss the advantages and disadvantages of each technique, as well as situations in which it provides the most benefit. A simple example, based on Internet shopping, is used throughout the paper to demonstrate the techniques.

Keywords: Mobile agents, system structuring, fault tolerance, exception handling, software engineering.

1 Introduction

From the early 90s the community working on mobile agent systems has been looking for a killer application to prove the usefulness of the concepts. Today, due to the fast development of the Internet, Grid computing, e-commerce, and due to the tremendous growth of the sizes of distributed systems and their proliferation to many new application areas, mobility is becoming a practical issue. Many companies are now building complex applications with some elements of mobility.

In this paper we will focus on code mobility [7], which is mainly used for providing a wide range of non-functional benefits, including on-line system customisation and upgrading, improvement of system performance and dynamic

N. Guelfi et al. (Eds.): FIDJI 2002, LNCS 2604, pp. 185–201, 2003.
© Springer-Verlag Berlin Heidelberg 2003

extension of applications. The term mobile agent refers to a software component (including its code and state) that can be moved from one location (node or host) of a distributed system to another where it will resume its execution. Mobile agent systems are often Internet scale systems. They presume application programmer's awareness of mobility, and cover a large variety of application domains, such as database access, network management or e-commerce [17][1].

Mobile agents are frequently mentioned in literature as being advantageous for helping to cope with faults in distributed systems, since they are able to perform local monitoring tasks, and to deal with network disconnection naturally. The use of mobile agents eases fault-management, especially in large-scale decentralised systems. However, there are still many errors that mobile agent-based applications have to face. The purpose of this paper is not to see how fault-tolerance can be achieved with mobile agents, but how fault-tolerance for mobile agents can be realised.

Mobile agent systems encounter traditional types of error that distributed software does, but also specific errors such as failures of migration requests, violations of security restrictions, specific communication exceptions [24]. The combination of the specific characteristics of mobile agents and the specific errors that they can encounter prevents traditional error recovery techniques from being fully efficient or directly applicable for building mobile applications. Indeed, traditional techniques for fault tolerance in distributed systems:

- are too heavy to be used in mobile systems;
- mainly focus on software tolerance of hardware faults;
- are not applicable for building mobile agents intended for execution on a number of different hosts during their life cycle;
- rely on hard-wired or permanent connections between system components;
- are not applicable for building applications consisting of moving entities scattered around several locations;
- are not suitable for systems whose structure changes dynamically, e.g., changes in system participants, their links and their locations;
- are oriented towards very different execution environments and computation paradigms.

There is a need for much more flexible and dynamic fault-tolerant techniques that are light in both code and communication exchanges. One of the important issues here is to involve application programmers that develop such mobile applications, in providing fault tolerance. We believe that it is inefficient to focus only on fault tolerance that the underlying middleware can provide transparently for the application. Application-specific fault tolerance incorporated at the application level is clearly a much more powerful approach to dealing with faults and abnormal situations of all possible types. In this paper we propose different techniques, not all necessarily meant for fault-tolerance, and show how they could be applied at this level to improve the overall dependability of mobile applications.

---

[1] Section 2.2 outlines major application domains in which mobile code is used.

2   Mobile Agent Systems

2.1   Characteristics of Mobile Systems

In this paper we consider mobile applications that can be built either as single mobile agents or as a number of co-operating mobile agents. We assume that each mobile agent can decide to move or can be forced to move depending on the application state, and that the agents move by moving both code and current state. Each host consists of a machine and an executing environment (a platform) which provides basic operations for mobility as well as access to local resources. The platform is usually based on a Java virtual machine, which provides full portability of the mobile agent bytecode.

The platform includes typical functions such as move an agent, resolve the name, dispatch, retract, and clone. In case of co-operative agents we assume that the platforms provide means for inter-agent information exchange and/or synchronisation. In this paper we are not focusing on any particular mobile environment as we would like to address general issues common for a number of them.

The most typical characteristics of mobile systems are as follows. These systems are very *dynamic* and *flexible* by nature, so agents join and leave platforms or groups of agents continuously. Usually they are *open systems* whose participants (i.e. the agents) can establish and change connections dynamically. The agents are *autonomous* and may decide to move from one host to another when necessary. This causes the application to be of a *world-wide scale*. Mobile agents usually *communicate* through blackboards *asynchronously*, and *do not know the location* of other agents. Usually a mobile agent application is *decentralised*, i.e., there is no central entity controlling the agents.

2.2   Application Domains

Code mobility is a means for developing flexible, customisable, adaptable, extendable and dynamic services in a number of application domains. In this section we give a brief overview of major domains that (can) benefit from employing mobile agents [11].

Network Management. The use of customised mobile agents for network management increases decentralisation and flexibility. Indeed, agents pro-actively carry out administration tasks, and can be dynamically replaced allowing, for instance, dynamic update of network policies. In addition, since mobile agents are located in network devices, they help reduce traffic around the management station, and make it possible to distribute processing load [1].

Remote Device Control and Configuration. Mobile agents are useful for performing monitoring tasks, such as information filtering, control functions and intrusion detection. The advantage of using mobile agents in this domain is that policies and itineraries of mobile agents can be modified dynamically [23] and can respond to an intrusion in real-time [6].

Active Networks. In an active network, nodes of the network - routers and switches - can perform computations [20]. On the one hand, it allows customised programs - mobile code - to be injected into the nodes of the network, making active network service management possible. On the other hand, packets, passing through routing elements, are no longer passive packets, because they contain small programs that are executed at each node. This approach enables dynamic optimisations, extensions and replacement of protocols [21].

Wireless Applications. Wireless networks suffer from low bandwidth and disconnection errors. Mobile agents help to overcome these limitations, since a mobile agent, roaming the connected network, can still work on behalf of a mobile user, even if the mobile user is disconnected. Dispatching a mobile agent close to a server reduces data transfer among information servers and the wireless device [14].

E-commerce, M-commerce. Electronic commerce (E-commerce) consists in buying and selling goods using electronic transaction processing technologies. Whereas traditional electronic commerce involves two stationary computers, mobile electronic commerce (M-commerce) involves at least one mobile computer. In both E-commerce and M-commerce, mobile agents are particularly useful in roaming electronic market places for discovering products, engaging transactions and negotiations on the user's behalf [5].

Distributed Information Retrieval. Agents, dispatched at remote information sources, can perform local searches, accesses to data and filtering them, eliminating network transfer of intermediate data [3].

Active Documents. Moving data with mobile code leads to the notion of active documents. Early forms consisted in interactive and animated web pages provided by applets running at the client side. Recent works enable complex documents, such as meeting schedules containing mobile code, to mediate communication among the participants, including notification of participants, and observation of workflow rules [8].

Workflow Management. Workflow, or business process, management systems consist in a set of tasks performed in a controlled order to realise a business purpose. Mobile agents embody a workflow by encapsulating the business process logic. Mobile agents permit the introduction or extension of workflows at run-time, since agents can dynamically uptake or replace components. Mobile agent itineraries (tasks and locations) can be altered at run-time, allowing just-in-time workflows to be realised [13].

Grid Computing and Global Computing. Mobile agents are particularly useful for efficiently monitoring distributed computational resources in Grid systems, since they help in coping with Grid large-scale size and discovering data [22]. Mobile code proved to be very useful for exploiting idle computing resources in a Grid system, for distributing data and computational tasks, for collecting computed results, as well as for charging and billing participants [2].

Emerging application domains. In addition to the domains listed above, experts foresee that application domains such as: IP Telephony, middleware service coding and service composition, are very likely to benefit from mobile code technology [10].

2.3   Abnormal Situations

There is a wide range of abnormal situations which mobile applications can face, which include: *migration requests failures, unavailability of resources* at the new location, *security restrictions, communication delays, failures of components* in the local (host) environment, *users' mistakes, agent programmers' mistakes, failures of the subsystems* of a complex mobile application to provide the required services, *node crashes, network partitioning,* and differences in the host environments on which mobile code is executed. These abnormal situations are mainly caused by:

1. failures of the underlying components it is using (i.e. their inability to deliver the required service);
2. failures of the agents it is co-operating with;
3. the agent own faults.

Type (1) includes a number of situations such as hardware faults of different nature (node crashes, lost or corrupted messages, disconnections), absence or malfunctioning of the required resources (main memory, disk storage, computation time, databases, information the agent is looking for, etc.), all types of errors reported by the underlying platforms (heap overflow, null pointer). Clearly some of these situations can be better tolerated by the underlying support (the platform) itself because this can be done transparently for the agent (e.g. using ordered delivery, group communication, replication) but in the situations when the support is not designed to do this all responsibility for recovery is left with the application. Very often local (i.e. involving only one agent located in this host) recovery can deal with such situations. Errors of type (2) include partner's failures and partner's inability to correctly communicate with the agent. They result in the agent inability to continue its computation and require co-operative handling involving several agents [9]. The abnormal situations of type (3) usually require local recovery at the agent level.

All situations that we have described above require application-specific handling. It is important here that depending on their type we can discuss the structuring issues of which part of the mobile application should be involved in the handling. Each agent first tries to handle all the abnormal situations of types 1 and 3 locally (generally speaking, the application-specific handlers will be developed for handling particular errors). When this recovery is not possible, a higher level recovery is applied, which involves a number of cooperating agents.

In a single-agent application, we should report a failure exception to a specialised component (a master waiting for the results, a guardian, a monitoring system, a client, an operator). When one of the co-operating agents is faulty a co-operative handling should be initiated in all of them. Proper structuring of multi-agent systems will allow us to find a subset of agents that have been recently involved in cooperation to avoid involving all of them in such cooperative recovery each time any of them signals an exception.

2.4   Challenges in Fault Tolerance

Mobile agents requirements with respect to fault tolerance include:

- the need to recover from errors encountered at remote locations;
- the need for light code, which can be easily moved among hosts. This imposes a light recovery scheme, if it is included into the mobile agent;
- the highly (world-wide) distributed nature of mobile systems make it impossible or difficult to maintain checkpoints enabling a group of agents to perform a backward error recovery;
- the highly dynamic nature of mobile systems is hardly compatible with the notion of transactions that forces several agents to stay in the same transaction as long as it does not commit or abort;
- abnormal situations are not known in advance, very often agents, cooperating within an application, are neither designed together nor developed by the same programmers. However, an agent should be robust enough to overcome them and continue its execution;
- very often mobile systems are executed in heterogeneous environments without agreed standards or communication interfaces;
- the location of each agent in a group of agents is unknown at run-time. Raising exceptions, having an immediate effect to stop the execution of agents, is impossible. It necessarily implies some delays;
- mobile agent systems are particularly sensitive to security concerns.

These points show that traditional techniques for fault tolerance in distributed systems are not directly applicable for handling abnormal situations of different types at the agent level. First of all, traditional techniques are mainly oriented on tolerating hardware faults (e.g. by using replication, group communication, transactions); but typically mobile systems have to face faults of a much wider range. Secondly, recovery based on rollback or abort cannot be always applied as the main recovery technique, because there are many application-specific modifications that cannot be simply 'erased'; this is why many abnormal situations have to be dealt with at the application level, using forward error recovery [12]. One more crucial factor for choosing forward error recovery is its comparatively low cost. Thirdly, mobile systems need flexible recovery (exception handling) solutions; in particular, it should be possible to change dynamically system configuration, structure, fault tolerance means to be applied and agent connections. One more reason is that, as we have explained above, there is a huge variety of abnormal situations of different types that can happen. The last reason is that mobile environments have computational models and communication techniques that are very different from the conventional ones (for example, they use asynchronous communication and dynamic binding).

3   Fault Tolerance Techniques for Mobile Agent Systems

The ultimate aim of this section is to propose a number of innovative ways of providing fault tolerance in mobile systems. All of the techniques discussed below rely on application-level forward error recovery as the most general way of dealing with faults of a widest possible range. The section starts with a brief outline of the criteria used in discussing and comparing these techniques. It then presents them using a working example, and discusses pros and cons of each technique with respect to the identified criteria.

3.1   Evaluation Criteria

The choice of the criteria is driven by our intention: to show the strength of each technique in providing typical fault tolerance activities; to analyse the ease with which it can be applied by the application programmers; and to understand how it fits the specific requirements of the mobile applications.

Structuring Fault Tolerance. As stated before, we focus on fault tolerance at the level of the application, and assume that low-level errors either are tolerated by the middleware components or, when this is not possible, are reported to the application at the appropriate abstraction level. Two structuring approaches can be distinguished here: either the fault tolerance code is separated from the functionality of the mobile entities or it is part of them.

- *Built-in Fault Tolerance.* In the case of a built-in fault-tolerant mechanism each agent is equipped with fault tolerance. Such a strategy enables the agent to be autonomous and independent of any other (e.g. a centralised entity) that is responsible for recovering from errors. The main disadvantage is that the agent is not flexible in providing fault tolerance, so, for example, it cannot tolerate unanticipated errors.
- *Separating Fault Tolerance from Functionality.* The alternative to built-in fault tolerance is provided by decoupling functionality code from error recovery code. The advantages of such a scheme are multiple: the error handler can be downloaded when necessary, it can be adapted to the particular error, several versions may be available, the agent can rely on a dedicated agent that provides recovery. The disadvantages are as follows: there may be some delay to move the error handling code; delegating the responsibility for error detection and correction to other agents may be not applicable for mobile agents that cannot always contact error handling agents; the decentralised nature of the application is compromised if the recovery scheme is in some sense centralised.

The fault tolerance techniques described below either use built-in fault tolerance (Coordinated Atomic actions actions, proof carrying code) or separate it from the functionality (meta-agent), or they allow programmers to flexibly choose these two (asynchronous resolution, self-repair).

Error Processing and Error Confinement. The essence of any fault tolerance technique is its error processing (error detection and error recovery) and error confinement capabilities. This includes the *way the errors are detected* when a particular technique is used, and the *information* that can be used for this detection (for example, internal agent states, input/output parameters of the calls, histories of event).

The area of error confinement defines the *damage domain* to be recovered after an error has been detected - this can be an agent, a part of an agent (e.g. its method) or a group of agents. This criterion is closely related to the structuring view discussed before.

Recursive Structuring and Scalability. Another vital issue is *recursiveness* of the technique: generally speaking, these techniques should allow developers to build recursive systems in which failure to deal with any error at a system level is transformed into an error that has to be handled at a higher system level [19]. This can be provided in different ways: action nesting, sub-agents, slave agents, client/server, action groups/subgroups, etc.

Scalability of a technique is related to the ease in which fault tolerance can be provided in systems consisting of multiple agents. We believe that from the fault tolerance point of view this issue is closely related to recursive system structuring.

Overheads. This criterion is used to compare the application-neutral (hidden) overheads caused by the techniques, which may include: a number of *additional messages* implying additional traffic; the *amount of code* to be moved to provide fault tolerance; etc.

Flexibility, Run-Time Reconfigurability. The flexibility of a particular technique is vital for developing fault tolerance means suitable for mobile applications. Code mobility itself provides a powerful support for implementing fault tolerance.

3.2   Working Example

In this subsection we introduce a small banking system that operates with mobile agents and requires fault tolerance. This example is used to illustrate the discussion of possible fault-tolerant techniques that could be used for mobile systems.

A user, wishing to acquire some product, launches a buyer agent that will roam the Internet searching for a seller agent offering the requested object. The buyer and seller agents will meet in an electronic market place, where they will exchange information regarding products that their respective users desire to buy or sell. Each agent is equipped with an e-purse holding some amount of electronic money. If the two agents have matching requests, they reach an agreement (the product is booked, and a contract is concluded), and the payment is then realised by transferring some money from the e-purse of the buyer agent directly to the e-purse of the seller agent. In this case the e-purse acts as cash money, there is no need to ask for a bank certification. If the payment fails, then the agreement has to be cancelled, and the seller agent releases the product.

In this scenario, the buyer agent can be either alone or composed of several agents roaming the Internet simultaneously. It may be difficult or even impossible for the user to contact the buyer agent or for the buyer agent to contact the agents distributed world-wide. Indeed, a mobile IP scheme enabling to contact mobile agents irrespectively of their position is difficult to consider when agents neither know each other nor participate in the same application.

We will consider the following errors in this scenario:

- there is no offer matching the request;
- there is a bug in the seller agent code: it is impossible to reach an agreement or to pay money from its e-purse;
- the buyer agent e-purse does not contain sufficient money;
- the buyer agent e-purse does not present sufficient privileges, e.g., a configuration error does not authorise money to be withdrawn from the e-purse.

3.3   Meta-agent

In the meta-agent scheme, the normal functionality is contained in the agent, while the fault-tolerant or resource control aspect is left to the meta-agent [25].

In our electronic market place, each agent has an additional meta-agent, as shown by figure 1. We will now consider the errors listed above. If the buyer agent does not find any corresponding seller, it informs its meta-agent that will take the appropriate decision: stop the buyer agent, let it move to another place, inform the user for changing the request, etc.

The bug in the seller code results in an internal error for the buyer agent. It will abort its current transaction, and try to find another partner. Alternatively, it may inform the meta-agent about the problem.

In the case (a) when the buyer has not enough money, the buyer agent raises an exception to its meta-agent (1), which is responsible for downloading money to the buyer agent e-purse. The meta-agent first contacts the user (2) for his agreement (3), and then the bank (4) for actually loading money (5), and finally uploads the electronic money to the e-purse (6). The payment can then occur (7).

For insufficient privileges (b), the meta-agent acts in a similar way, it simply asks the user for more privileges, and changes the code of the agent accordingly (4).

Discussion. Meta-agents offer the advantage that the error handling code (actually contained in the meta-agent) can be downloaded or changed at run-time, thus favoring flexibility and adaptability with respect to errors. More than one meta-agent can be related to an agent, thus enabling several exception handling. Meta-agents may either come with the agent or be only requested in case of problems or simply be stationary at some well-known place. There is no overhead at the level of the agent itself, even though at the level of the application, there is a certain amount of code dedicated to the meta-agent, and some message transfer is necessary between the agent and its meta-agent.

The meta-agents are useful for an asynchronous recovery from local errors (i.e., the meta-agent can deal with the error and then inform the agent), when there is no need for a cooperative resolution scheme at the level of the agents and when exceptions are raised in isolated agents. This may be the case for wireless applications and active networks.

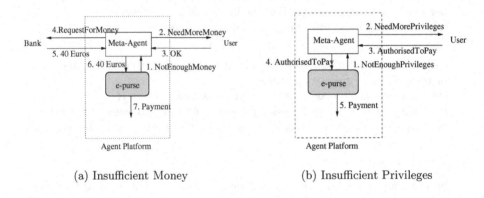

(a) Insufficient Money   (b) Insufficient Privileges

Fig. 1. Meta-agent

3.4   Coordinated Atomic Actions

Coordinated Atomic actions (CA actions) [26] are a structuring mechanism for developing dependable concurrent systems. CA actions generalise the concepts of atomic actions and transactions. Atomic actions control cooperative concurrency among a set of participating entities (e.g., processes, objects) and provide forward error recovery using cooperative exception handling. Transactions maintain the coherency of external resource competitively accessed by concurrent actions. CA actions can be nested and when an action is not able to provide the required result an exception is propagated to the containing action.

Regarding the market place example, figure 2 shows a buyer and a seller agents entering a CA action, called CAAgreement, for realising the agreement. This CA action contains a nested CA action for the payment, CAPayment.

Whenever the payment fails, either (a) the buyer agent enters a recovery phase, where it asks for more money, and the payment finally succeeds; or (b) the buyer cannot recover, leading to the failure of CAPayment, which in turns causes CAAgreement to abort. We notice that before aborting CAAgreement releases the booking of the object that had been previously realised.

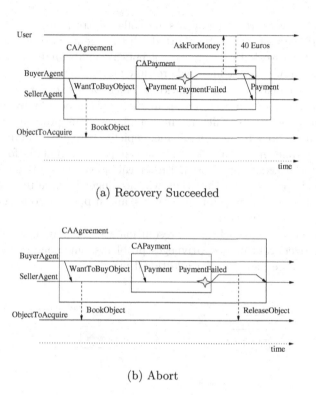

(a) Recovery Succeeded

(b) Abort

Fig. 2. Coordinated Atomic Actions

Discussion. CA actions offer the most general way of providing fault tolerance in concurrent systems: they clearly define the damage area (i.e., the CA action scope) to be recovered and are intended for recursive system structuring. The hidden overheads are caused by additional synchronisation of the agents participating in an action on the action entry and exit.

CA actions are especially well suited to complex applications involving cooperating agents; for large-scale applications in which agents are aware of other agents, i.e., active documents; for systems in which we need cooperative handling of exceptions, i.e., workflow management applications or when we need recursive structuring of complex mobile applications for fault tolerance. However, additional work has to be carried out to make this concept more applicable for mobile applications. This in particular includes better understanding of the underlying principles of agent participation in a cooperative activity, requires introducing location-independent and location-aware actions, as well as open actions, and developing a specialised support based on the existing Java RMI support [27].

3.5 Asynchronous Resolution

In some cases, several roaming agents act collaboratively for the resolution of a given task. If the task has to be aborted, all the agents have to be informed in order to stop their work. However, those agents are unattainable by asynchronous exceptions, since we do not know where they are.

Consider, for instance, the scenario in which we want to cancel purchasing a series of stamps, where each stamp in the series is bought by an individual agent, possibly located in different market places. This problem can be solved using an asynchronous resolution scheme, depicted by figure 3: individual agents, from time to time, may consult some agreed place (AgentPlatform_3), where messages for the agents are stored. Either this place contains no more money that the agent can use, and thus they will no longer be able to buy stamps; or it contains directives to stop buying stamps, and if possible to re-sell those that have already been purchased.

This collaborative asynchronous resolution scheme may also help the buyer agents to recover from money/privileges problems, since one of them may ask the others for more money or for additional privileges.

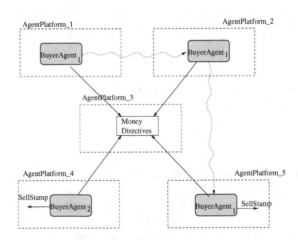

Fig. 3. Asynchronous Resolution

Discussion. This approach naturally scales to large-size systems because the fault detection and the recovery solutions employ the mobile agent mechanisms (blackboard communication, and mobility). The flexibility of the recovery mechanism and the overhead depend on the way the agent code related to the recovery mechanism is managed. If additional meta-agents are used, then flexibility increases and the agent can cope with new directives, in this case the additional code is stored in meta-agents. Otherwise, flexibility is limited to the original code present in the agent.

Asynchronous resolution is well suited to asynchronous recovery (i.e., when there is no need for all the agents to recover at the same time) and for collaborative agents in the situations when they can be individually recovered from the same exception in their particular locations. Grid computing and e-commerce are good candidates for this kind of fault tolerance technique.

3.6   Self-Repair

In this case, the agent does not consult its user (neither through a meta-agent, nor directly). It tries instead to solve the problem autonomously by asking other agents, not necessarily involved in the same task, for help.

For instance, in the case of the electronic market place, if the buyer does not find any matching offer, it may ask other agents if they know about possible sellers.

As shown by figure 4, if the buyer agent has no sufficient money (1), and provided it is authorised to spend more money than the e-purse holds, it can ask all other agents present in the market place to borrow it some money (2). If an agent agrees to lend money to the buyer agent (3), they conclude a contract (specifying interests and delays). Then, the buyer agent receives some money, that it will use for buying the initial object (4). The agent that lent the money will be refunded afterwards, once the buyer agent will have downloaded some money directly from its bank. This scheme can be very convenient in case of urgent decisions. Borrowing money from another agent present in the market place may be realised more quickly than entering a remote communication with the bank.

Discussion. It is worth noting that this kind of resolution can be undertaken with meta-agents as well as with CA actions. However, it suits better for the situations: when the agent is given full autonomy or crucially needs to recover even partially from abnormal situations, e.g. wireless applications; when control of the application is decentralised both for the functionality and the fault tolerance requirements; and for situations requiring a quick resolution, i.e., remote device control or active networks.

This technique scales to large-size systems since the error is confined to the agent itself, which autonomously tries to solve the problem. Obviously there is an overhead in the size of code necessary to carry resolution schemes and in execution time needed to overcome problems.

3.7   Proof Carrying Code

Before trying to reach an agreement and then realising that the buyer has not enough money, the proof carrying code alternative enables both parties to expose

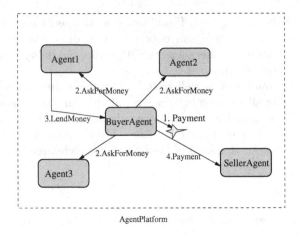

AgentPlatform

Fig. 4. Self-Repair

some of their internal information, that will prove or not that they are able to enter the transaction. In the example of figure 5, the buyer and seller agent exchange information regarding the amount of money contained in the e-purse, the privileges they have (buy or sell), as well as the minimum and maximum price requested or allowed for the object. Given the values, we see that the buyer has not sufficient money (only 4 Euros), even if an agreement is reached for a price between 5 and 7 Euros.

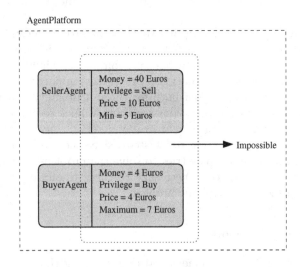

Fig. 5. Proof Carrying Code

In the case of bugs in the seller agents, an additional proof carried by the seller agent code may allow for them to be detected.

This is a simplified version of the original proof carrying code [16]. We can easily imagine how to actually replace specification values with code.

Discussion. Flexibility of this approach is limited since the proof, used for error detection, is part of the agent and not customisable at run-time. There is a clear overhead in code size due to the proof that has to be carried by the agent and in execution time required to execute it.

This scheme is particularly well adapted for mobile agents that enter interactions with unknown agents, i.e., agents that have been designed independently and that may use different standards, and for discovering and composing unknown services proposed by potential partners.

4   Related Works

The main body of research in fault tolerance of mobile systems focuses on software techniques oriented towards tolerating hardware faults. For example, an approach to developing consensus protocols to be used for achieving an agreement when agents crash is presented in [18]. A novel algorithm for ensuring that a message is always delivered to a mobile agent is proposed in [15]. The particularity of this algorithm is that it does not enforce continuous connectivity with the message source. Our intention is to build on such techniques when possible to allow tolerance of faults of a wider range. The techniques we are considering usually use such services as the underlying middleware supports (which promotes separation of concerns). Moreover, when some of them are either not capable of delivering the required service or not used or very expensive to use, the agents can deal with such problems in an application-specific fashion using the techniques discussed in Section 3.

There are two techniques which are related to this work. Paper [9] introduces an agent service (called Electronic exception handling institution) dedicated to detecting and solving exceptional conditions in software agent marketplaces. This service collects information about typical abnormal situations and uses AI techniques to find out the best way of handling them. It is interesting that the authors recognise the needs for involving several agents in cooperative handling of complex exceptions (in a way similar to CA actions). In the scheme proposed in [24] each mobile agent has a guard agent - comparable to meta-agents - that handles all exceptions propagated from it. This scheme is very important, as it is the first scheme dealing with the specific characteristics of the mobile environment.

5   Conclusion

Mobile agent systems have specific characteristics (they are highly decentralised, dynamic and made of roaming entities) and encounter specific abnormal situations (migration errors, resource and security problems, partner's failures). These particularities impose requirements for fault tolerance that traditional techniques hardly succeed in meeting. This paper discusses several approaches to providing fault tolerance, at the application level, in the framework of mobile agent systems. It is worth noting that the same ideas could be well applied to other decentralised systems, such as biologically inspired ones, and to applications running on portable devices and facing physical mobility. Our future work includes proposing a scheme combining proof carrying code and light specifications for agent programming, developing a flexible support for open mobile CA actions and establishing patterns of exception handling for Lana [4], a mobile agent platform incorporating a support for security, coordination and disconnection of nodes.

Acknowledgment. Alexander Romanovsky is partially supported by European IST DSoS (Dependable Systems of Systems) Project (IST-1999-11585). Giovanna Di Marzo Serugendo is supported by Swiss NSF grant 21-68026.02.

References

1. M. Baldi, S. Gai, and G. P. Picco. Exploiting code mobility in decentralized and flexible network management. In K. Rothermel and R. Popescu-Zeletin, editors, *Proceedings of the 1st International Workshop on Mobile Agents 97 (MA'97)*, volume 1219 of *LNCS*, pages 13–26. Springer-Verlag, 1997.

2. W. Binder, G. Di Marzo Serugendo, and J. Hulaas. Towards a Secure and Efficient Model for Grid Computing using Mobile Code. In *8th ECOOP Workshop on Mobile Object Systems: Agent Applications and New Frontiers*, June 2002.

3. B. Brewington, R. Gray, K. Moizumi, D. Kotz, G. Cybenko, and D. Rus. Mobile Agents for Distributed Information Retrieval. In M. Klusch, editor, *Intelligent Information Agents*, chapter 15, pages 355–395. Springer-Verlag, 1999.

4. C. Bryce, C. Razafimahefa, and M. Pawlak. Lana: An Approach to Programming Autonomous Systems. In *16th European Conference on Object-Oriented Programming, ECOOP'02*, 2002.

5. P. Dasgupta, N. Narasimhan, L. E. Moser, and P. M. Melliar-Smith. MAgNET: Mobile Agents for Networked Electronic Trading. *IEEE Transactions on Knowledge and Data Engineering, Special Issue on Web Applications*, 11(4):509–525, July-August 1999.

6. N. Foukia, S. Hassas, S. Fenet, and J. Hulaas. An Intrusion Response Scheme: Tracking the Source using the Stigmergy Paradigm. In *Proceedings of Security of Mobile Multiagent Systems Workshop (SEMAS-2002)*, 2002.

7. A. Fuggetta, G. P. Picco, and G. Vigna. Understanding Code Mobility. *IEEE Transactions on Software Engineering*, 24(5):342–361, 1998.

8. F. Kilander, P. Werle, and K. Hansson. Jima - A Jini-based Infrastructure for Active Documents and Mobile Agents. In *Proceedings of the Personal Computing and Communication (PCC) Workshop*, November 1999.

9. M. Klein and C. Dellarocas. Exception handling in agent systems. In O. Etzioni, J. P. Müller, and J. M. Bradshaw, editors, *Proceedings of the Third International Conference on Autonomous Agents (Agents'99)*, pages 62–68. ACM Press, 1999.

10. D. Kotz, R. Gray, and D. Rus. Future Directions for Mobile Agent Research. *IEEE Distributed Systems Online*, 3(8), 2002.

11. D. B. Lange and M. Oshima. Seven good reasons for mobile agents. *Communications of the ACM*, 42(3):88–89, 1999.
12. P. A. Lee and T. Anderson. *Fault Tolerance: Principles and Practice*. Dependable computing and fault-tolerant systems. Springer-Verlag, 1990.
13. S. W. Loke and A. B. Zaslavsky. Towards distributed workflow enactment with itineraries and mobile agent management. In J. Liu and Y. Ye, editors, *E-Commerce Agents, Marketplace Solutions, Security Issues, and Supply and Demand*, volume 2033 of *Lecture Notes in Computer Science*, pages 283–294. Springer-Verlag, 2001.
14. Q. H. Mahmoud. MobiAgent: A Mobile Agent-based Approach to Wireless Information Systems. In *Proceedings of the 3rd International Bi-Conference Workshop on Agent-Oriented Information Systems, held with the 5th International Conference on Autonomous Agents 2001*, 2001.
15. A. L. Murphy and G. P. Picco. Reliable communication for highly mobile agents. *Journal of Autonomous Agents and Multi-Agent Systems*, 5(1):81–100, March 2002.
16. G. C. Necula. Proof-carrying code. In *The 24th ACM SIGPLAN-SIGACT Symposium on Principles of Programming Languages (POPL'97)*, 1997.
17. G. P. Picco. Mobile agents: An introduction. *Journal of Microprocessors and Microsystems*, 25(2):65–74, April 2001.
18. S. Pleisch and A. Schiper. Modeling fault-tolerant mobile agent execution as a sequence of agreement problems. In *19th IEEE Symposium on Reliable Distributed Systems (SRDS'00)*, pages 11–20. IEEE Computer Society Press, 2000.
19. B. Randell. Recursively structured distributed computing systems. In *Proceedings of Third Symposium on Reliability in Distributed Software and Database Systems*, pages 3–11. IEEE Computer Society Press, 1983.
20. D. L. Tennenhouse. Active networks. In *Proceedings of the Second Symposium on Operating Systems Design and Implementation (OSDI '96)*, pages 89–90, Berkeley, CA, USA, 1996. USENIX Association.
21. D. L. Tennenhouse, J. M. Smith, W. D. Sincoskie, D. J. Wetherall, and G. J. Minden. A Survey of Active Network Research. *IEEE Communications Magazine*, 1997.
22. O. Tomarchio, L. Vita, and A. Puliafito. Active monitoring in GRID environments using mobile agent technology. In *2nd Workshop on Active Middleware Services (AMS'00) in HPDC-9*, August 2002.
23. A. Tripathi, T. Ahmed, S. Pathak, A. Pathak, M. Carney, M. Koka, and P. Dokas. Active Monitoring of Network Systems using Mobile Agents. In *Proceedings of Networks 2002, a joint conference of ICWLHN 2002 and ICN 2002*, 2002.
24. A. Tripathi and R. Miller. Exception handling in agent-oriented systems. In A. Romanovsky, C. Dony, J. Lindskov Knudsen, and A. Tripathi, editors, *Advances in Exception Handling Techniques*, volume 2022 of *LNCS*, pages 128–146. Springer-Verlag, 2001.
25. A. Villazon and W. Binder. Portable Resource Reification in Java-based Mobile Agent Systems. In *Proceedings of the Fifth IEEE International Conference on Mobile Agents (MA'01)*, December 2001.
26. J. Xu, B. Randell, A. Romanovsky, C. Rubira, R. Stroud, and Z. Wu. Fault tolerance in concurrent object-oriented software through coordinated error recovery. In *25th International Symposium on Fault-Tolerant Computing Systems (FTCS-25)*, pages 499–509. IEEE Computer Society Press, 1995.
27. A. F. Zorzo and R. J. Stroud. A Distributed Object-Oriented Framework for Dependable Multiparty Interactions. *ACM Sigplan Notices*, 34(10):435–446, October 1999.

The Role of OCL in the Model Driven Architecture

Jos Warmer

Klasse Objecten, Netherlands
`j.warmer@klasse.nl`

Abstract. Within the Model Driven Architecture (MDA) models and model transformations play a central role. At the model level OCL adds the precision that is lacking in plain UML. A model that combines the use of OCL and UML is perfectly suitable for MDA transformations. At the meta-model level, OCL is used to define validation rules for models. These can be executed against a model to automatically check whether the model conforms to the validation rules. The third use of OCL is as part of the transformation language in which MDA model transformations will be defined. The OMG has issues an RfP for such a language.

Presenter: Jos Warmer is chief consultant with Klasse Objecten. He works as trainer and mentor, as architect and systems analyst in client projects, and advices companies regarding the use of object technology and component based development. Earlier he was employed by IBM, where he was a member of the European Object Technology Practice group. Since 1997 he is a member of the UML core team, the team that made this OMG standard . He was chief architect of the most precise part of UML: the Object Constraint Language (OCL). He is the author of the book "The Object Constraint Language: Precise Modeling in UML" and is a regular speaker at international seminars and conferences.

N. Guelfi et al. (Eds.): FIDJI 2002, LNCS 2604, p. 202, 2003.
© Springer-Verlag Berlin Heidelberg 2003

Requirements Elicitation with Use Cases

Shane Sendall

Swiss Federal Institute of Technology in Lausanne
Shane.Sendall@epfl.ch

Abstract. Nowadays, the complexity of the software systems that needs to be produced is staggering. Developing such systems requires that the development team first understands the problem, i.e., they have a global picture of what is required to be built, before they can make a sensible judgment on an architecture for the solution. Use cases offer a simple, storytelling-like way to capture the requirements. They provide a means for facilitating the capture and validation of requirements from stakeholders, technical and non-technical alike, which makes them an important tool to have in one's development kit. The simplicity of the use case concept is nevertheless deceptive, because writing effective use cases requires much practice and experience. In fact, there are many issues that must be addressed on the road to mastering requirements elicitation with use cases. In this tutorial, a number of these issues will be raised and addressed, giving the participants a better understanding of what an effective use case is, how to produce them, and where use cases in general can be appropriately applied.

Presenter: Shane Sendall is currently a senior research and teaching assistant at the Software Engineering Laboratory, Swiss Federal Institute of Technology in Lausanne (EPFL), Switzerland. Previously to joining EPFL, Shane worked at the Centre of Software Maintenance, University of Queensland, Australia. Shane recently completed his PhD at EPFL, which was related to improving the current state-of-the-art in software requirements specification. He has been lecturing on use cases for over two years.

N. Guelfi et al. (Eds.): FIDJI 2002, LNCS 2604, p. 203, 2003.
© Springer-Verlag Berlin Heidelberg 2003

Java Threads Can Be Very Useful Building Blocks

Claude Petitpierre

EPFL, Laboratoire de Téléinformatique, 1015 Lausanne, Switzerland
claude.petitpierre@epfl.ch

Abstract. A thread is often considered as a very delicate feature that introduces more troubles than solutions in a development. Actually, this idea is not correct. In this tutorial, we will show that threads can be friendly even in simple applications, provided they are embedded in the right communication structures and are used to separate the data structures from the behavior of an application. In that case, they simplify debugging and maintenance. In the presentation, we will introduce the basic concurrency concepts offered by Java and discuss several typical uses of threads. In particular, we will show how to establish a communication between the threads and the GUI (graphical user interface) implemented with the Swing library, how to handle simultaneously GUI, client and server accesses in the same application and finally how to code the various UML diagrams that define the behavior of an interactive application.

Presenter: Claude Petitpierre has received his diploma of Electrical Engineer in 1972 from the "Ecole Polytechnique de Lausanne". He spent the next 5 years in industry, where he participated in the development of realtime cement plant control. He went back to the EPFL, obtained the title of Doctor in 1984 and then spent one year (1985-1986) at the AT&T Bell Labs in Holmdel. He was appointed professor in 1987. He is interested in the theories and techniques that can support the development of complete and reliable software products and in the formal modeling and analysis theories. The work pursued in his laboratory led to the development of Synchronous C++, a parsimonious superset of C++, supporting concurrency in a way that provides the new language with modeling capacity similar to the one provided by formal languages such as CCS or CSP. The approach has now been extended to Java and a framework with several program generators and libraries is available. He is also interested in computer aided teaching and has developed a computer aided programming course that is used by the first year students.

N. Guelfi et al. (Eds.): FIDJI 2002, LNCS 2604, p. 204, 2003.
© Springer-Verlag Berlin Heidelberg 2003

Author Index